T0304856

The Tidal Year

The Tidal Year

Freya Bromley

CORONET

First published in Great Britain in 2023 by Coronet
An imprint of Hodder & Stoughton
An Hachette UK company

4

Copyright © Freya Bromley 2023

The Tidal Year Journey map on pg vi © Malaika Francique
Image on pg. 20 © Liz Seabrook
"THIS IS THE SEA"
Words and Music by MICHAEL SCOTT
DIZZY HEIGHTS MUSIC PUBLISHING, LTD. (PRS)
All rights administered by WARNER CHAPPELL MUSIC LTD

A CIP catalogue record for this title is available from the British Library

Hardback ISBN 9781399709675
Paperback ISBN 9781399709705
eBook ISBN 9781399709699

Typeset in Bembo MT by Hewer Text UK Ltd, Edinburgh
Printed and bound in Great Britain by Clays Ltd, Elcograf S.p.A.

Hodder & Stoughton policy is to use papers that are natural, renewable
and recyclable products and made from wood grown in sustainable
forests. The logging and manufacturing processes are expected to
conform to the environmental regulations of the country of origin.

Hodder & Stoughton Ltd
Carmelite House
50 Victoria Embankment
London EC4Y 0DZ

www.hodder.co.uk

That was the river,
This is the sea.

– The Waterboys

THE TIDAL YEAR JOURNEY

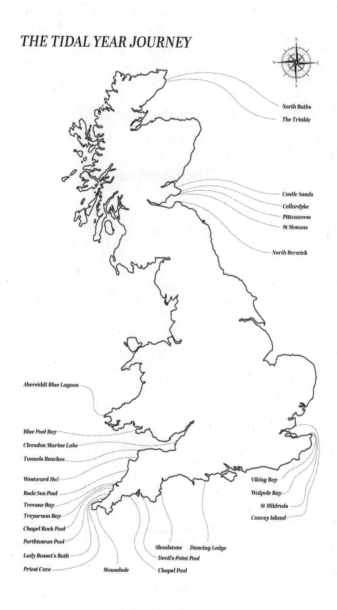

North Baths
The Trinkie

Castle Sands
Cellardyke
Pittenweem
St Monans

North Berwick

Abereiddi Blue Lagoon

Blue Pool Bay
Clevedon Marine Lake
Tunnels Beaches

Westward Ho!
Bude Sea Pool
Trevone Bay
Treyarnon Bay
Chapel Rock Pool
Porthtowan Pool
Lady Basset's Bath
Priest Cove

Mousehole

Shoalstone   Dancing Ledge
Devil's Point Pool
Chapel Pool

Viking Bay
Walpole Bay
St Mildreds
Canvey Island

Author's Note

Names, places and moments have changed as I've tried to bring Tom into the present of my life by recreating the past. Writing about our time together has perhaps taken me further from facts. Memories of him are poems I tell myself, to bring him closer to me. And closer to meaning. Meaning that has contextualised everything I do, everyone I love and everywhere I swim.

Prologue

When I saw the bench for the first time I thought, *Rohanna really is doing grief better than me.* It's a simple bench. The view from it seems to radiate outwards like the layers of a conker. At the centre there's this gorgeous, burned-chocolate seat encased by Alexandra Park. Then beyond there's the B106 and Hornsey train tracks and further still you can see Canary Wharf, the Gherkin, the Shard and – on a very clear day – the London Eye. That day the silver birches glowed white-hot and a Turkish hazel dangled its mustardy catkins. Cherry trees were flowering too, their petals like pink candyfloss across the park. Ally Pally seemed the first place to offer spring's promise. Maybe it had been happening for a while; I just hadn't been looking. I even saw a nuthatch, its steely grey head working its way down a tree trunk. I would've said it was a sign, if I believed in that kind of thing.

Everyone arrived with food and alcohol and daffodils. One of the boys began laying the flowers out in

1

an S beside the bench, but before he could finish a passing Boston terrier tore through the display. The dog shook his daffodil-stuffed muzzle until the petals were shredded like yellow confetti. Cradling the dog, the owner apologised profusely and walked away back-wards. Another stranger stopped to ask, *what are you doing?* Rohanna replied, *it's my sister Sami's birthday. She would've been twenty-three.* The stranger nodded then walked on. I wondered if he'd think about it later. Maybe he'd even call his sister, just to say hi. Probably not. Even I didn't do that, and I should really know better. I stood on my own for a while and looked at the plaque:

*How lucky we are to have something that
makes saying goodbye so hard.*

Bloody hell that's good, I thought. Tragic yet profound. The combination of a Winnie the Pooh quote and a Monotype Corsiva font was nostalgic and moving without being pretentious or mystical. It was perfect.

People were passing around a big bag of lightly sea salted Tyrrells and plastic cups of cava. I took two glasses. It was a trick someone at work taught me once. Take two and then, if you're done with a conversation, you can nod towards the drinks and pretend you're delivering one to a friend. This wasn't so subtle in a park; I just looked like an alcoholic. I tried to get out of a conversation with Sami's trampoline instructor, but there was nowhere to hide so walking away meant striking up a conversation with someone new and offering them the other cup. The woman who accepted it was wearing a pair of cotton dungarees and tiny koi carp earrings that swished like they were swimming when she talked. She said she'd recently moved to a canal boat near Little Venice so she could get some peace and quiet to finish her screenplay. *Unfortunately,* she said, *it's not quiet. Living on the river means constantly hearing the same two things. People walking past saying the name of your boat aloud ('Oh* Darjeeling'*) and couples breaking up.*

Rohanna was busy being hugged by people. I got jealous again watching all the embraces. She was the pièce de résistance at this death party and wore it well. Her smile put other people at ease. She was wearing grey trousers and this black turtleneck; I wondered if she'd planned that. Looking down at my own denim coat and green slacks, I berated myself for dressing so colourfully at a memorial. I considered how many cups of cava it would take for me to ask a stranger for a hug. Probably only three. Then again, I knew three would make me angry before they made me affectionate. As if I'd manifested him, a man appeared beside me with the bottle and stack of cups. He had a squashed packet of menthols in his breast pocket and a ginger moustache, which needed a trim as the hairs were curling over his upper lip. Since he had both hands full he peeled a cup from the others with his teeth and nudged it towards me. On a different day, I might've put it back and taken one that hadn't touched his mouth. He did an inelegant pour that was all foam, so I chased the bottle when he tried to pull away to let him fill it up once the bubbles died down. We stood in silence for a while, then he asked me how I knew Sami.

I know Rohanna, her sister. We met at a bereavement retreat. How about you? I asked. *Cello lessons*, he replied. That she was exceptionally musically talented was one of the things I knew about Sami from what Rohanna had told me. I also knew her favourite meal was macaroni cheese; she was the life and soul of any party and she played piano too. Beautifully, apparently. Sami died while travelling in South America. It was an allergic reaction. She wasn't alone when it happened. There were people sitting outside on plastic chairs playing cards. When organising her things, Rohanna and her mum discovered her vibrators and had a good laugh about it. I held an image of Sami in my mind but couldn't remember if Rohanna had shown it to me in a frame or on her phone or from a small print folded up in her wallet. I thought about Sami's face so often that it was as clear in my mind as if it were a memory.

4

A bereavement retreat, he said the words back as if wanting to hear how they sounded coming from his mouth, *so strange. I've never heard of that before. What was it like?* Someone took a cup from his stack. *Whatever you're imagining, probably that.* I looked around. There were maybe thirty to forty people there. I'd endured small talk with three. I could probably leave soon.

And everyone's . . . This guy wasn't fast. *Bereaved? Yes,* I confirmed. We were quiet again. He sipped and some of the bubbles lingered on the hair above his lip. I'm not sure why, but I felt the need to add, *I met a girl whose brother had choked on a sausage at the dinner table and died in front of his whole family.* He swallowed. *Death by bangers and mash. Can you imagine?* he said. Clearly imagining it. *And what happened to you?*

I could've replied that my brother died from a rare bone cancer four years ago, but the thought of saying his name made me feel sick, so I decided to put my sunglasses on instead. It was rude, but the sheer effort it took to be stood up, existing in that moment while holding a plastic cup in my hand felt monumental. I wished he'd leave me alone. Eventually, I caught Rohanna's eye and gave her a look that I hoped said: what an awful fucking day.

How have you been? She downed her cup and extended her hand to allow someone to refill it. *Fine,* I lied. Rohanna's eye twitched and I could tell she didn't believe me but wasn't sure she could take on asking for the truth. We were both doing our best. She let out a low sigh. *Every year, I tell myself it's just like any other day and just like any other day it will pass and be ok. But it's not. It's just shit.* I took her hand and agreed: *unbelievably shit.*

Somehow Sami's birthday did the same to me. It punctured my calendar like a storm in an otherwise cloudless sky. For weeks I'd watched it loom on the horizon, reminding me of this thing I was trying to forget. Then that morning I woke with exceptional clarity and told my boyfriend I wanted to break up and would be moving out. It was both entirely related and had nothing to do with Sami's birthday. I had hoped that things to do with living – boyfriend, flat, job, drinking, friends – would make me feel better. Sami's anniversary reminded me that I needed to be better at the things to do with dying.

I hugged Rohanna goodbye and left the party. Then I left the park, and then London. I wasn't sure how long it would be before I'd return. My mum had agreed to drive from Wales to pick me up. If she could have, she would've said *I told you so*, but I don't think she'd seen this one coming. Anyway, that doesn't matter. What matters is that she came to get me. She pulled up in a Honda that still had the mud spray of the Brecons on the wheel rims. It was a miracle we'd found each other while I was walking the streets around Ally Pally, because I'd long given up trying to explain Live Location to her. *Get in*, she said. *You know how much I hate the North Circular.*

Spring

Spring

Chapter One

Am-Nawr: 51.85996° N, 3.13642° W

For a long time being in my family has felt like living in a waiting room. We were seven for many years before my older brothers moved out and we became five. Then Tom died, and we returned from the hospital as a four for the very first time. I had hoped that moving out would mean moving forward. Emma did too, so we both left. Two. Then I started the sequence in reverse and moved back home with my parents. Three. Though I knew we would never reach seven again.

Being part of a family as large as ours meant fighting to be seen, heard and fit in a five-seater Honda Civic. We are therefore a chaotic unit of loud voices and colourful personalities. My parents are the outdoors type. They have a National Trust membership and listen to a lot of Radio 4. Dad is a smoker – Marlboros outdoors, vaping indoors – and my mum looks like she's recently quit, though she's never had a cigarette in her life. Lawrence and Howard are a decade older than me and were the best, and worst, babysitters. Once they said that if I told our parents about their party, they'd tie me to a picnic bench and cover me in strawberry jam so bees would eat me alive. They're my half-brothers from Dad's first marriage, but I never considered them anything less than fully mine. Then there's me. Although I'm technically the middle child, I have all the qualities – confident, conscientious and bossy – of being eldest as Lawrence and Howard left for university during my preadolescence and I took on the role of telling my younger siblings what to do. They're the twins: Emma and Tom. Except Tom is missing, of course, so uniting as a family always feels like we can't quite start the party. There's still one guest to arrive and we're all hoping he'll walk through the door again one day.

After Tom's death, Mum and Dad moved away from the house where we had spent our childhood, which felt like a complicated relief. I'd thought that being somewhere new would stop it feeling haunted, but Tom's things and pictures were still there. Sometimes it was nice to be haunted. I welcomed his ghost and got frustrated that I didn't believe in that kind of thing more; that I didn't have the faith. Their home is a long, low house half in the clouds in the Brecons. Nearby there's the Sugar Loaf Mountain, a mining tourist attraction called Big Pit and a ring road that leads to a large Waitrose. The house is called *Am-nawr*, meaning 'for now' in Welsh. My parents always speak about it like it's an in-between place, yet they've been there for a few years. Jobs need doing but stay on the list. The storms rattling over the River Usk tug the windows away from the sills and there are nails left in the walls from hanging photographs of a family we never met, the wallpaper a different colour around the frame's shadowy outline. *Am-nawr.* After Tom, everything felt temporary, everything felt transient.

Six weeks after Sami's anniversary, I was still in Wales. I was beginning to tire of circling around my parents and their everydayness; the way Dad left teabags in the sink and Mum left every cupboard and drawer open. I floated from my laptop to making tea to staring out the window and then to bed where I searched 'Lesbian Oil Massage' on Pornhub then fell asleep to Stephen Fry-narrated audiobooks. I wondered when I should return to London.

Rohanna texted to ask how I was. I labelled it 'Unread' in the hope that I might have the strength to reply later. My younger sister, Emma, phoned too and said she'd come visit at the weekend. She lives in Solihull with her Staffordshire boyfriend Dan, who likes to post about carp-fishing on Instagram. They met when she tapped him on the shoulder in a chicken shop and said, *I like your accent.* They travel around the country watching darts tournaments. She does her food shopping on a Sunday and has a meal plan for the week ahead, including packed lunches that she takes to the office. She knows how to use grout cleaner and regularly drives to my grandma, just to check in. She has her life together in a way I fear I never will. Since I'd left London, she'd been messaging me things like *are you eating* and *how is it being alone in Wales.* In my replies, I usually compensated for my lack of vulnerability with exclamation marks and *Bake Off* GIFs. I texted back to say I was leaving Wales that weekend, which wasn't true, because I couldn't handle the thought of her big brown eyes worrying at me.

My commute to work was the twenty seconds it took me to walk from my bedroom to Mum's desk. There was a mug of tea waiting for me beside the keyboard. I could tell it'd been there a while from the brown tannin film on the surface. I'd overslept again. Grief was a hole I walked around during the day and fell into at night. I looked out the window and saw Mum loading boxes and a broken toaster into the car. Guessing from her muddy leggings, bum bag and anorak she was going horse-riding after the dump. Going to the dump is one of my parents' favourite pastimes. I wondered if that was something to do with their age or unique to the type of people they are. She waved and I waved back, with the study window a passive spectator between us. Mum tipped her hand towards her mouth to gesture drinking tea. Giving a thumbs up, I mimed: *yep, got it thanks*. I took a sip then realised it was cold and dribbled it back into the mug. I'd microwave it later.

Mum slammed the boot shut and drove away. Last week I'd had to explain to a colleague that 'boot' means 'trunk' while localising a country album review from American to British English. *Boot like shoe?* she'd asked and I'd said *yes, but also no*, which felt like an explanation I gave a lot at work. My job was writing album reviews and artist biographies. It involved spending an inordinate amount of time on thesaurus.com. I could do it from Wales; in fact I could do it anywhere there was Wi-Fi, Wikipedia and enough time for me to sit and have an extended period of self-loathing where I contemplated deleting everything I'd written before realising I was too close to deadline. My therapist said I worked so hard in an attempt to impress my parents. She often said things like this, and I wondered if in therapy there should be an ache of resonance in my belly when she talked. Instead, I felt she'd deeply misunderstood me. Perhaps it was less active than misunderstanding. Simply not seeing or looking in the wrong direction. It was clear, to me at least, that I worked so hard to avoid thinking about Tom. I was mostly successful in my attempts.

I opened my laptop. Two unread emails. The subject line of the first read: 'Thank you team xoxo'. I knew then it would be from Annie as she's the only colleague I have who would actually write xoxo. Many of my Monday mornings have been spent watching her choose a Quote of the Week for her email signature from hellogiggles.com. Annie's dog, Rocco, had died and she was writing to thank us for the flowers. Attached to the email was a poorly composed photo of the bouquet beside a framed print of the dog's paws. I wondered if Annie had that made after the dog was dead and if the vet had put its paw in a special kind of ink to make it. She wrote: *only time will heal my broken heart,* and she was, *sad to miss the planning review but still coming to terms with my new reality*. The second email was a follow-up from a different colleague asking me to contribute to the flowers and explaining that Annie would be off till the thirteenth. I looked at my calendar. A week?! I tried to calm down by reminding myself that it was a very big Icelandic sheepdog, and its absence must be noticeable in the house. Then I remembered that Annie was grieving for an animal that regularly ate its own sick. I was so livid that I walked into the bathroom, stuffed my mouth with a half-finished loo roll and screamed as loud as I dared.

It wasn't uncommon for me to be angry when I felt misunderstood, and it wasn't uncommon for me to be misunderstood when talking about grief, so I suppose for a few years I'd been quite an angry person. Nothing triggered me more than hearing people talk about their pets' deaths. Dead grandparents usually set me off, but I could muster some sympathy for a human loss. Cats or dogs, however, I could not tolerate.

Losing her dog was incomparable to the loss I had suffered and yet I couldn't stop myself comparing. I kept thinking about the memorial pawprint. If I could have a cast of Tom's handprint on my desk, I would. I felt rage, but mostly jealousy. I was jealous that she'd felt able to ask for the time and space she needed. I was jealous that she'd had all these words to articulate how she felt. I was jealous that people acknowledged her grief. I was jealous that she had asked for help and that people had helped her. I was jealous because what Annie showed me was that I'd wasted time I could've been loved and cared for, being alone and misunderstood instead.

My phone pinged. *It'll be a long week with Annie off! Post-work pint at The Blue Posts tonight?* Not everyone had realised I wasn't in London. This wasn't surprising. People aren't always good noticers. When Tom died, I'd gone back to work very quickly, and I hadn't stopped since. I was worried what would happen if I did. I learned a lot when I returned. At first, I said I was not well when people asked how I was. *Not well at all.* Then I found myself either apologising for upsetting them or rejected when they gave a reply that only lasted the time it took from pressing the coffee machine to an americano appearing in their mug. *I suppose everything happens for a reason*, one said and retreated to their desk. *Oh Freya it's a good job you're so brave*, another commented, *must go. This pitch won't write itself eh!* The one I really couldn't handle was, *he's in a better place now*.

I learned to say, *I'm well thank you*, and watched a lot of reality TV for somewhere to go from there. That made everyone feel fine. Nobody spoke to me about Tom, but they all carried on emailing. They signed off, *best wishes*, and I started my replies: *hello, hope you're well*. For a while, I hoped nothing for no one. Then I thought that hoping was the only thing that would save me.

From there, I leaned into the positivity movement. I carried on contributing to a corporate culture insistent on smiling, as if capitalism was what would save me. My office hours, then happy hours, became the medium with which I was yoked to reality. I spent my time safely losing it in predictable ways. There was something familiar and cosy about working too hard, drinking too much and having sex too often. Sometimes I needed to feel another person's weight to feel my own. Sometimes I needed to swim to feel weightless. It was good to go between feeling my body was everything and nothing. I learned to unbuckle myself like that.

I replied to the text: *out of town. Sorry!* then leaned back into Mum's office chair and spun around. Her desk is cluttered with trinkets, photos, a roll of sticky tape and a dish full of feathers. When Tom died Mum started collecting them whenever she went for a walk. She likes the white ones best. I suppose because they look like angels sent them from the heavens. I've resisted telling her they're probably pigeon feathers. Rubbing one between my fingers, I thought about Sami's bench and wished I had a place to feel Tom. I typed a message to Emma: *pictures of Tom everywhere in this house*, then saw how it looked with the heart-eyes emoji, crying emoji or face with steam from nose emoji. Typing Tom's name was the only way I saw him in the present these days. Seeing it made me feel as empty as a scorched-out crater. I backspaced the message and the cursor blinked at me.

I wondered if Tom would recognise the person I'd become after his death. Probably not. There was the duty I had to him, to be the person he knew. Then the duty I had to myself, to be whoever I needed to be to keep going. Someday soon, there'd be time for both. For now it was: *hello hope you're well* and *best wishes, Freya.*

The tidal pool in Margate

Chapter Two

Walpole Bay: 51.39339° N, 1.39960° E

That afternoon, I called Miri. She was the only person I could explain my dog-death rage to. My sister probably could've related to it all, but she was too tangled up in my own guilt. When I thought about Emma I thought about Tom and the promise I made him before he died.

I told Miri I was distressed by how hateful I felt. Now as well as my own grief, I had these hideous emotions putting a chasm between me and the people in my life. She said I had a habit of having one mean thought and deciding I had the moral backbone of an éclair. *The proof is in the pudding*, she said. *Mean people don't worry they're mean.* We laughed about the paw print for a while, then Miri added quite seriously: *you should try to feel gently sorry for her. When people care so much about losing a pet, it's probably because they find relationships with humans quite hard.*

You might assume certain things if I tell you that Miri and I met on a wild swimming retreat in Cornwall. You're probably right about all of them. I saw her on the platform of Truro station. It was September, in the more optimistic weeks when COVID-19 looked like it might go away. She was wearing a scarf to cover her face. It was gorgeous swirls of blue and cream, like the mottling of a shell, and fell below her cropped, brunette bob. I first noticed how incredibly small she is. She'd hate it if I said that but there it is. You're very small, Miriam.

The second thing I noticed was the doorstop of a book in her hand. I was surprised it didn't weigh her down. I remember thinking that anyone who reads books like that must have all the answers. Since then, Miri has lived up to my expectations that she knows nearly everything.

There were ten women on the trip. Each day we ate breakfast together at a long wooden table then went on swimming trips around Cornwall. We did underwater handstands at Godrevy Cove, collected sea glass at Grebe beach and picked blackberries in just our swimsuits and sandals at Maenporth. Every night, we took a winding path to a nearby creek for a swim. We had to be careful to keep an eye on a spot on the shore as the current out to sea moved quickly and a few times we found ourselves drifting towards the estuary while we lay on our backs with the sound of the sea in our ears. Someone told me that it was where Daphne du Maurier set *Frenchman's Creek*. I've always liked to believe that's true. It was too perfect for it not to have been. I could imagine the pirates smuggling loot on a small rowboat moored at the steep stone wall tumbling into the water.

The house we were staying in was a charred timber structure with two floors, large enough to have an east and a west wing. Miri and I slept in a shared room in the rafters with four single beds. One of the other guests was a very loud snorer. Each night I rushed to get to sleep before her, but her irregular piglet-like snorts woke me up anyway. I sighed loudly. Miri rolled over and rested her cheek on her palms, which were pressed together like a prayer. With her eyes still closed she said, *tell me something you've never told anyone before.* And I did.

While Miri was in the shower the next morning, I studied her things, hoping they'd reveal clues to how I could become a woman as quietly in control as she was. I flicked through a small notepad with a magenta elastic keeping a pencil attached. Inside there were ratings out of ten for the books she'd been reading and on the days of the week she'd noted how much water she'd drunk. I picked up her grey reusable bottle and looked at the brand, then made a mental note to buy it as soon as I returned to London. Miri is the kind of woman who knows what a kohlrabi is and how you cook an artichoke. It was a surprise when she told me she was thirty-five as she always looks so well rested.

I rested too that week. I took off my watch and counted time only by the tide and gaps between meals. I left with a tan across the small strip of pale skin on my wrist. It was bliss to be shoulder to shoulder with women and to have water everywhere. From all of that came my friendship with Miri and the agreement to begin an adventure.

On a Thursday morning in April, I woke up to baaing. I peeled back the curtain to see a flock of sheep munching my father's flower beds. *For fuck's sake*, he shouted, *Elizabeth, the sheep are back!* then marched out in his Y-fronts and wellies waving his arms as if that would encourage them to cooperate. The sheep blinked at him unknowingly, and I got the impression that was how Dad thought we all looked at him most of the time.

I opened Instagram and scrolled for a while, putting off venturing outside to help. Annie had a new dog. Two, in fact. She'd shared a photo smiling with them both. They appeared to be just as happy, with their big wet tongues lolling over their canines. I wished I could get a new brother, but even then I wouldn't want one, or two. Tom was irreplaceable. I closed the app and spent the morning attempting to herd sheep away with Dad. Surely it was time to go back to London.

⌇

Most days I sat at a desk in the mountains, staring at the sea on my computer. Dad said it's typical of my generation to always want to be somewhere you're not and I said it's typical of his generation to say something like that. My laptop screensaver was a photo of Walpole Bay tidal pool. Every day I stared at it and thought, *I could be swimming right now*. In the photo, the water is as blue as a whale's back and the metal ladder curving over the pool boundary shimmers like some kind of starship.

It must've been four months since Miri and I had both needed to get away. Miri had been caught up in the panic of job-hunting during a pandemic, and I had been escaping my ex-boyfriend who'd asked me when I would stop being sad about my brother. A search for 'Swims Near London' had offered up Margate, so Miri borrowed a car from her neighbour, and we left the city.

Tidal pools are pools of saltwater left on a beach by an ebbing tide. I'd never swum in a tidal pool before that trip to Margate and the ability to enjoy the salt of the sea in a safe watery cradle was sublime. If I looked at the screensaver long enough, I could almost hear the lulling shoosh-shoosh of the waves against the pool wall. I closed my eyes and dreamed that I was there again, only to open them and realise I was at my desk.

Then one day – staring at my screensaver – I started searching online for other tidal pools. I spent hours researching them and found very little concrete information connecting this constellation of pools around the country. I called Miri and told her about all of this. I told her about the mining history connected to many of the pools and the funding issues of the local councils who struggled to conserve them. What I didn't tell her was that I needed to spend a year on my way somewhere. That it was not about arriving but moving. I said that we could collect the information and she said, *could is a big word*, but agreed without much persuasion. That was how we decided that we would try to swim in every tidal pool in mainland Britain and do it in one year.

Chapter Three

Scafell Pike: 54.45424° N, 3.21154° W

Miri had agreed to come and visit me in Wales to begin our adventure. I was warmed by the prospect of seeing her again and feeling like less of a foreign object. I didn't sleep much the night before that first swim. I kept waking up thinking I'd forgotten to pack a spare pair of socks or wondering if I should bring an emergency foil blanket. I did, in the end.

Still sleepy, I opened the hallway cupboard to get my hiking boots. The top shelf was lined with five shoe boxes, each labelled with Sharpie: Elizabeth, Gordon, Emma, Freya and Tom. His box was on the bottom, and I wondered if the boots had started on top but ended there by rotation now there was no one to wear them.

We always were a family of walkers. Hikers, in fact. His feet would still be the biggest. Size eleven. I remember staring at Tom's boots and their grey-green laces while we ate cheese and pickle sandwiches on the Snowdon summit. He was grinning because he'd beaten me to the cairn, though I reassured him it wasn't a race. It would've been, if I'd have been faster than him, but somehow my little brother had gotten tall and gangly and fast.

I studied Tom's boots. They were once fine nubuck leather. Now the laces drooped, the tongue lolled. I wanted to smell them, to see if they held a scent memory. But I knew from his sheets, his jumpers, his coat that they wouldn't. Salt lines charted a map on the shank. I wondered when we last went to the sea together. There was still dirt in the outsole.

The soles were worn by years and memories. Imprinted by a life that had rubbed the tread heavier on one side. There was one hike that weighed the heaviest on me. Scafell Pike. That night he'd screamed in pain. *My legs*, he kept shouting. *My legs!* I stood in my pyjamas with a glass of water. *Growing pains*, Mum said, then instructed me to fill a hot water bottle. That was my first memory of 'it'. How many times had they sent Mum away? How many times had they told Tom it was growing pains? How long was it before a doctor had finally told us that it was bone cancer? It was everywhere. That would be it.

The cancer burrowed through his bone marrow like a weevil. An oncologist said Tom's spine was like balsa wood. Snappable. The scaffolding of his body had let him down. We tried to build him stronger, hammering nails here and there. Before he collapsed in on himself.

I stared at the cupboard and thought about the GP. Someone later told me he'd quit, couldn't handle the guilt anymore. I thought that seemed a shame. Another life.

My own laces were thinning, like climbing rope across a crevasse. The fibres around the lacing hook were fraying. I pulled them out of each eyelet – these long-woven worms – and swapped them for Tom's. I threaded in and out, in and out like the tide. I took it as a symbol of sorts, an attempt to weave his life into mine again, but inside I felt unchanged.

My boots sighed open. I put them on and headed outside where Miri was already sitting in the driver's seat fiddling with the buttons of the rental car. She'd said she didn't mind driving the whole way, but kept rearranging her short hair behind her ears, which was her tell that she was apprehensive.

Mum was waiting to wave us off. She was funny with goodbyes like that: never missed them, however early. Standing barefoot in her dressing gown, she leaned against the door frame with her arms folded. I turned around to wave. Then swallowed. The waving is a small part of us acknowledging that a goodbye could really mean goodbye. I don't think we'd ever thought about that before Tom, but I noticed she'd started hugging me tighter whenever I left to go somewhere. I wanted to say, *I won't leave you too,* but I just said, *you should put some shoes on,* and got in the car.

Blue Pool Bay is a turquoise jewel nestled on the Gower coast. The natural rockpool is bordered by cliffs and the cove can only be reached by a winding clifftop path. It's named after its stunning lazuline water and is cited as a 'hidden gem' compared to similar spots in Cornwall. It all seemed too good to be true, too beautiful. And just an hour and a half's drive from my parents' house.

I'd prepared myself for our first tidal swim to be quite disappointing and anticlimactic. When we'd looked at pictures of the bay online it reminded me of the Blue Lagoon in *Peter Pan,* like if we blinked we might see a mermaid sunning herself on the rocks with a conch in her grip. Miri and I said things to each other like, *I bet they upped the contrast for that one* or *they must have taken that on a really nice day.* It was therefore a surprise to us that – after a week of grey skies and seemingly endless rain – there was not a cloud in sight when we travelled from Gilwern to Gower.

I always felt guilty when Miri drove and it was my job to just sit there. I tried to make up for it by coming ready with 'Would You Rather' questions, but we eventually ran out of enthusiasm. *Do you mind if I put a podcast on?* Miri was already fiddling with the aux cable. Before the intro was even playing, I knew it would be a *Desert Island Discs*. When we first met, she'd been making her way through every episode starting from the 1940s. She said she'd learned far more about what it was actually like in Britain historically through the people who were invited on the programme, the music they picked and the conversations they had than anything else. Miri uses words like *values* and *postmodern* a lot. I rarely listen to the episodes she recommends. I prefer to watch her talk about them and the way she moves her hands, touching the hair at the back of her neck.

Miri glanced in the wing mirror, then shook her head and said, *Sue Lawley wouldn't have let him just monologue like this!* Eventually the closing music played out and Miri wiped away a tear with her shoulder, hands still on the steering wheel. She released a closing sigh, *that was a good one.* I agreed and we watched traffic turn in to a car park while a family jostled a pram off a bus. Miri is an exceptionally resilient woman. I find what people often mean when they say 'resilient' is that they want people to be good at suffering in silence. Miri is certainly good at carrying on, but when I watch her listen to *Desert*

Island Discs, every possible emotion flashes across her face. Forty-three minutes later, she lifts her chin and continues her life.

What would be your luxury item? I asked and Miri nibbled her bottom lip, though I expected she'd thought about it before. *If I've got the Bible and Shakespeare I have every story ever told. So it'd have to be booze, an endless supply of ice cold, perfectly mixed dirty martinis.* She looked between the road and her phone while she put on the radio and turned the volume up.

It's beautiful here, Miri said as we sped past a field full of cotton-wool sheep. *Your walks must be lovely.* I shrugged. I didn't want to admit that I'd barely left the house for weeks, paying no attention to the tapestried landscape and instead sulking in the office or stewing in the bathtub until my fingers puckered. *No?* Miri nudged. *I haven't been out much to be honest.*

She indicated and we followed a sign for The Mumbles. *The most exciting thing that's happened while I've been here was when the man who digs holes in the garden touched my arm when I brought him a cup of tea. Not sure I could adjust to this pace of life.*

Miri did a thing with her eyebrows that was our shorthand for go on. *Well, I dunno. I guess he was initiating something, but he's not been back since. Chose the day he was finishing. Shame, really. He was quite cute. Imagine a Welsh Timothée Chalamet in muddy overalls.* I'd clearly been in Wales too long. *Not why did he touch your arm, why was he digging holes?*

Pond, I confirmed. We slowed down at a zebra crossing and a parade of dog-walkers bounded towards the coast. *Must be hard being around Tom's things.* I readjusted; the leather seat was slick on the back of my arms. The seatbelt wouldn't let me pull it, so I gave up and let it straitjacket me. *Less that, more the pace thing. I don't know how to do quiet.*

Good reason to start? Miri moved her hand from the wheel and rested it on my arm. *It was nicer when Timothée did that,* I said.

Blue Pool Bay

Chapter Four

At high tide, both the beach and pool at Blue Pool Bay are completely covered, so it's a trip that needs careful timing. In between talking there was a nervous energy between me and Miri. An unspoken agreement that we should get there as soon as possible before the weather changed, but it didn't. The stretch of coastal path between Rhossili and Broughton was a dream. Dunes of golden sand and light bouncing off the ocean like shattered glass. The campsite where we parked was dotted with caravans and tents. It was exciting to see families making memories and witness the simple pleasure of people buying ice creams with 99 Flakes and zipping their children into windbreakers. It smelled of holidays, sweet and fresh like sun cream and salt breeze.

To reach the pool we passed Three Chimneys Arch and Spaniard Rock, locations of shipwrecks from the 1600s where timber and silver coins have been discovered and where metal detectorists still trudge along the beach looking for treasure. We walked on the shore, kneeling to look at mussel beds smattered among boulders with their blue fingernails reaching towards the sky. The tide crept closer and we were in danger of getting our boots wet so we scrambled up the cliffs in search of a footpath above. It was steep and I needed to dig my hands into the earth until it sank under my nails. It was as dark, rich and moist as chocolate cake.

Miri and I took our time to point out and agree on a route together. We set off in one direction, then found ourselves stranded at a steep edge with no clear footholds and realised we could no longer see the course we'd planned. Then it was time to go back a few steps and scurry on our bottoms. My hands were raw from gripping the rocks, but it felt good to climb and descend, to only focus on the step ahead and nothing past it. When the beach was finally metres away the rocks drooped and we had to jump. As I landed my boots sank into the sand, still wet from high tide.

There was no one else on the beach. Even the seagulls, who'd been mewling, were quiet. We placed our bottoms on the barnacled rocks and put our feet in the water. It was cool. Cold, in fact. The hair on my arms bristled to gooseflesh. Miri and I weren't so delicate that we wore wetsuits, but we weren't brave enough to jump straight in either. *It's cold isn't it?* I said. *Quite*, Miri agreed. Then we laughed, knowing that we hadn't come all this way just to, quite literally, dip our toes in. After a few more moments of trepidation, we took our first strokes across the water. There was that euphoric glow. That adrenaline! My body began to tingle.

The pool was so small that I floated more than I swam. Gripping the edge, I inspected the new home I found myself cocooned in. Below the limpet-scarred limestone was an underwater forest. Leathery twigs of bladderwrack branched out next to thick ribbons of treacle-brown kelp.

Clumsily, I stepped out of my swimsuit and fumbled with my knickers while I was still seabitten and damp. My hands quivered as I passed Miri the flask of coffee. We'd done it! We sat wrapped up in our coats and scarves with the sun beaming on our faces but chests still rattling. Although it couldn't have been the first time that year it was sunny, it was the first time I'd stopped to appreciate the warmth on my skin, the radiance of April's light and how golden and hopeful it was.

The journey back was a calm one. We'd completed our first swim and the sun was still shining. The headland fizzed with wildflowers, and we even spied yellow whitlow grass. Gower Peninsula is one of the only places where this flower can be found in the wild. It was a flash of yellow cushioned between two rocks. There was juniper too, and lots of it, hugging the limestone with its tangle of barbed arms. I picked up a dandelion clock and presented it to Miri. *Wish?* She puffed up her cheeks and leaned in before I pulled it away. *The job will happen, I promise. Don't waste your wish on it.* Miri had recently been made redundant from a graphic design role for a London art gallery. The search for another job was not going well. I raised the dandelion again and she gave an upturned smile. It took her a while to decide on something new, but she wished on it hard. I could tell.

I walked with my dandelion for a while. The wind stole a few wishes, but I felt confident that I still had enough in there. When was the last time I'd made a wish? I didn't bother with birthday candles anymore. It must've been years ago, sitting on the sofa with Tom, when he presented me with an eyelash and instructed me to blow. I knew from films that cancer meant losing hair, but I'd never considered the eyelashes or eyebrows. A familiar face doesn't look as familiar without them. Most of my memories of Tom are like that. Sans eyelashes, sans eyebrows. A big, bright moon face, swollen from chemotherapy. I wished I could remember his face more from before. There, a wish. That one would do. I blew and dropped the stem.

~~

Not wanting the day to end, we drove to Rhossili Bay, where the headland was packed with families in anoraks and groups dismounting racing bikes. We sat with a view out to the sea, eating whitebait with our gloves on, determined to sit outside in this first flush of spring. I made a promise to myself that, later in the year, when it would become increasingly difficult to plunge into cold water, I'd remind myself of this day and that it was a sign we should be doing this.

To a year of swimming in tidal pools, Miri said. *The tidal year!* We toasted our Bulmers together and they gave a satisfying clink. *Do you think we can really do this?* I picked at the bottle label. Miri paused and her eyes followed a man chasing a napkin down the path. *I think we should do this. And we can.*

When I had agreed to the adventure, I'd made an unwritten pact with myself that I'd do everything I could to complete it. Sat on Rhossili Bay, I was suddenly aware of the scale of it. The journey stretched out ahead of me and I imagined what it would be like. I thought first of the sense of achievement when we'd completed it, then secondly the challenges: rainy days, cancelled trains and hypothermia.

What if we miss a tidal pool? Can you imagine if we travel all the way to Scotland, then discover we forgot one in deepest darkest Glasgow or something? Or say we've done every single pool, then realise we missed a load and the whole thing's been a sham?

Well, it could happen. Not in Glasgow because there's no beach, but it could happen somewhere else, she laughed, *all we can do is commit to the research. And it's not like this is about right or wrong. Right?* I nodded. *Anyway, I'm more worried about taking time off. Not sure what's happening about work yet,* Miri trailed off, *so yeah, there's that.*

We'll do weekends. We can get most done if we get up early enough and time it right with the tide. Then there's two longer trips we'll need to do. Scotland and Cornwall to catch all the tidal pools on the southwest coast. We can manage that.

She nodded. *We'll need to time the journeys right. Think about the sea temperature, midge season, if the life-guarded pools will be closed over winter.*

That's the bit I'm looking forward to most, I said. *The route-planning? You're mad.* Miri scratched her forehead. With me not driving, she'd already taken on the burden of most of the directions. *No. The time in the car, chatting.* She smiled and her tooth that is whiter than the others flashed.

I pulled my coat around me a little tighter and contemplated our adventure in the rear-view mirror.

Something we said we'd do once but forgot about and it never actually happened. I didn't want that.

Yes, I said finally and nudged her with my elbow, *we can do this*. What I didn't say was that I needed it. I needed it so badly, and from the way Miri stayed close, I think she knew that all along.

Chapter Five

Myatt's Fields: 51.47370° N, 0.10386° W

I moved to a one-bedroom flat that I chose for its proximity to Myatt's Fields, which was full of Japanese anemones and lilac alliums that spring. Most mornings, I had my coffee on a bench and watched small birds or damselflies dance on the telephone wire. At the same time, my neighbour would emerge in pyjamas to walk his dog and we'd wave at one another with the bandstand between us. It quickly felt like home.

On moving day, Mum arrived with her toolbox to help me unpack. She's brought that same yellow metal toolbox to every flat I've ever lived in. It's full of unusual contraptions that only she knows the uses for, and it jangles with a silvery mystery that follows her everywhere. Dad likes to joke that he's never had to call a plumber, because he has Mum. That joke undersells her quiet power. She can fix a sink. And just as likely mend a boat, start a car, trim a hedge, re-chain a bike and gut a fish. She's never tried to teach me any of these things. Not because she thinks I can't, but because these acts of service are the truest way she knows how to express love.

Bubble wrap was strewn across the kitchen floor like debris covering a beach, books were liberated from their boxes and I was reunited with possessions I'd forgotten I owned. Mum unwrapped the bubble wrap from around my photo frames and paused. It was clear she'd found one of Tom as her shoulders came up close to her ears and she started crying. She released her grief in loud, velvety shudders. *Handsome boy*, she said with her fingertips touching the frame. I agreed quietly and tried to stop myself from visibly stiffening. Her grief beside mine felt like pulling on a coat and my jumper getting bunched up beneath it. I rested my hand on her back in what could only be described as a performative manner and felt myself leaving my body.

You're never sad, she wiped her tear-stained cheek with the back of her sleeve. *That's not true*, I shifted on my feet and unpacked a serving bowl that I only ever used for crisps, not salad like I suspected it was intended for. *Why do you never cry then?* I wanted to joke that I wished I knew, but she didn't appreciate my jokes. *Not everyone feels in the same way*, was all I could muster.

She blew her nose on a rolled-up tissue from her sleeve and said into it: *I miss him so much. You don't get it.* We were quiet while we stared at the pile of bubble wrap. *I do get it,* I replied finally. Something inside me began to fizz. Digging my fingernails into the fleshy part of my palm, I added under my breath, *it didn't just happen to you.*

At that point Mum left to get something from the car and didn't return for forty minutes. I stood in the empty flat Tom would never see. My insides felt like a long-burned cigarette. A stick of ash waiting for someone to tap once and turn to dust. When he'd died, I'd been so sad I'd worried I'd never feel better. Now I wished I was sadder again, because feeling nothing made me worry I was broken.

That night, I lay awake and ruminated on how things could've gone differently. I was angry that our conversation made me hold her grief in one hand and mine in the other, weighing them for size. Maybe I was wrong; maybe it *had* happened to her more than me.

Cancer had been my mum's job for three years. She became a chemist, a carer and a bookkeeper of treatments. I remembered her shiny black notepads, thick with dated logs of every appointment with every oncologist. She shielded me from all of that. I had tried once to be better. To play a larger role in the Fuck Cancer play our life had become. This was still in

Act I, when we had something that resembled energy to fight this thing. At nineteen, Tom was technically an adult, so we shouldn't have been allowed to stay overnight, but the nurses were kind and knew that the rules of Visiting Hours couldn't apply to a cancer this brutal, on a boy this young. I'd asked to sleep over in the hospital with Tom. When that night came, the nurses brought extra blankets and set up a chair for me. It must've been around 3 a.m. when I woke to the light twitching. Tom was standing by the bed, which wasn't easy for him unassisted. He leaned against the metal bars and wobbled like a spinning top.

Are you alright? I asked, then thought what a stupid question that was. *What can I get you?* I corrected. Tom shuffled to the open suitcase where there was a plastic box full of neatly organised pills. *Let me!* I jumped up. *Any of these?* I began raising packets to him and noticed my hands were shaking. I didn't know what any of these were or what they did. If he said yes, could I give them to him in the middle of the night without understanding? Was that responsible? I glanced at Mum's notepads. Her writing was a chunky, curved mess I couldn't understand. Was that 'two doses' or 'low doses'? I suddenly hated her, hated myself. *How about some water?* I suggested.

No, Tom replied and brought his hand to his forehead so it covered his eyes. He did that when he lost in *Grand Theft Auto* or Dad told him what to do. He was pissed off. I didn't know what to do, and Tom knew that. I wondered who was more embarrassed: him or me.

It's fine. I'm just going for a wee. Offering my arm for him to grip, we shuffled together to the toilet. Then I waited for him. It took a while. I walked him back into bed and went to the light switch. *Anything else I can get you?* I asked and felt it was probably the emptiest question I'd ever asked in my life. He shook his head and the fluorescent hospital lights flickered off. I wondered if he was trying not to cry. *You can cry,* I wanted to say, *I'll hold your hand.* But I didn't say that. And I didn't hold his hand either. We just went to sleep in silence, and I tried not to cry myself.

Mum arrived in the morning and seemed to magic everything away. I took for granted that mothers have this innate ability to kiss things better. She did that as much as she could. There were circles under her eyes the colour of bruised fruit. She looked tired. I'd fantasised that she'd return well-rested and grab me by the shoulders, *I really needed a good night's sleep. Thank you, darling.* In my fantasy, me staying over was to help her. Afterwards, I realised how deluded that was. It was a favour she did to let me feel like I could help.

Maybe it did all happen to Mum more than me. She'd shielded me from so much, and that shield remained opaque and concrete. Even then – as we removed bubble wrap from around my photo frames – we were still trying to find letterboxes of connection through which we could peer at one another.

Chapter Six

I'd known that a consequence of living alone was that there would be times when it would just be me, but when Mum left and it happened for the first time, it still felt strange. When I met Miri, she was living alone. I thought that seemed incredibly grown up, but also very lonely. Now that was me too. I wondered if I'd orchestrated it that way, then decided that was the romantic in me searching for reason in everything.

Miri told me that she rarely feels lonely because Kirsty Young keeps her company. She also said I had ways to meaningfully spend my time and that was a good antidote to the aches and pains of single living. Miri was right, as usual, but that didn't stop a certain melancholy creeping in some days. From my flat I could hear the bells ringing from St John the Divine. The sound of my neighbours' footsteps through the ceiling was also loud. I'd drawn out an imaginary floorplan in my mind based on how they moved and decided their flat wasn't the same layout as mine. I slept with three pillows. Two for under my head and one to hold like it was a person. On the nights I had a guest they'd use that pillow, and then I'd have a few nights of disturbed sleep because the smell made it not right to hug.

It rained all of May. I wrote that on the eighteenth but was positive that the weather wouldn't improve. The sound of it trickling down the gutter became a soundtrack of sorts. I went on lots of dates and walked there in the rain. Arriving wet gave me something to talk about for the first five minutes. I smoothed my hair down and tried to look like my pictures.

Before each date, I looked in the mirror and wasn't sure how I felt about the person looking back. She looked tired. I *was* tired. I have raven black hair that falls below my shoulders and thick dark brows to match. My hair is never styled, just brushed, because I'm busy. I have a patch of vitiligo on my left cheek that resembles the pattern on a Holstein-Friesian cow. My nose is aquiline – my least favourite thing about my face – and my smile became my favourite after I had Invisalign. Muscle memory, however, forgets that I have new teeth and I still instinctively bring my hand to cover my mouth when I laugh. I exercise my laugh lines often and tell myself their deepening around my mouth and between my brows is the only true sign of beauty. My eyes tell a slightly different story. When I started dating again, I Googled things like 'sun damage' and 'how to avoid crow's feet'. I panicked that my best years were behind me, then panicked that I was panicking about it. I was twenty-six. Miri was thirty-five. I thought she was resplendent and elegant and gorgeous and smelled of Aesop creams, COS knitwear and sophistication. I wanted to be as kind to myself as I was to her, but that felt somehow impossible.

Most of the time – on these dates, that is – I felt like I was interviewing for stand-up in the graveyard slot. Of course, I had my own routine and practised being self-deprecating about my work to show I didn't take myself too seriously, which I did. Or wasn't too intimidating, which I was. I had rehearsed punchlines about my dating history and living alone, too. Men liked to ask questions about that. *Don't you get lonely? Don't you have friends?* Then, *what's your type?* they'd ask. *Men with great taste*, I'd reply. I spoke about Tom on every date, but never in my real life. Surface-level conversations were the safe space I could say his name. Part of me was always curious to hear the reply. Most went quiet. One said, *you don't have to talk about it*, which was odd as I'd brought it up. Another cupped my left

breast and said he'd kiss it better. It was a study, a socio-
logical test, and I never enjoyed the data being
presented back to me. Really, it was a string of first
encounters designed to stop me from developing more
meaningful friendships where I'd be asked how I truly
was. There was, however, one man who I returned to
more than the others that false spring.

Marlowe was a DJ and music producer who had a
mind of cupboards and drawers that I liked to pull
open and empty, ransacking him of his wisdom like I
was packing to leave town right away. Haruki
Murakami novels, baroque instruments, bell hooks
essays, the perfect negroni. He was quick to distance
himself from any scene considered 'hip' or 'cool' while
doing things that established him as the epitome of
both: wearing men's jewellery, an apartment in New
York, friends in Tbilisi and a recording studio in Berlin.
*I've been producing a record with Shura. Have you heard of
her?* He didn't wait for a reply, then moved on to talk
about things like the transformation of trauma in the
body. I listened to him, and it was a break from myself.
I was bored of myself. He overshared, and I confused
that for intimacy. He told me about a sister who was
having IVF, but he didn't think she should. *Not on her
own.* We did that at each other. Started conversations

we should both be taking to therapy, but knew we wouldn't. Instead, we got drunk on warm saké from Brixton Market and shared too much, too quickly and concluded nothing.

I often found myself orbiting creative people like a crazy, spun-out planet. The shadow-artist in me craved what they had: confidence to share their art with the world. I was writing full-time but was too self-conscious to call myself a writer. I became an expert on an album for five days then filed the assignment and moved on to the next one. I enjoyed the bizarre specificity of it. I practised serial monogamy when listening to musicians while I wrote about them. It was a fidelity I practised nowhere else.

I love words, I love putting them together, but I didn't think I had anything to say that wasn't about someone else's art. When I tried to write stories, they came out Tom-shaped and I worried that just made me bereaved, not a storyteller. Being romantically near people I considered 'real artists' was near enough for me. Being near Marlowe felt very near.

His childhood was something from an Enid Blyton book. Seven siblings tearing through Oxfordshire countryside and retreating to a country manor full of dusty books to have tea and learn to play the harpsichord. His father was an organist and conductor. The patriarch of a brood of eccentric children, all with bizarre occupations. I liked the idea of having so many siblings that missing one wouldn't be quite so bad. Four hadn't been enough for me. Maybe six would've done it. Maybe six in-laws could make up one Tom.

Marlowe said family get-togethers were always tense because he couldn't shake the feeling that his mother was disappointed he wasn't a professional organist. I laughed, then realised he wasn't joking and rearranged my face. Shame was a big word for him. I noticed how his mouth moved when he fashioned an 's' on his lips into a noose for his own ego. Shame in society. Shame in education. Shame in masturbation. I asked if shame was his love language, and he bristled. I said boarding-school boys had been my downfall before. *Good. We should all be aware of our own red flags. Mine are women talking about astrology or wanting to cuddle.* I asked why. *Think about what they can't give themselves that they need from you*, he replied, and I've thought about that a lot ever since.

On our second date, Marlowe wore the same shirt and jacket as the first. He was living out of a suitcase and calling it a lifestyle. A rootless travelling man with no permanent residence. I thought I could be his home for a while. He was filthy and delicious; all made more tempting by him being a former chorister. I couldn't help myself. He was direct and said he'd come back to mine, but only if I knew he wouldn't stay over.

It felt like something I wanted to know about myself. Could I detach that much? The answer was yes. But I wouldn't do it again. My orgasm was shallow and meaningless, delivered by someone who'd already tried to set my expectations low. He didn't let me hold him. We said goodbye, and I slept alone again, listening to the rain fall down the drain outside my window. I promised myself not again. And he said: *no, not again. Until next time.*

I enjoyed our conversations over oceans while he was back somewhere else. *How's your album?* I'd say. *How's your writing?* he'd reply. *When will I know it's done?* I asked him about a story I was working on. *When it resonates more as the end of something than the beginning.* I waited for the feeling to come.

That was how it went. We messaged, then didn't. There was no accountability or continuity to our relationship, which seemed to comfort and pain us both. There was a distance in him I related to, and rubbing up against one another felt like I might get closer to myself. He rubbed me like I was a lucky coin. Rubbed me like his thumbprint might disappear. His body was a shell I put to my ear, waiting for the sound of the ocean. Nothing. We echoed into one another, our mouths caves to these deep empty parts of ourselves. *Not again,* I said. *No, until next time,* he replied.

Chapter Seven

Brockwell Lido: 51.45298° N, 0.10614° W

I cut a fringe as if new hair might make me feel better. Using the kitchen scissors, I hacked at it while listening to FKA Twigs. It looked awful. This was something I did. When feeling restless I tried to force a change. Usually a new hairstyle, new man or new flat. I like packing up and leaving. I've never completed a tenancy at any place I've ever lived, and I'm incredibly motivated by newness. New desk, new flowers in a crisp porcelain vase, new curtains to open instead of the old roll blinds, new address to click Remember for Next Time on Safari.

Once the lido reopened, Miri and I resumed our routine of swimming followed by coffee. Those mornings were the signposts in the week for me to stop and take a moment. A pause that I enjoyed sharing with her. I chained up my bike and got frustrated by the lock, glancing up at Brockwell Park sloping before me, running long past the hill and tennis courts out of view. Squashing my body and swimming bag through the turnstiles, I directed a lot of physical anger towards the slidey metal thing that never recognised my lido pass. Miri was already waiting by the poolside. There was a momentary twitch in her eye when she saw me. She was surprised by the fringe. *Don't ask*, I covered it with my hand. I'd hoped it would effortlessly part like Jane Birkin, but I looked like a budget Noel Fielding at best. Miri pulled me in towards her and whispered into my hair, *you look fabulous*.

One of the small delights of lockdown was that the changing rooms were closed so everyone stripped by the water. It created a sense of community that we'd all been missing. I enjoyed the normality of nudity. Seeing a flash of skin that wasn't sexualised. Just a body about to do the amazing thing of moving itself across a fifty-metre pool.

Although our lido passes said we were out of winter season, I wasn't finding the water welcoming. Standing in the shallow end, we stared at one another and laughed. *Please, I insist . . .* Miri gestured to the water, inviting me to take the plunge. *No no, I insist! After you.* Keeping my arms folded, I pushed her with my hips. Miri looked around the pool, as if worried we had an audience. *Come on, we'd better get going or we'll freeze.* This hesitation was part of our routine, and it was always Miri who started swimming first. Once she got far enough away from me, I fretted about keeping up and waded until I had to start swimming. We were quiet for a while as the cold gripped our lungs tight as a clenched fist. Then my mind cleared of all thoughts.

After the first length, my body was no longer covered in pins and needles. Rolling back my shoulders to relax my neck, I breaststroked alongside Miri and we took up the width of the slow lane. *Can you do another?* I asked and she nodded from the pool edge where she was gripping the concrete. I pushed the wall away with my feet and glided onto my back. Bare branches swayed above the low brick building; the sweeping pale concrete lintels formed a rhythm like the lido went on forever.

We bundled ourselves into the Lido Cafe, stocky and layered as if wearing every item of clothing we owned. The adrenaline of the swim wore off fast and was replaced by vicious shivers. We waved at Pete, who gestured to our usual table under the heater. *Coffee?* He chewed his pencil. He was the only waiter who swam. Sometimes in winter he'd take our order then come back five minutes later and ask again, too cold to remember after a pre-shift dip. Pete shuttled over our coffees and two fat golden croissants that we tore apart with our fingers hiding beneath our knitwear. Miri pulled her sleeves over her wrists and held her flat white. *How's the unpacking? You settled?*

Just about. Not been in much. I scratched the back of my neck where my hair was still wet. *Where've you been?* I shrugged, *out*. Miri sipped. She tended to sip or chew when she was trying not to display any judgement on her face. I sensed this line of enquiry would lead to her finishing her coffee quite quickly. *I went out with Marlowe again this week.*

How was that? I nodded, and she asked what I liked about him. Pursing my lips together, I wondered why the easiest questions always seemed so hard to answer. *I suppose he's interesting. I feel like he could talk about anything.* Miri sipped again. *He did say something I've been thinking about.* Miri moved the menu out the way. *We were talking about red flags . . .*

Miri butted in, *interesting date topic. Was this four?* I proudly clarified that it was our sixth, which, by London's dating standards, was quite monumental. *And he said his were astrology and someone who wants to cuddle.* I tried to ignore Miri scrunching up her nose and continued, *he said that it's a red flag because it makes him wonder what they need from him that they can't get from themselves.*

Well, a hug. Clearly, Miri blinked, *you literally can't give yourself a hug.* She caught Pete's attention and ordered two more coffees. They arrived quickly, but this time in bowlish green cups, and were plonked down. Pete wiped the spillage with his linen apron. *I mean, that's ludicrous. You know that right?* I didn't look up. *Such flawed logic, it's astounding.*

Maybe he has a point . . . I started to defend Marlowe, but Miri interrupted. *It's ok to want a hug though. Isn't it?* She was asking not because she wasn't sure, but to hear me agree. I nodded blandly.

I hope this won't be another 'be careful because you only get twelve chances with me' situation. I wriggled my jaw and Miri reached out to touch my arm. *Oh, I'm sorry. I love that you give people chances! He sounds smart and . . . interesting, but he's clearly scared of something. Being close to people maybe?* I thought back to him making excuses to leave and talking about his seven siblings with such distance that he could've been talking about characters of a book he'd half-finished and left on a holiday home bookshelf.

I decided I would see him again, just to be sure, then changed the subject. *This weekend, shall we leave early? Then we can travel there, have a swim and still have time to walk into town for lunch.* We paid for our coffees and left the lido, with a plan to visit another tidal pool.

Chapter Eight

Devil's Point: 50.36124° N, 4.16124° W

Miri and I visited Devil's Point shortly after it had its first spring clean in two years. Over lockdown the pool had filled with seaweed, grit and stones and the locals were beginning to complain about the scummy layer of green and accompanying smell. By the weekend of our visit in early May, it had been restored to a shining rectangle of water nestled on the pebbled beach. I'd hoped the tidal pool would be a metaphor of sorts and I'd leave feeling renewed.

The tidal pool was a forty-minute walk from the station, which led us through an unassuming part of Plymouth. We passed a Kwik-Fit, a takeaway called Union Jack and World Cuisine and a large discount furniture warehouse selling settees with the sunken imprint of the families who'd sat on them for over a decade. The smell of salt on the breeze let us know we were getting closer. We approached a row of painted houses and thought of names for each colour:

tangerine, lavender, sky. I said I'd live in the purple one and buy a matching raincoat. Miri chose the charcoal grey. Then finally the terraced houses fell away, and the sea was laid out before us.

Resting on the southern tip of the Stonehouse Peninsula, the concrete tidal pool has been there for nearly a hundred years. It's a simple structure made of four concrete walls. The treacherous tides converging on the shore made it clear how this part of the coast got its name. Miri gave me a look that hinted that it was smaller than she'd expected. Despite being only a few metres wide, Firestone Bay was busy. A family with flasks of something hot were sitting against the limestone sea defence while a dog-walker threw a stick into the waves and watched his springer spaniel retrieve it again and again. By the pool, a collection of friends chatted with their hands buried deep in their pockets, and in the distance stand-up paddleboarders skated past, jeering when the first of their group fell in and shrieked at the cold. It was good to see everyone having their own spring clean. It would've been easy to stay inside and yet there we all were, outside and hoping for something new with spring's arrival.

Two young girls were in the water. They politely stopped jumping long enough for us to climb in. Both were wearing shortie wetsuits that came just below their knees and elbows with nifty-looking waterproof boots. *So we don't step on the stones at the bottom*, one of them told us. *You look like my cousin*, the other added. *Is she nice?* I asked, to which she shrugged. They dipped and dived, submerging their heads and kicking their legs up. Miri and I neatly lapped the pool in measured breaststroke, circling the girls while they played. A sudden chill swept over the water. The youngest turned to the other, *is wind made when the birds flap their wings?* Spitting a stream of water into her face, the other replied. *No, silly. It's God blowing his nose.*

When we were done admiring the view from our infinity pool, we waved goodbye. They paused from jumping in long enough to shout, *see ya*, then clasped hands and leapt back into the water. We returned to our piles of clothes, shivering, and found them soaked. I pulled on my soggy socks while my chest hummed from the cold. As we left, the youngest turned onto her back and looked up at the sky with her arms and legs splayed out like a starfish. *Floating is like flying*, she said, and I thought that it was.

My sister wanted to come and visit me in London, which was a sure sign that she'd been talking about me with Mum. I spent a lot of my adult life avoiding Emma because she knew me better than anyone else.

She had this way of looking at me where her eyes turned to mirrored pools and I never liked what they reflected.

I played the role of fun older sister and took her out for pizza, then the Prince of Wales rooftop because on Fridays they have a live saxophonist who plays over dodgy R&B music. Somehow, in this alternate night-life reality a sweaty man in a Burton shirt and brown shoes was a god. I was happy for him that he'd found a place to exist like that.

I pushed the laminated menu across the bar towards Emma. *Cottontails?* I asked. When Emma was little, she'd mispronounced cocktails and it's been our joke ever since. There was so much about our grief that was unsaid, but between siblings there's also lots that doesn't need saying. You understand each other in a way that's instinctive and historical. Rohanna once told me that when a sibling dies you lose a part of your past, present and future. I wasn't sure what the future looked like for Emma and me. I hoped there'd be a bench for us, but that wish felt difficult to share. Keeping our conversations in the past was somehow more comfortable.

Emma raised her eyebrow at the drinks list. *Jeez Louise, London is pricey*. I paid for two of whatever she wanted, which I instantly regretted as the double vodka slimline tonics tasted like firewater. We danced to music I remembered having on our shared battery-powered MP3 player and Emma talked for too long to a group of people wearing matching fluorescent golf visors until I pulled her away by her bag.

When Fergie's 'London Bridge' started playing, Emma leaned in close and tried to tell me something. Her breath, rancid with alcohol, was hot on my neck. I couldn't tell if she was shouting because of the loud music or because she was angry about something. *No one ever said Tom was going to die.* My breathing became ragged. I put my hand to my ear and pretended not to have heard. The saxophonist was strolling towards us with his instrument hanging from him by a stupid nylon neck brace. I was suddenly exceptionally irritated by him. *Why didn't you tell me he was going to die?* Emma pushed. I felt lightheaded and wanted to sit down. I thought about what to say: I didn't know, I'm sorry, I still can't believe it, no one told me either. My hand moved towards her and hovered in the space between us. *Let me get us some more drinks,* I said and escaped to the bar.

I just need a minute, I thought, then allowed everyone else to be served first to buy myself some extra time. I thought about the promise I had made Tom the last time I saw him. I tipped back a stranded glass of wine. Swallowing stopped me crying. I leaned on the bar – which was a mistake as it made my forearms sticky – and texted Marlowe: *I'm an awful sister.* I don't know what I expected him to say, and apparently neither did he as three dots appeared then vanished. Eventually, I returned to Emma with Apple Sourz. She liked those. They were sweet. Emma took both and shot them, then wiped her mouth with the back of her hand without looking at me. We didn't speak about Tom again.

As quickly as the dates we'd had sped by, Marlowe ghosted me. I grieved his disappearance like it was some kind of death. Somehow it was easier for me to lose myself in feeling lovesick than anything Tom-related. Heartache was a predictable emotion that those around me could understand. I mourned the loss of our imagined coupledom, then called Miri daily with updates, although there were none.

Tunnels Beach

Chapter Nine

I woke to the sound of the door banging. Rubbing my tongue over my furry teeth, I glanced in the mirror. I had mascara on my face even though I'd scrubbed eco-friendly bamboo pads under my eyes until they'd turned red. *Thanks*, I mumbled as I accepted a delivery then closed the door. It was *Grief Works: Stories of Life, Death and Surviving* by Julia Samuel. It was probably a kind but passive-aggressive invitation to open up from Mum. I tossed it onto the sofa and put the kettle on.

Towards the end of last year, I'd finished the first draft of a novel I'd been secretly working on. When I was editing the manuscript, I realised that any time a character had to do some thinking, I'd write that they put the kettle on. Every time I made a cup of tea I thought about that. I didn't know which was more daunting: giving up on the manuscript or working on it for another six months only to find it was still awful.

Sitting in front of my laptop, I opened the usual tabs – Twitter, Pitchfork, Poetry Foundation and the *New Yorker* – to start my day with caffeine and a humming, low level of inferiority and social anxiety. I looked at last night's search history to find an article I'd intended to read and despair about humanity titled 'With the Clock Running Out, Humans Need to Rethink Time Itself'. At 2:04 a.m. I'd searched: *Sad or depressed, Depression grief same thing, Grief books, Books on grief not old, Wet look lingerie.* Apparently, I thought a latex suspender belt would fix everything. Maybe it would. I'd find out in three to five working days.

Swim? I texted Miri. She sent me the *Sex and the City* GIF where Carrie's dancing in her closet. I scratched my crotch, which was unusually itchy, then put my swimsuit on under my jeans. I texted Miri again, *can you get chlamydia from fingering?* She replied instantly, *you can get chlamydia from nearly anything. Google it.* I saw three dots. *But fingering? Retro. Good for you.*

A final gift from Marlowe? We'd used condoms, but what about hand stuff? I tried to retrace our actions like the ball and cup magic trick. Suddenly I was paranoid. After inspecting my knickers and WebMD, I concluded it was either thrush or BV. I shuffled into Boots and searched for the 'Feminine Hygiene' aisle then stared at the bacterial vaginosis or thrush test kits. £10.49. Fucking hell. Why did we put up with this? I'd have to come back and spend another tenner on a tube of Canesten. I stared at the Femfresh soap and deodorant bottles in the shape of pink shells and felt a wave of cunt shame wash over me. I put the test in my pocket and walked out the shop. *Fuck you, Big Pharma.*

It'd only been two and a half hours since messaging Miri for a swim, and my attempts to distract myself from Marlowe hadn't worked. While waiting at the lido, I turned my phone off and on again then texted Miri to check it was definitely working. Of course, it was. Finally I turned it from Silent to Sound On, which I hadn't done since I'd bought it. Marlowe wasn't getting in touch again.

When we arrived at the campsite Doug, the owner of Owl Valley, greeted us. Miri and I had taken a long weekend to camp in North Devon so we could tick Tunnels Beach, Bude Sea Pool and Westward Ho! off our tidal pool list. Doug looked like he'd come close to being cast as Hagrid, but they'd decided to go with someone more human-sized. Despite a chill in the air, he was wearing shorts, Velcro sandals and a Chelmsford Sausage & Cider Fest '06 t-shirt with a hole under the armpit. His belly was rotund, his beard scraggly, and he had a bald head like a newly washed potato. Doug helped us unload our bags from the car and threw them into a trailer, which his son-in-law pulled behind a quad bike. *I'll walk you to the cabin*, he nodded.

What a gorgeous place you have here, Miri said and asked Doug how long he'd been in this corner of the world. The path narrowed, and I let them walk ahead. I enjoyed showing up at places with Miri; she was good at making generic small talk feel genuine. Perhaps it had something to do with her ability to maintain eye contact without blinking much. Doug told us that when his mother died he'd decided he wanted to change his life with the money, so he'd bought this plot of land with no planning permission and persuaded his daughter to move, along with her children, from Essex to North Devon.

Although we'd booked a tent, we were staying in a cabin as an internet outage, common at Owl Valley apparently, meant they'd accidentally double-booked. The upgrade was fine with us. The cabin was built on timber stilts and beneath it the woodland sloped into a babbling brook. Nettles and bracken had grown tall, so it was entirely secluded from anyone and anything, except the sound of the stream. A wooden deck wrapped around one central room, with a kitchen and bathroom built on the outside walls. The furniture consisted of a bed (inside) and a table (outside) that had a mosaic sun in the centre. Outside, there was a steel unit with a hob, sink and nails hammered into the wood that served to hang kitchen utensils. I'd only known Doug for fifteen minutes, but I felt incredibly proud of him to have built this place. Everything I'd ever achieved suddenly felt insignificant and I wished I'd worked towards something as tangible and satisfying as an outdoor kitchenette with a nail that perfectly fits a spatula.

I thought about a life where my family started a campsite. It wouldn't have occurred to me to dream about moving away together until Tom got ill. I wondered if it was the same for Doug. Once, I'd been donating blood and the nurse had said to me, *what's your story then*, and I wasn't sure what he meant. *No one comes here without a story*, he said. I had returned to the office and told my colleagues about my exchange with the nurse. *I hate needles*, one said and the other agreed. I worked with them both for two more years and I don't think either ever signed up, despite one bragging that he had a particularly rare blood-type. If I was able to view Tom's death as something that could deliver me perspective, as much as it delivered me pain, I wondered what I could do. Tidal pools had seemed a good place to start.

Chapter Ten

Our first tidal pool in North Devon was Tunnels Beach. Lots of the research for this trip had been guess-work that left us unsure if we'd find a swimmable pool (or anything at all), but Tunnels Beach was quite the institution. There was a website with pop-up information boxes, ticket office that charged the £3 entrance fee and leaflets with high- and low-season prices for weddings. We could even hire a striped deck chair for the day. Tunnels Beach was man-made in the 1820s. It was hand-carved by Welsh miners hired to create a network of six tunnels through the Ilfracombe hillside. It took them two years to carve the tunnels. As we entered, I noticed the pickaxe marks still visible along the walls.

In Victorian times, there was gender-segregated swimming and horse-drawn boxes called bathing machines, which were wheeled to the water's edge to protect the modesty of the ladies. Women were allocated Wildersmouth Beach, and the men got a boat to Crewkhorne Cove where they could swim nude. Lucky them. There was a bugler who sat between the pools and if anyone attempted to spy on the women, they'd blow an alarm call.

The tidal pool was formed by damming back the water, so it's covered by the sea twice a day and is always kept full of clean water. That meant we should've checked if the tide was spring or neap, but it was only when we arrived that we realised we'd got the timing all wrong. *Damn it*, Miri said. *Wasn't it about this time yesterday?* I replied.

Miri turned around. *You know the tide is a different time every day, don't you?* The wind disturbed her hair, but she stood still. *Don't say that like I'm stupid*, I said defensively. *The moon and sun are the same every day, why is the tide different?* She thought about it, *good point. I don't know*. I've since learned that most shorelines experience two high and low tides within a twenty-four-hour period. The first high tide is caused when the sea is closer to the moon and its gravitational pull creates a tidal bulge. The second is created by the rotational force of the Earth and moon orbiting a common centre of mass, which is worth knowing if you're travelling around Britain to swim in tidal pools.

Accepting failure, we went into town for flaky battered haddock from The Ilfracombe Fryer, where we had a disagreement about whether to pay for a whole bottle of ketchup because they didn't have sachets for takeaways. I won, as I refused to eat my chips without any condiments, but in many ways I was the real loser, as I spent the rest of the weekend worrying that the bottle of Heinz in my backpack would explode. We passed a parish church with a clock tower sign that read: *It Is Time To Seek The Lord*, then towards the harbour we saw the Damien Hirst sculpture, *Verity*, piercing the clouds with her sword. I admired it for a while, and my chest inflated in awe of the female body and its strength. This feeling didn't last long as a tanned, meaty man pointed to the sculpture's exposed, pregnant breasts and said, *put 'em away love*.

My maternal grandmother's name is June, and when the smell of the first fallen apples fills the air and I start sitting in the shade rather than the sun, I always think of her more. During the war, she lived in Ilfracombe. Her father was a chef in the Merchant Navy and worked on the North Atlantic run bringing food back from America in a convoy. In 1942 he came home with an address written on a slip of paper and told my great-grandmother to go to Devon where they'd be looked after. She travelled with her two small children to Mrs Jewel's Guest House, which was taking in families fleeing London. By 1943 my great-grand-father was invalided from the Navy for ulcers, which Grandma said was from the stress of being chased by German submarines. They stayed in Ilfracombe as a family for three years before they ran out of money and returned to London, where my great-grandfather worked in a restaurant in Argyll Street. Before I visited, I asked Grandma June if she'd ever been to Tunnels Beach and she recalled a vague memory of boys being whistled down when they tried to climb the cliffs. She later went to a convent school so was not keen on swimming. *It was a mortal sin to wear a swimsuit*, she told me.

I've never met anyone who can pull off a pair of leather driving gloves quite like my grandmother. Unfortunately, I don't possess her ability to cook a honeyed ham and new potatoes for twelve. I did, however, inherit her mistrust in men. This seemed to skip a generation and only presented itself as mild caution, then wild abandon, when my mum fell in love with Dad.

When Mum was nine and her brothers ten and fourteen, her father left for a woman twenty years younger. Before their separation, their family life is well documented. There's cinefilm that shows the three children and immortalises my grandmother's gorgeousness, her hair organised in curls on her head and the way she held a box handbag. There are few photographs, and certainly no cinefilm, from afterwards. Mum didn't see her father until she walked to a phone box to call him many years later. I've often thought about visiting the phone box in Wales as a significant artefact in her life. Her father is a character that can do no wrong. Because of this, she views love as unconditional. In accepting that, I've come to understand her. If she were to think too much about the phone box, there would be no father in her life.

On our second trip to Tunnels Beach the pool was visible. I bought the guide from the kiosk and smiled at the attendant who recognised us. The swim was worth the wait. Clear water, blue sky, body tingling. I put my head under and it was the brain freeze of a hundred ice creams in one plunge. The real majesty of Tunnels Beach isn't the water, but the view from the tidal pool wall as you look towards the rocks, carved in the rough shape of the coastline. The boundaries are sensitive, gentle. They respond to the environment: boulders and lime mortar all as one.

There's a story to tell there and I could feel the past lives around me as I swam. The tunnels have told many stories. Before they were carved, the coves were used by smugglers and William de Tracy even took refuge in a cave here after the murder of Thomas Becket, Archbishop of Canterbury. The pool is surrounded by basin-like rockpools made famous by Philip Henry Gosse, a biologist and friend of Charles Darwin, who found new seawater species there. After his discoveries, tourists flooded to this beach to collect seashells and search for crabs. It was nice to watch children continuing the natural urge to pick up unusual things and turn them over in their palms, to stick their noses into nature and marvel at the weird and wonderful creatures hiding in Tunnels Beach.

We swam for far too long, taking breaks to sit on the tidal pool wall and look back at the beach. Swimming in early spring was an exercise in knowing my own limits. The day was dizzyingly beautiful, but the water was still cold and I needed to be careful not to stay in too long or I'd risk hypothermia, which can happen even on sunny days. *I'm done for now*, I said and was nudged along by the waves on my way back to shore. There was enough of an edge that I needed the zip of my coat done right up beneath my chin, but when I leaned back and the sun hit my face, I could pretend it was summer. Couples, families and friends were doing the same, sitting on deck chairs or picnic blankets in layers of winter clothing to enjoy the beach. *I adore British people*, I thought.

The Tunnels Beach guidebook was at the bottom of my bag and the corners were frilled where my swimsuit had dampened the pages. Miri got changed under her towel while I read it to her. It said that, back then, swimming wasn't something for pleasure but more a sea-water cure. I asked Miri if she swam for pleasure or for her ailments. She peered over her sunglasses, *entirely for the ailments of modern life*. An excerpt from the *North Devon Journal* in 1859 said a Mr Charles William Clarke travelled from Clifton to Ilfracombe as he was recommended sea swimming 'for the benefit of his health, having recently suffered from indisposition.' He wasn't a strong swimmer and the swell carried him out of his depth. His body was found a few hours later. It said, 'the deceased was bereft of his wife about two years since, and leaves an only child, a five-year-old girl.' His 'indisposition' made sense then. He was grieving, like me, and someone had thought the water might do him good. Not waving, but drowning. I recalled making jokes about my dead brother on my date with Marlowe. I closed the guidebook, which hadn't given me the distraction I'd hoped for, and looked out to sea.

Chapter Eleven

Westward Ho! Tidal Pool: 51.04082° N, 4.24309° W

Westward Ho!'s exclamation mark really jumped off the signage when the village carefully pootled into view from the A39. The name comes from Charles Kingsley's 1855 novel *Westward Ho!*, which was set in nearby Bideford. When it became a bestseller, local entrepreneurs renamed the village to attract tourists. I'd intended to read the book before our trip, but when I found it in the library and skimmed past lines like 'in the glorious fight of 1588, what had we been by now but a popish appanage of a world-tyranny' I decided I'd rather not. The town still felt rather dusty. There was a caravan park, Tesco Express and a carousel amusement and adventure golf. Perhaps 'dusty' was an unkind retelling, as we visited on a quiet evening when the sky was paper white and I wasn't in the mood to enjoy much. I was always searching for ways to satiate my appetite for future promise. It kept me from being present because the present was a place that'd been too painful for too long. I loved being about to go to the tidal pools and I loved being nearly there, but visiting our second in North Devon, knowing they'd be behind me soon, made me melancholy. I wondered if I'd destabilised myself so much from life's bad stuff that I couldn't feel the good stuff either. I was just stuck in the middle.

Although it was Saturday, the beach was quiet that evening. England were playing Ukraine in the Euros and everyone was inside watching the game. Houses had their windows ajar and every now and then we'd hear a cheer or groan. Miri and I sat cross-legged on the tidal pool wall and waited for the water to boil on our Trangia so we could make pesto pasta. Steam furled out of the stove and I took a moment to appreciate how the nature had organised itself. Westward Ho! tidal pool is a square painted with neat white lines stamped with 1.2M DEEP END in black. It's surrounded by boulders, rocky shelves and the nearby Pebble Ridge. Spring tides wash the pebbles back. Each year locals meet for 'potwalloping' and throw them back to restore the bank, followed by food and festivities.

A cheer came from the houses beyond the coastal path. I thought about World Cups past with my family crowded around the TV. Once the cheering had subsided, the beach was quiet again. It was just us. The waves were so far away, protected by the rocks, that I couldn't hear them lapping against the shore. I wanted to speak the memory into existence, but suddenly my tongue felt swollen like a sea mollusc, white-grey and lolling.

Tom liked football, I said and Miri looked surprised, like she hadn't expected me to say that. *Did he?* I didn't answer, because it didn't feel like she meant it as a question, more buying time. *What else did he like?* I thought about it. Sailing boats, Robinsons Barley Water, dancing to McFly, his red car, bright orange life jackets, *Ice Road Truckers,* Calippo lollies. Instead, I said, *dunno. Boys seem to just like football don't they,* though that wasn't really true. Tom had been more into boats than football. It was just too painful to think of things he liked that were no longer touched by his existence.

I'm not a football person. Believe me when I say I've tried. For a while I thought it was the great life-hack. Pretend to be into football and all the men in your life will adore you. It was a way to get uninterrupted quality time with my dad or brothers, but I wasn't really a fan and they knew it too.

Football games from our childhood feel hazy to me too, which is a shame, because there are finite matches

I ever experienced with Tom. I can't get more, and I wish I could remember the ones I had, but back then I'd been wishing for half-time once Lawrence had corrected me enough times when I called it the interval.

I remembered one match for everything but the game. It must've been World Cup 2010 because I remember there being a general unease from Tom because the identity of The Stig had been revealed and he wasn't enjoying *Top Gear* the same. Everyone came to our house so we could feel the full extent of our seven-person brood, plus friends and family. There were so many of us that we'd moved the television and wooden stand outside where everyone went to great lengths to remind people to: *watch the cable*. Tom was wearing one of Howard's old football shirts that had BECKHAM on the back, though these were the Gerrard and Rooney days. It was a bit small for him and he kept having to pull it down. Everyone shouted at the TV so loud that the three littlest of us didn't know what was going on, but we didn't need to because the swell of family directed us to joy or misery, and we mimicked their expressions in turn by jumping up or sitting solemnly with our hands besides our cheeks. When the ball slipped through Rob Green's hands, Tom tried to copy Lawrence and swear at the television, but Mum quickly put an end to that.

Whenever the twins played football in the garden, they used their jumpers as makeshift goal posts and would shout *Green!* when they missed. That's what's so special about siblings; you have a shared language, a shared history that you can rely on to speak to one another. Emma and Tom had a language as twins long before ours as siblings. I remember them babytalking to one another from their cots. I'd peer over and see them both babbling, having full conversations before they even knew words.

It could be lonely, being a sibling to twins. There were moments when I felt excluded or outright forgotten, like I'd entered a party and everyone was in on a joke I didn't understand. I learned early that rather than feeling jealous, it was better to watch this special thing I had a close relationship to. This special, strange, awesome thing that is twins.

More often than Emma called Tom her twin, she called him her Soul Twin.

That Sunday, I called Emma and asked her if she remembered watching the 2010 World Cup together. She said she didn't, so I asked if she remembered shouting *Green!* when we missed a goal. She didn't. Emma'd stopped playing quite young, though she'd been good at it. I had a suspicion it was because she knew Tom hated his twin sister being the footie star. Instead, she took up rugby and was selected for the county team, then later played for the firsts at university. This is the kind of person Emma is. Always putting others first. Always trying to make everyone else happy. Even on the phone that day, I could hear a tug in her voice as she tried to join me on a recollection which I didn't often invite her on. *Maybe I do remember*, she said once we'd moved on, *I'm probably not remembering hard enough.*

Chapter Twelve

Tom's Bedroom: 51.27198° N, 0.40136° W

The night we visited Westward Ho!, I woke up during the same dream I always have. I didn't like to call it a nightmare, because I believed that gave it too much power. If anything, it was more of a memory. Alcohol usually made me feel fuzzy enough to fall asleep again, but we didn't have any in the cabin. I walked outside to the makeshift bathroom, squeezed toothpaste onto my finger and sucked it. The bitter taste stopped me thinking about my dream for a while. I let my weight sink into the mattress and tried to stay still so I wouldn't wake Miri. She had a job interview in two days and needed rest.

There was no window in the cabin, but I imagined all that was outside to help me sleep. There was fizzing cow parsley, which would be heavy and weighted by rain. Water droplets falling from the flower heads, momentarily unbalancing them before they'd spring back to upright. *I should start a journal*, I thought. Then

I worried the page would be full of this stirring in my chest that woke me up and left behind a general unease and mistrust of the world, so I thought best not write for now.

People told me *the memories will be yours forever* and *you'll never forget*. But you do. I did, at least. Survival had meant shutting out all of the pain and in doing so, I'd shut out Tom's memory. I didn't want to admit to myself that I couldn't hear his voice or remember his face so clearly anymore. He was fading. I knew that if I practised, the images would regain strength. I should hold him in my mind and map his face, chart his movements and plot our shared history. Closing my eyes, I tried to remember. A hot pain seared through my sinuses. I clenched my eyes shut to block the tears. It often felt like I had to choose between moving forward and losing him forever or remembering and living in pain. I hoped one day it wouldn't feel like such a choice. When it didn't, I'd write.

The memory that arrived in my dreams was from a day I'd visited my parents. Mum was exhausted. She'd been up with Tom for a period of sleepless nights. *Come back with me to London*, I said that afternoon, *we can go for lunch somewhere nice and it'll take your mind off things for a bit*. Instantly, I regretted it.

She poked her tongue in the inside of her cheek and exhaled sharply while continuing to organise pills into day-of-the-week boxes. *My mind's never not on Tom. Today's not a good day. We'll get lunch another time.* I was acting like I knew best, because none of us knew what we were doing. Dad agreed it was a good idea and said he'd look after Tom, which was a kind but empty gesture. Although no one would admit it, we all knew Tom only wanted her. Eventually, Mum said fine and told me to say good-bye to my brother. I didn't know then that it would be the last time I saw him at home.

Tom was in his bedroom and when he heard foot-steps on the landing, he called out for Mum. *It's me,* I smiled as I opened the door. He looked visibly disap-pointed, and I tried not to be offended. I walked to the window and started talking about taking Mum for lunch, asking him not to make too big a deal of it so she could get out for a while. When I opened the curtains he screamed. Tom pulled his duvet over his head and cried. I froze with my hand on the curtain, shocked. Pulling them shut again, I returned to the bed where I pressed my hand to the arch of his shoul-der beneath the covers. His body moved up and down against my palm. It rattled as he exhaled. I thought about how much his body was failing him, and keep-ing him going. I considered hugging him, but was too scared to feel him crying against me. I removed my hand and went back downstairs.

Mum asked how Tom was doing. My throat felt tight so I said nothing and just nodded. We went out for lunch. I don't remember what we ate. I don't remember having a particularly nice time.

Tom died a week later, and I've always felt that Mum resents me for losing time with him in those final days. When we were all more exhausted, she's said as much. I know she didn't mean to. Mostly because we both know it's true so there was no point hurting my feelings over it.

I had a new relationship with that memory all the time. First, I felt bad for my mother, then I felt bad for Tom and I knew one day I would feel bad for me. When Tom was ill, I'd never thought about what it felt like to have cancer. I don't think my brain would've let me wonder. It would've made it all too difficult. I couldn't cope with knowing Tom's life would end. It was too awful and too strange. Tom was sitting in bed lifting a glass of water that I'd filled to his lips. And he'd be gone? Gone where? I couldn't comprehend it.

Then the dream started and it became impossible not to imagine the pain. His scream when the light flooded the room was the worst part. I thought a lot about why he cried out and what was happening inside him. Did the light hurt his eyes? Was it a headache? Was he nauseous?

There was a deep shame on my chest like an invisible, unshiftable boulder. Guilt that I'd stolen precious time from my mum, but also guilt that I hadn't offered Tom compassion. I hadn't sat with him and witnessed his pain. I hadn't asked if he was scared of dying. I hadn't been a sister who held his hand the day he was born and wasn't afraid to hold his hand when he was dying. Instead, I walked away.

I wondered how different that day would've been if I'd taken the time to sit down on Tom's bed and ask what hurt or how I could help. I wondered how different my life would be if I'd kept the promise I made to him the next time I saw him, the last time before he died. Would I be able to offer myself compassion, knowing I'd given it so generously to him? Instead, I struggled to accept compassion from anyone, including myself, knowing that I had never truly offered it to Tom.

Bude Sea Pool

Chapter Thirteen

Bude Sea Pool: 50.83274° N, 4.55403° W

After a bad night's sleep, I knew the best possible place to be was the sea. The only thing that could cure me was saltwater. I thought of Tunnels Beach and how it cured the ailments of so many. I was quiet beside Miri on the journey to Bude Sea Pool, itching to get my hit. The tidal pool was built beside Summerleaze beach in the 1930s and is a semi-natural pool, carved into the rocks. It's large (about the size of a football pitch) and rugged. Its spot just under the cliffs reminded me that, one day, this place on the coast will be gone. Crumbled to dust, ash, nothing. How many years will that take? Was a year the same for sandstone as it was for me? I tried to put my life in relation to the nature around me. I was happy we'd touched one another. For now – in this special moment in place and time – there was a tidal pool at Summerleaze and there were people enjoying it.

As we approached, we were greeted by a 'BUDE SEA POOL' sign and steel-fence enclosure. Further along was another that read 'No Lifeguard on Duty', then 'No Diving and No Dogs in the Pool'. Further still one simply shouted 'Danger' in hard-hat yellow. Around the pool, I noticed many instructions: 'NEVER DIVE OR JUMP into Bude Sea Pool.' 'STAY AWAY from the cliff.' 'DON'T RUN around Bude Sea Pool.' 'TREAD CAREFULLY around and in Bude Sea Pool.' Shielding my face from the sun with my hand, I looked towards the beach where the waves roared. The tidal pool meant swimmers could dive into the saltwater of the Atlantic, while protected from its ferocity. On the beach there were no safety signs but here, where it was safer, there were rules. It didn't make sense.

I stripped by the side and tried to shake the temptation to jump in. I'd been forewarned. My eyes were weary from lack of sleep and a lump in my throat reminded me of my dream. I held my nose and leapt where the water looked deepest. The diamonds on the surface scattered, my skin blazed and I felt human again.

Back on the poolside, we had an opportunity to admire the pastel beach huts and volunteers look-out. There was a trestle table laid out, with volunteers crowded around selling tea towels and mugs with a lino-cut design of the pool. It was easy to see, and feel, that people really cared. I felt momentarily bad for disobeying their signs and jumping in. Rule-breakers' remorse led me to buy a postcard and tea towel. We stopped to chat with a volunteer who told us more about the work she did with Friends of Bude Sea Pool. In 2010, public funding was withdrawn so the organisation campaigned to keep it open and took on management the following year. They've since made repairs and invested in facilities, all while keeping it free. *Did you know we have to raise at least £100,000 every year to keep the pool open?* she asked. *I didn't,* I said and bought another tea towel.

A new man appeared in my life like rain in July. Unexpected, perhaps not arriving at the most opportune moment, but glorious. Suddenly, the air is made an ocean. You're sprinting through a storm, laughing and running. Rain lashes your legs and you feel it all over, you feel it everywhere. You find a place to stop and listen to the musicality of it pummelling parched grass, leaving behind the scent of wet earth. How rich and new and promising it smells. You realise you're hopeful for future seasons. For future.

This new man was travelling to film a short surf doc so we were unable to meet and had been speaking on the phone for weeks. I'd collected few solid facts about him. He lived near Hackney Marshes in East

London, made documentaries for a living and had an older brother who lived far away that he didn't see much. *We have that in common*, I thought. His name was Jem, and we seemed to have decided to skip the *where did you grow up* and *what do you do for work* and gone straight to the kinds of conversational specificities that implied we'd known one another for years. He sent me a video of a man named Marc Ornstein at the Midwest Freestyle Canoeing tournament in 2006 then one of a starling murmuration over Folkestone, and we talked about the parallel collaboration of birds. Later, he sent me a YouTube by a man from Tokyo titled 'Grow the Tiger Prawn Bought at the Supermarket' where he showed viewers how to make the sand just right for his new pet. As the prawn burrowed into the sand the video was captioned: わが家にまさる所なし – No place like home! I was initially mystified, but eventually found the fifteen minutes of subtitled aquarium-cam to copyright-free Japanese music quite hypnotising.

I read Jem's last message again then stared at the small picture by his phone number. He'd recently been to Bude and Ilfracombe and sent me pictures of beaches to visit and things to do. He was laughing in all of the photographs and looked like the kind of person who laughed a lot. Jem joked that he was an aspiring retiree, and it surprised me that I had a physical reaction to that. Perhaps it was disapproval, perhaps it was jealousy. The thought of giving myself permission to be liberated from the confines of the career I'd created for myself was inconceivable. We messaged about tidal pools, and I sent him a picture Miri had taken of me making tea in our cabin. *Very cosy*, he said, *no place like home!*

～〜

Everyone was out to enjoy the water that day at Bude. Busted up campervans had their doors open, couples jostled surfboards onto their roof racks and kids ran after one another in the queue for Phil's Whippy. On the horizon of Summerleaze beach a collection of surfers waited for waves. I thought about Jem and his surfing. Would I have recognised him if he were here? This man from the internet that I had a picture of in my mind? From photographs, I knew the surfboard he'd rented while he was in Devon and imagined how the muscles of his forearms flexed to carry it across the beach. I knew the sound of his voice from the phone and imagined the way his lips moved around the word Summerleaze. I knew he had boughs of soft brown curls and imagined them dancing in the breeze. Already I was painting around the details I'd been given to create a remarkable portrait of a man I barely knew.

It wasn't uncommon for me to feel disappointed when things weren't how I'd dreamed them up. Even if they were better. I was always hoping to be anywhere but where I was. I considered saying this to Miri, but decided that materialising Jem's name into the real world, there in Bude, might break some luck I didn't yet possess.

The tide was coming in and sweeping water across the walkway between the tidal pool and the beach. Miri and I removed our shoes and waded through the water, circling a washed-up jellyfish that we peered over cautiously. It pulsed in the shallows like a blue vein. I told Miri that in Japanese mythology it was Ryūjin, dragon king of the sea, who took away the jellyfish's bones. Ryūjin lived in a coral palace and controlled the tides with magical jewels. Long ago, the king's wife was sick and he believed the only cure to be a monkey liver, so he sent his servant, Jellyfish, onto land to find one. Jellyfish found a monkey and told him to ride his shell out to sea but made the mistake of revealing his quest. Clever Monkey told Jellyfish he'd left his liver in a jar in the forest and offered to go and fetch it. When Jellyfish returned empty-handed, Ryūjin delivered his punishment for being so gullible by beating Jellyfish until its bones were crushed. Jellyfish was condemned to float in the ocean, forever.

Chapter Fourteen

Burgess Park Lime Kiln: 51.48217° N, 0.08795° W

Leaving North Devon left me with an intense case of future nostalgia. A particularly inquisitive robin stopped at the cabin table to wish us farewell as we took our still-damp swimsuits off the washing line and packed our bags. We said our goodbyes to Doug. I wished him good luck and truly meant it.

London felt a million miles away. It was two-hundred and fourteen, but I didn't want to travel the distance. Before every weekend away I told myself I wouldn't check my inbox, Instagram or dating apps. It was only a few days, and no one would even realise I was offline. Miri and I used the phrase constantly, motivating one another to unplug, then I heard myself and was disgusted by the mere implication that online was our default.

As Miri reversed out of the campsite and waved to Doug, I was struck by a regret that I'd not kept the promise to myself. An ache set in that we were leaving, and I'd missed an opportunity to feel more at peace. Instead, I'd carried all my grief, rejection and frustration all the way to Westward Ho! and its bloody stupid exclamation mark, unpacked it, and was dragging it all the way home again.

I closed my eyes as Miri merged onto the motorway and we sped beside a lorry. It always made me want to hold my breath, as if it might help squeeze the car into the lane. I opened them and saw Miri watching me. *You get used to that bit,* she readjusted the mirror, *when you go from stationary to seventy miles per hour, it takes a while to speed up. It's the same for slowing down. You need time to transition.* I murmured something about booking driving lessons soon.

When we were in Wales, I noticed you took your iPad into the shower. Like you didn't even want quiet for the time it took to wash your hair. I looked out the window and saw a dead rabbit on the hard shoulder. *I know you want to slow down, but don't get frustrated with yourself when it's not as easy as you'd like,* she indicated and passed the lorry again, *we all need time to change lanes.*

Jem said there was a lime kiln at Burgess Park and that we should go see it, so I agreed to meet him that Wednesday for our first date. He was not far from the lime kiln when I saw him. He'd been looking down at his phone, sharing his location, before he looked up and saw me. He was wearing a once-red t-shirt, bleached pink by the sun, and had curls in his hair like hyacinthine locks. I still had a while to walk before we'd be in front of each other. Suddenly I couldn't remember how normal people walk. How do you walk when you're striding through a park, on your way to meet someone who your body knows is going to change your life?

We strode around Burgess Park like bizarre power walkers, watching our shoes hit the path and talking loudly. Jem pointed to the lake then the woodland area and set off in new directions. It woke a part of me that had been hibernating. The part that liked to explore and climb and play. Out of nowhere, we started running up a mound of dirt. Dust flew from our feet and my breath knocked at my ribcage. I slowed down as I joined Jem at the summit. Sweat laced my scalp. He'd beaten me. I placed my hands on my hips to open up my chest and breathe for a while. I noticed the intensity with which the Earth held me.

There was a familiar tension in the back of my legs. I wondered if walking up the escalator on the Bakerloo Line used the same muscles as hiking up a mountain and if so then why did it feel so completely different?

Jem shielded his eyes from the sun and surveyed the landscape ahead of us. A sooty blue butterfly flitted then settled in the long grass. Suddenly I was far away from London and all the experiences that had kept me down. I was on top of every mountain I'd ever climbed. Jem's chest rose and fell as he caught his breath too. *There'll be time to beat me*, he said.

We kept walking and occasionally I looked up at Jem then forgot what I was saying, or smiled and worried my teeth were obvious in my mouth. He told me about his experience with a ghost, something that, coming from anyone else, would've made me laugh in their face. *Drink?* he asked.

When we arrived at The Camberwell Arms, he said *Jem at 7 p.m.* and I was delighted that he'd made a reservation. I berated myself for being so easily impressed by basic life tasks when completed by men. Why did a man who could use OpenTable always seem so utterly self-sufficient? He could've left after the walk, so could I, and yet we seemed to have both optimistically hoped for more. There was a soft glow from the candles and ranunculus on the table, which was quickly too small once wine, water, plates and bread arrived. We ordered grilled lemon sole with lardo, sage and pickled citrus. Borlotti bean & tagliolini minestra, artichokes and parmesan. Marinda tomatoes with bagna càuda, walnuts and marjoram.

Did you know tomatoes could be this good? I asked. He said he grew his own. *These ones are particularly good. But the bad ones have to exist to make these ones taste so amazing.* I thought he was right, and every bad date I'd been on had only ever existed to make this one so wonderful.

I said I was worried about watery tomatoes after Brexit, and he said that was funny. I said funny was the last thing it was. Then he said some real things that should make me worry about Brexit, and I felt sad. *You look pretty*, he said. And I wondered if he meant especially when I looked forlorn.

Chapter Fifteen

St Gabriel's Manor: 51.47478° N, 0.10552° W

It's not common to be neighbourly in London, but St Gabriel's Manor did it well. There was a long shelf above the postboxes where people swapped books, the WhatsApp group was often abuzz with invites to play tennis, and there was a corkboard with flyers about how to become a volunteer gardener in the park. In the hallway, there was a seating area where people left furniture they no longer wanted. I didn't need new chairs, but when I passed four mid-century dining chairs in a gorgeous brushed walnut I saw an opportunity to make some money. Selling them online was a relatively successful attempt to spend time on my laptop while avoiding working on my book. That afternoon, a man called Felipe messaged: *are these still available?* The generic, one-tap response followed by, *hello. Could I collect tomorrow evening?*

When Marketplace Man arrived, I was taken aback by how handsome he was and instantly regretted that

I was wearing my glasses. He was tall with dark skin and wearing casual but expensive-looking trousers paired with socks and Yeezy sliders. He looked like the kind of man to be cast in a De'Longhi coffee machine advert. Misinterpreting my surprise, he said, *sorry, I thought we said eight o'clock,* then took a step back from the door. *No, no we did! Sorry the time ran away from me today,* I lied. *Please come in,* I added to stop us apologising at each other. He said I could call him Flip then dragged his feet on the doormat when I told him not to worry about taking off his shoes, though I wasn't sure that sliders really counted as shoes anyway. I shut the door behind him and then it was just us in the flat. He said I had a nice place and I recited the facts I knew about the building's history as a seminary. Flip nodded while his eyes drifted from the windows to my bookcase, giving me an opportunity to notice how when he put his hands in his pockets the fabric became taut against his buttocks. I tried and failed at not looking.

He looked around as if any movement might damage my furniture. *Ted Hughes,* he read the spine of *The Hawk in the Rain* then recited from memory, *I imagine this midnight moment's forest . . .* I didn't know much poetry by heart but hearing the line aloud I recognised it from 'The Thought Fox'. It gave me a jolt to hear it aloud, like we shared a memory from a time we hadn't known each other. I expected him to check I looked impressed, but he was still studying the books. *Then it goes something something something and ends . . . the page is printed. That's how I remember that one. Is that right?* I admitted I wasn't sure and said, *I thought for too long that that poem was actually about a real fox.* I knew a lot about Hughes, but for some reason decided to play myself down. *It's about whatever you want it to be about,* Flip, as I now knew him, said with a shrug.

Do you mind if I . . . he gestured towards the chairs. *Please, go ahead,* I said and he sat down. It felt odd to be standing above him, so I sat too and we stared at one another across the table. I thought it was strange of him to sit, but I supposed it would be stranger to buy chairs you hadn't sat in. To break the silence, I mimed eating and moved an imaginary knife in my right hand. *What's for dinner?* he asked. *Trifle,* I replied and he precariously picked up an imaginary spoon as though it were loaded with wobbling jelly and custard. *Very realistic,* I laughed. It was the first time I'd laughed with someone at this table. Maybe I shouldn't let the chairs go. *Thanks. I'm an actor.* I raised an eyebrow and regretted it as he looked embarrassed, shy maybe. *Do you do words? Or just mime eating pudding?* He looked coolly amused, *I do all of the words.*

I said: *I'm words too. Writing, not acting though.* Although it was true, it felt like a lie. I always thought someone would expose me as a fraud if I called myself a writer. I usually said something nondescript like 'copy' or I work 'in music'. *Words*, he confirmed. *I could've guessed that. You have poet energy about you.* I hoped what he saw in me was something everyone did. Then I remembered he was an actor and was probably good at delivering lines.

£230, wasn't it? I nodded and passed him my bank details on my phone. We remained seated while he typed them into his banking app. *Nationwide*, I noted to myself in case it might be a detail I could read into later. *Let me help you carry these out*, I stood up. *No need. I've got it.* He stacked two then bent his arm into a right angle. Something inside me jolted. I was sad he was leaving. Then it would just be me in the flat again, with no laughter at the table. I thought about asking Flip to stay, but couldn't think of a way it wouldn't sound desperate. It was too late for coffee. Could I offer him wine if I only had a third of a bottle left? *You could*, he hesitated, *give me your number though?*

You already have my number, I said. *I have your number for the chairs. This time I want it for . . . talking to you.* The subtle upward quirk of his mouth punctuated the end of his sentence. I picked up my phone and dialled the unsaved number above his last message. He brought the phone to his ear, still clutching two of the chairs. *Here's my number, for talking purposes*, I said into the receiver, then hung up, and we smiled at each other in what was quickly becoming a habit.

Chapter Sixteen

Dancing Ledge: 50.58939° N, 2.02361° W

Plotting our tidal pool adventure pulled me into the world of local conservation societies and library archives. I spent a lot of time on websites like watchet-conservation.co.uk or Dorset Talk Forum reading long, often rambling posts about volunteering for litter-picking, pleas for local historical photos or complaints about over-foraging of wild garlic from out-of-towners. My paper-crowded kitchen table had only two chairs again and was covered by maps marked with potential connected journeys in Scotland. The rigorous planning was a way to avoid thinking about a bench that didn't yet exist for Tom.

My research on Dancing Ledge revealed that the tidal pool was part of an abandoned quarry where stone was transported from the coast by flat-bottomed barges. After the Great Fire of London, Christopher Wren chose to rebuild St Paul's with Purbeck stone and it became increasingly popular. In the twentieth century, a small pool was blasted into one of the ledges by the masters of nearby Durnford School for swimming lessons. A biography of a former pupil claimed Durnford 'epitomised the strange British faith in bad food, plenty of Latin and beatings from an early age.' It's rumoured that the school was brutal for young boys and the headmaster enforced Strip & Swim at the pool each morning, whatever the weather. The school closed in the Second World War and the building was later demolished, but the pool remains. I enjoyed reading about famous former pupils. Filmmaker Derek Jarman titled his biography *Dancing Ledge* and novelist Ian Fleming found inspiration for his Bond series in the local history. Not far from the school was an East Holme estate owned by the Bond family called Creech Grange. One of their ancestors was John Bond, an Elizabethan spy. Their house was inscribed with the motto *non sufficit orbis*, meaning 'The world is not enough'.

From Wareham train station, Miri and I boarded the No. 40 Breezer and travelled through the hollows and fullness of the Dorset landscape. The bus rolled over the contours of the Purbeck hills, dipping and winding around Corfe Castle. Miri had got the job she'd interviewed for and spent most of the journey telling me about her new role. She'd be working as a packaging designer for Danone. *It's so much more than just milk though*, she said and started talking about drinkable yoghurts. I wondered if art galleries to dairy felt like an odd gear-change, but the enthusiasm with which she told me about the increase in plant-based alternatives and resurgence of milk deliveries didn't hint as much. *Milk is having a bit of a renaissance*, she looked out the bus window, *it's very exciting*. Miri was good at quickly getting onboard with how things were.

At Durnford Drove we began our walk and crossed a track with a stone sign shaped like a tombstone, I thought of graves and memorial benches, then Emma. Earlier in the week I'd said I'd call her. It was now the weekend, and I hadn't. I always expected better of future me. Miri saw me frowning and tried to start a conversation about Tom, but I quickly changed the subject to the wildflowers. The chalk grasslands were a kaleidoscope of spring colour: yellow of kidney vetch, pink of herb robert and green of the long, tall grass, all dancing with the movement of pale blue butterflies. I glanced upon a starry patch of white stitchwort. Folklore says picking these flowers will cause a thunderstorm, so I passed and let them be. When their seed capsules ripen they noisily fire their seeds across the field, popping like fireworks. Eventually, I ran out of new flowers to spot or, more accurately, ones I could name. I brought the conversation back to milk.

When we arrived at the coast, the sea was laid out before us. I stepped forward to peer over the ledge and there was the pool. A speck among the limestone. From this height, I had a chance to assess the tidal pool's size. It's small and mimics the shape of a natural rockpool. There are two stories for how Dancing Ledge might've got its name. Some say it describes how the water dances over the rocky ledge at changing tides while others say the pool is the same size as a ballroom. Miri looked over at the last twelve feet of our journey. It was vertical. *There's no way. I can't go down there!* I pretended to be confident and took the most accessible route, which was on my bottom. I slid down, fingers gripping the stone as I went, and finally my feet hit the ground with a thud. I turned back to look at the vertiginous landscape and tried not to think about whether we'd even be able to climb back up. Lifting my arms up, I helped stabilise Miri on her way down. Her legs were only slightly shorter than mine, but enough that it made finding places to step and grip more difficult. Miri's knuckles were as white as the limestone. For the last part, I put my hands under her armpits and pulled her from the cliff to the ground.

Finally, it was time to swim and we clambered into the limpet-studded pool. I ran my fingers over their conicals, fingering the grooves where they were rasped to the rocks. *You know limpets move to feed at night, but always return to the same spot.* I imagined them waking by starlight to tongue algae from the rocks before strolling home. *It's nice to think they have a home they remember. They're the luckiest limpets to have their home here.*

I pulled the water over me like a blanket. It was warmer submerged in the water than exposed on the wind-lashed coast. Just metres away, the waves tugged at their leash like a hungry dog. We lingered a while and the tide bounded towards us, ready to swallow the stillness of the pool. It broke over barnacles and fossils, then showered us with seawater like a blessing. Dancing Ledge was how I experienced my friendship with Miri, a safe space within otherwise turbulent times.

Chapter Seventeen

Crown & Greyhound: 51.44939° N, 0.08503° W

I woke up and allowed myself a few moments in bed to think about Jem and the way he tugged at the belt loop of my shorts to kiss me in the park when he walked me home. I imagined his finger hooked around the denim and the sensation of being caught by his body. The soft evening air was resin in the moment his lips touched mine. Something hardened inside me.

My alarm went off. I pulled myself out of the daydream. I had a habit of holding onto things too tightly while hoping they wouldn't slip through my fingers. To avoid the Marlowe-shaped mess I'd got myself in I decided it would be a good idea not to get attached to Jem too quickly. I called Flip and asked him on a date. Hopefully the juggling would make me less fretful. I was doing too much fretting. Miri had even noticed and said I'd looked 'preoccupied' recently.

It must've been a Sunday when I went on my first date with Flip because the pub was closing early. He lived in Crystal Palace and chose a place in Dulwich, remarking that it was equidistant between the two of us, which was an early sign of his even and considered nature. When I arrived he was already there, sitting outside the Crown & Greyhound at an umbrellaed table in the rain. He was holding a half-pint of Guinness and rubbed his hand over his shaved head before he stood to greet me: *poet! It's good to see you.*

He described himself as a playwright, as if wanting to clarify his earlier introduction as an actor. With his number and full name from his bank transfer I'd had a good amount of information to occupy myself with. This wasn't my finest sleuthing as it was easy to find his IMDB page and biography on the Royal Shakespeare Company website. He'd written and directed a few plays. I'd not seen any of them, but Miri said his show at the Royal Court theatre was all anyone talked about in 2018. I had, however, watched an HBO dramedy where the running joke was that Flip's character was incredibly attractive. I wondered if it was awkward auditioning for a role where the main trait was good looks, then remembered that men don't get awkward about thinking they're fantastic. Now he was working on his directorial debut, which he described as a British *Get Out*. Experience told me that Flip would be an awful show-off, but somehow he wasn't. I told him that he was handsome, and his eyes crinkled at the corners but he didn't seem to register the compliment too much. This quickly became a dance we did. I expressed admiration, and he smiled then asked me a question about something in my life nowhere near as impressive.

Flip had gone to a good school and hadn't really intended to be an actor, but it had just kind of happened. I liked that his work evolved with him, and he still wrote about growing up black in his hometown. He still lives there now. A real South London boy. He's far from a boy. He's a man. A man with a knee that gave him trouble who liked debbie tucker green plays and Jude's ice cream and had spoonfuls of self-discipline because he wrote most mornings and only ever ordered pints by the half. He said his mum was a therapist, so I folded that piece of information away to analyse later. He told me about swimming lessons at school. *Maybe I'll get back into swimming*, he said. *You should*, I agreed and we made plans I wasn't sure we'd keep to go to Lewisham leisure centre together. I liked the way he told stories, and had to remind myself they weren't stories, but his life.

I've not been on a date with someone this much younger than me, he said. *How much younger do you think I am?* I leaned over my crossed arms on the table. *Well*, he looked intensely uncomfortable, *I'm guessing you're in your twenties?* I nodded and asked him if he was on dating apps. He said he was new to them and hated it. *Everyone feels they have to say they hate it. It's a necessary evil.* I asked him to show me his profile. He was thirty-nine and his parameters were set to: Women, Aged 27-32, Radius 3 miles. I smirked. It's frustrating when men virtue-signal their alliance to women then move towards the same patriarchal structures they claim to want to dismantle. My head wanted to make a case for rejecting outdated gender norms but the hungrier animal instinct in me just wanted him to think I was gorgeous and viable.

I thought that if I dated someone younger, I'd be able to have a few years before I have to think about kids. My eyebrows twitched. *Just because I'm twenty-six doesn't mean I don't want a baby straight away . . .*

Do you? he interjected. It felt like a trick question. *No. But the two aren't connected. You could just ask,* I sipped, *but I suppose that's what you've done here in a roundabout way. What's the story there anyway?* He sipped, longer this time. *Whatever you're probably thinking, I guess that.* I didn't say anything. *My ex was the same age as me, we weren't right together for various reasons, but now I'm also thinking about time.*

Flip paused, then continued in a new direction. *She thought I was away a lot,* I nodded, *and we worked in similar fields, so I ended up hiding things from her that were going well for me when they weren't going so well for her.* He gripped his pint glass and I noticed he cut his fingernails so there was only the faintest sliver of white, a shoreline. I thought of Jem's hands and the tomatoes he grew.

That must've been very sad. For both of you, I wondered what her version of that story would be. Nothing made me as suspicious as a date talking about a 'crazy' ex-girlfriend. I more often met sensible women pushed to their limits than patient men who had the self-awareness to know that two people make the dynamic in a relationship. When my female friends claimed to be at the 'end of their tether', it often transpired that they were somewhere around the middle and found previously undiscovered resources for accommodating the bad behaviour of their boyfriends. I couldn't be sure that I wouldn't side with Flip's ex if I heard her version. There was a first time for everything, I supposed.

We talked for a few hours and did that thing people on first dates do where we drank the equivalent of over a bottle of red wine, but all in small glasses as we danced around being unsure if the other person wanted to stay longer. Then, as the waitress shooed us out long after last orders, Flip waited for me to get in a taxi, and I kissed him goodnight. It was easy and surprising how softly my body surrendered into his. On the journey home I thought a lot about 'The Thought Fox' poem and its *midnight moment's forest.*

When Emma called, I'd been thinking every possible thought about Rohanna and her sister's bench while pretending to myself I was watching a documentary about The Velvet Underground. We chatted about things for a while, then I decided to broach the B word. *Have you thought about a bench?* Emma replied no then said, *wait what?* I scratched my head. *Why would you say no if you don't know what I'm talking about?* I turned the TV from muted to off. *No because I can't have thought about it if I don't know what you mean. And I don't know what you mean most of the time but that's not really the point of chatting, is it?*

I pinned a photograph from Dancing Ledge on my kitchen corkboard and tried to start again. *We could have a bench for Tom. We could go and . . . sit on it.* Emma didn't reply so I asked if she was still there. *That would be nice*, she said generously. *It could be somewhere significant to us, significant to Tom.* She asked where, and I paused. *Maybe the school?* As soon as I said it, I knew it wasn't great. The school field backs onto a public park and is a mishmash of football pitches, metal climbing frames and dog-waste bins. I was jealous of Rohanna, not just that she had Sami's bench, but that it was in

116

North London where the parks were much better. I brushed the thought away, *we can think about the details later. But we don't really have anywhere to go right now. And maybe somewhere would be good?*

The photograph was too heavy for one pin and fell from the corkboard. *I don't mean like a grave or anything.* Emma agreed, *no not a grave,* then we were quiet. I'd never liked the thought of Tom being underground. It felt dark, cold. *What do we have instead? Were we planning something?*

There was a cremation, remember. I shifted my weight onto the other foot, *obviously I remember, but I don't remember us talking about what we would do with . . . it.* Were ashes it or them, I wondered. *Did someone pick them up?* I imagined them lost in the post or returned to sender after no one replied to the Royal Mail 'We Missed You' slip.

Mum and Dad have them in Wales. I was annoyed that Emma knew this, and I didn't. She added, *I helped them move,* and I remembered that she'd taken a few days off work to help. My excuse had been that work was busy because the thought of packing up Tom's things was too much.

What does it look like? I asked. *A tube,* Emma paused and tried to think of a way to describe it. Descriptions weren't really her thing. *Kind of like the one Bellever was in.*

Bellever? Bellever was a cat! I could sense Emma shrug through the phone. *Still ashes though.* I decided to plant a stake in the ground. *I would like somewhere to go. So I think a bench is a good idea.* Emma put the phone down to make tea. *I agree*, she said eventually. *How's your day anyway?* I blurted out that I went to see Sami's bench, and she asked me when. *About six weeks ago.*

Oh that makes sense, Emma replied. It had taken me months to get the courage to discuss it. She knew that and didn't seem to mind. *Anyway, I've got to go. Chat to you later.* Emma said, *I love you.* I said, *goodbye*, and hung up.

Summer

Chapter Eighteen

Silk Road: 51.47385° N, 0.08919° W

I'd been getting to know Jem at a pace that alarmed me. We saw each other often, but it never felt soon enough. Sometimes I wrote things I wanted to tell or ask him on Notes, but then when we met a million other things occurred to me first. The train journeys east were exhausting. I set off excited then rattled across London as a ball of nervous energy. His texture was familiar to me now. He was quiet yet energetic, playful yet reflective, gentle yet passionate, self-assured yet questioning. There with me in London, but wild in spirit.

We spent most of our time outdoors. I took him to Brockwell Park, Myatt's Fields and Camberwell Old Cemetery, then he showed me Hackney Marshes, Victoria Park and the deer at Clissold. We pressed our palms against tree bark and rubbed petals between our fingers while we talked. Jem stuffed my pockets with pinecones and taught me how to blow blades of grass between my thumbs like a kazoo, then put the grass up my nose to tickle me until I started sneezing. The first time he tried to show me how to identify birdsong with the BirdNet app I said, *we live in London. Just Google pigeon,* then we heard a blue tit, a sedge warbler and even a ring-necked parakeet so I had to admit it was quite cool. When I slowed down to notice, nature surprised me. It felt like the first summer I'd truly lived in London.

That weekend, I'd deliberated on the perfect itinerary then suggested it as though it were spontaneous. A walk with ice cream through Herne Hill followed by a swim at Brockwell Lido then dinner at Silk Road for charcoal red snapper, fried dumplings and black fungus with cabbage. We talked about work and ambitions because those were the kind of questions I enjoyed answering. He continued slurping hand-pulled noodles before leaning back into a swig of Tiger beer, *my ambition is to have more time. I do everything around that.* That wasn't an answer I understood straight away, and we talked around it for a while. He continued, *I'm not sure I want to be a film editor. I'm a director, but right now I'm editing a lot to make money. I make money to have more time to work on my own projects or to have time when I don't have to work,* he pushed the plate with the last dumpling towards me, *so I can spend more time away with friends, go surfing, have more days like this.* He rubbed my shoulder, *it's all about time.*

What were my ambitions? To get a promotion, write and publish a book, own a house. In many ways, they were about time too: how to fill it, how to rush it, how to prove that I deserved it instead of Tom. My ambitions were all products of being preoccupied, ways to keep me going and avoid thinking about how hurt I was inside. Busyness was my preferred anaesthetic. I wondered when it would stop. If my ambition would run out of steam or if I would first.

Jem seemed to sense I was somewhere else as he moved his thumb over the patch of vitiligo by my mouth. *You have chilli on your face, you beautiful goose.* I felt lightheaded, an inhalation of helium. Looking down at the white lake of my plate to pick up my chopsticks, I was surprised to see I was still sitting at the table and not bouncing about the ceiling.

Our conversation was soundtracked by a bell that tinkled whenever someone came in. A Deliveroo driver shuffled in to collect a takeaway order and was followed by a calico cat with a corner missing from its ear. Jem cooed at it and put some fish on his palm. The man sharing the table with us looked up from reading the news on his iPhone to hiss and say, *get away*, in a low voice. Jem shot him a look then tickled the cat behind its ears while it mewled.

The cat wound itself around Jem's calves when we paid and even followed us as far as Myatt's Fields park, where it looked bored and slinked off. Jem's parents have two cats called Jelly and Bob, which is funny because of course there's Jem and Rob, his brother. Once, he'd asked his mother if she'd intentionally tried to replace them when they'd left home and she'd said it was a coincidence. *Sounds like they miss you*, I offered. Jem didn't reply. *Sometimes I miss you when you're not around. Is that crazy?* I asked. *No. That's nice*, he said and held my hand. I waited for him to say he missed me too, but it never came. I followed his eye to see what he was watching and tried to guess what Jem was thinking, but neither was clear to me. There was a space there that I desired to inhibit, a withdrawn reserve, a whole universe within him. Much of the time, I felt that I had no idea what he was thinking or feeling, and I was never sure if that was because he didn't either, or I wasn't invited to know.

It was then, on our walk through the park in the night, that he told me he'd be going away for a while. *Where?* I asked. *Sweden*, he said. *How long for?* I asked. *I'm not sure*, he replied. *Probably not long.* Jem shrugged, and I wished I was the shrugging type. The cat reappeared, as if to remind me that things could go away and come back.

The following week, Jem and I had what would be our last night together for I didn't know how long. He lived in a terraced house near The Crooked Billet pub with two flatmates. The kitchen was full of bags of rice, pasta, lentils, orzo and jars in all shapes and sizes including a tall hexagonal container of Jem's home-made kimchi. There was a sunset-orange Le Creuset kettle that whistled on the hob and on the kitchen table – which was folded against the wall like an origami future-teller – there was mimosa in an old green bottle with the label scratched off. Everything was sticky because they didn't have an extractor fan. When I arrived, Jem presented me with a broccoli like it was a bouquet of flowers: *I'm going to nourish you with homegrown vegetables*. He served it up with a salad of his own lettuce and yellow courgettes topped with olive oil, toasted pine nuts and parmesan. It was delicious.

Jem's bedroom was right at the top of the house beneath the gable roof. When I walked around the bed, I had to stoop my head a little where the ceiling yawned. I took a hungry inventory of his possessions. Guitar, stack of old film reels, free-standing mirror and a book on growing tomatoes. He'd carefully placed a collection of rocks on the windowsill. I picked one up and pressed it into my palm.

There was a skylight that reflected us at night. I'd watch him on top of me in the semi-darkness and it was as though we were making love in the stars, there among the constellations with Cassiopeia, Virgo and Andromeda. In bed, he was passionate and generous and talkative. Our limbs tangled like weeds as we practised every way our two bodies could fit together. We fell asleep without closing the blind and in the morning the sun shone on our naked bodies like a blessing.

Pockets full of pinecones

Chapter Nineteen

The Trinkie: 58.42883° N, 3.07019° W

On the flight to Inverness, I held a book open for an hour and forty minutes while I thought about Jem in Sweden and whether I'd forgotten to pack a travel towel. Occasionally I glanced sideways at Miri turning the pages of *Middlemarch*. George Eliot seemed a bold choice for a long weekend away. Even with the words printed in the tiniest font, it was chunky. At least if we got in any trouble she could use it in self-defence. When we descended, I dog-eared the same page because I knew I hadn't taken any of it in.

When I wasn't messaging Jem, I was messaging Flip, and when I finished alternating between the two of them, I allocated time to feeling guilty about not being in touch with Emma, then half-heartedly constructed a text that didn't have much substance beyond: *Any fun plans for the weekend!!* or *How's Dan?! Keeping well, I hope!* What I lacked in thoughtfulness, I compensated for in exclamation marks. She replied promptly with a recipe she intended to cook over the weekend and told me that she and Dan had gone on a fishing trip outside Staffordshire but slept in the car when they'd heard rats scurrying outside the tent. Dan is mortally afraid of rodents. I said this was the perfect excuse to never go fishing again but Emma said it was ok. She liked having the peace and quiet while they sat on foldable chairs beside the water. I tried to imagine being so kind that I'd sleep by a rat-infested river to make my partner happy.

Inverness Airport looks like the lovechild of an Austrian shopping centre and a Cash & Carry car park. It's a large hanger-esque building with 'INVERNESS' protruding from the flat roof in blue letters. We drove to Edinburgh over four days, stopping to visit tidal pools in Wick, Moray Firth, Macduff, Cellardyke and North Berwick. I'd never been this far north. I'd intended to connect with my Scottish roots, but my ancestry.com trial expired before I'd learned anything beyond the name of the town my paternal grandma grew up in: Kirkcaldy, Fife.

The tidal pools we'd previously travelled to were never far from a coffee shop, car park or place to stop for lunch. Our trip to Scotland was wild. It was rugged and involved long drives following the curves of the coastline. Houses had miles between them, villages even more. We took it in turns to exclaim *wow*, as we looked out the window. Passing fields were bathed in mysterious shafts of light and across the clifftop roads I could see the widening of the world.

Our first swim was the Trinkie. It was late on Friday and a storm was threatening to break. The clouds were skull-white and the air had a chaotic movement to it, like it was drunk on bottled lightning. From inside our black Kia, we couldn't feel the wind, but I watched it tear through fields, rattle gates, pull at branches and whip waves into the cliffs.

We stopped following the sat nav when the road signs began to mention Wick. First eight, then five, three, then just half a mile away. We arrived at where we suspected the tidal pool might be and pulled up onto a verge to investigate. There, we found an information board that let us know that the pool had opened in July 1932 and generations of Wickers have learned to swim there since. It was blessedly unmobbed. Even the sign – which had a black-and-white photo of the pool in its 1930s heyday – said that 'only a few hardy souls use it now'. It was cold for August, although maybe cold was the usual here.

Trinkie is an old Scots word for 'trench' as this pool used to be a quarry, with the stone being used to build many of the homes in Wick as well as its harbour. The tidal pool slopes gently into the water, which made me think of tectonic plates and glaciers and how this coast must've been connected land once. To the right of the pool I saw the Grey Bools, a jumble of giant sedimentary rock loosened from the cliffs in the last Ice Age. Just like this coastline had changed before, I knew it wouldn't keep its current formation forever.

Two low walls had been added and a perimeter painted in white to force some order onto this place. Force is perhaps the wrong word as it didn't feel forceful at all. The construction was entirely embracing. It's hard to explain how so much love can be seen in the painting of white walls, but I experienced it at that tidal pool. Every year, Friends of the Trinkie gather to scrub the boundaries and give it a fresh lick of paint. The paint was a white so stark it couldn't have been Eggshell or Wevet but only Brilliant White.

While we swam, the wind assaulted the horizon, crushing the distant sea with its fist. With only our heads peeking out from the water and our fingers clutching the painted wall, I felt entirely protected. It was that safety that led us to staying in minutes longer than we should've.

Bundled into the car, we returned to Wick for our second Scottish tidal pool. It seemed pointless to remove our wet swimsuits, so we sat wrapped in our towels. Miri turned the heating up, but I barely felt it. This was, perhaps, our second mistake with the weather that day.

Chapter Twenty

Wick is a curious and small place. It has a Guinness World Record for the world's smallest street and in 1868 Robert Louis Stevenson wrote a letter saying, 'certainly Wick in itself possesses no beauty: bare, grey shores, grim grey houses; not even the gleam of red tiles; not even the greenness of a tree'. I read that before we visited and thought it was harsh but when we crawled into town I glanced at a derelict pub graffitied with *Repent and You Will be Saved* and thought Stevenson was probably being fair then and he would've been fair if he said it now. And yet, Wick has two tidal pools. I wondered if there was a name for the phenomenon of a town seeing another with a tidal pool and thinking: we'd like one of them. Miri said the modern equivalent was solar panels. None for miles, then a town with more converted energy than Silicon Valley.

North Baths tidal pool can be found below an estate of bungalows set into the cliffs. A tall wire fence made us worry we were trespassing, but we continued at the sight of water. It was built into the harbour and isn't as naturally stunning as the Trinkie. I felt bad for it in comparison, like it was an ugly sister. I needn't have pitied it as the pool was clearly loved. Along the old port wall 'North Baths' had been painted with great care in thick white-and-blue lettering.

When I'd started planning our Scotland trip, I'd searched online archives and libraries but never found much. Facebook Groups had quickly become my secret weapon. Spending time on my phone usually made me feel sad and empty: adverts for clothes I didn't need and couldn't afford, pictures of plastic in the ocean, problems I didn't know how to fix but felt responsible for and updates from friends who didn't keep in touch or exes with new girlfriends. These groups were different. The posts arrived as reminders that I should be outside. I asked for information about the two tidal pools around Wick. Were they still there and were they swimmable? Did anyone have any pictures from their childhood or even when they were built? I added a swimmer and blue heart emoji, then clicked 'Publish'. After only an hour, I had a flurry of responses including a message from Eileen who'd recently posted a photo of a very large tub of mayonnaise asking friends: *if you have any spare fifteen-litre buckets could you please bring them to help whitewash the pool.* We'd messaged back and forth for a few days. She'd told me she'd never been a strong swimmer but during lockdown this place, centred in her community, became a way to be outside, to have a break, to meet people. She said North Baths tidal pool saved her life.

Then life got in the way and I forgot about Eileen and her swims at North Baths. It was so distant in my memory that when we started swimming beside two women in their fifties; I didn't recognise Eileen at all. We were telling her we were visiting from London when she exclaimed, *oh ay! You're the wee girl from Facebook.* I said I was and when she abruptly exited the water I wondered if I'd offended her by not replying to her last message. She pulled out her Motorola and started recording. *You need this captured!* I looked at Miri, who self-consciously rearranged her hair while treading water. It was beaded with rain, as if sewn there. I was used to people raising their eyebrows at our adventure and I didn't blame them when it came to swimming in the rain sixteen miles from John o' Groats on a Friday night, but Eileen understood that this was about more than that.

Hypothermia is hard to explain. Perhaps that's because I completely forgot it. I read that the brain does that with pain sometimes. It just forgets. I suppose it has to or why would we continue to do things that risk us getting hurt like climb trees, fall in love or swim in Scottish tidal pools? For a while, the cold felt like the cold always does. All-consuming. There was nothing other than that. It was only when I could no longer hear or connect my thoughts to moving my arms or opening my mouth that I knew something was wrong. My body was shutting down and it was happening in slow motion.

I was slumped by the car and jumped when the headlights flashed. Miri had unlocked it. There must've been a sound – a beep-boop – but I didn't hear it. I saw her mouth move but I couldn't hear what she was saying. What was happening in the outside world wasn't connecting to anything inside me. I was all hollowed out and the cold was in my bones. I wanted to move my hand towards the car door. I knew warmth, and survival, were inside but my body was paralysed. My fingers were skin candles: cold, waxy, clumsy.

There was a blur of colour. Miri pushed me into the car and shut the door behind me. Then everything went dark.

Chapter Twenty-One

Portknockie Harbour: 57.70437° N, 2.85976° W

Perhaps an hour later, I looked up at Miri driving. *That was weird.* She gave me a lopsided smile, then looked serious: *don't ever do that to me again.* Later, she told me that she'd had to take off my wet swimsuit in the car and rush to dress me then place a coat over me. The heaters had been on full blast, but the cold had got in deep. She'd tried to feed me chocolate, but I dropped it in the footwell when my claw-like hands still didn't work. It was like emerging from a dream. I mostly remember hypothermia through what Miri told me. Maybe I did forget. I think my brain has gotten quite good at that.

I remembered the sleepless nights after Tom's death. I remembered asking Emma if I could sleep in her bed then lying awake, wondering if she was asleep, for hours each night. We were curled up like leaves waiting to be swept off the pavement; dry, brittle. We were careful not to touch, wanting to touch, not touching. The slow and distant hum of our bodies, shivering under the duvets. There were tears constantly, then no tears. I wondered if it was possible to cry any more. Looking in the mirror, my face seemed different. Not just because my eyes were pink wet swells and the skin between my nostrils and lip was broken, red and raw from rubbing, but because I was a changed person.

The drive to Portknockie tidal pool that Saturday traced the triangular inlet of Moray Firth, past where the River Ness and Findhorn flowed into the sea. It seemed as though the coastal roads looked out to nowhere, just water then the edge of the world. Around Buckie the sky cleared momentarily and, if I really squinted, I could see back to Wick, more than fifty miles away. We descended the cliffs to follow a tight circular route that felt more like a marble chute than a road. Down and down. Round and round. It was one of those days so flat and cold that even the birds looked fed up. A black-legged kittiwake hid its beak beneath its wings, a puff of cloud-grey feathers. Cold or not, it was busy. Family-sized cars waited by the water's edge with their boots open. Parents sat on camping chairs, sipping from flasks while they watched the kids and shoved Fruit Shoots into their hands when they returned from the water, dripping onto the tarmac. When we got out of the car, our mistake was clear. This was very much a paddling pool.

There was a Portknockie Harbour sign that read 'YOU ARE HERE', though it wasn't large enough that you could get confused about what you were looking at. It was very harbour-like. Beneath said sign was a 12 x 9m pool painted Play-Doh blue. Water and sand sloshed around up to ankle-depth, and beyond was a sand runway into the second of two basins. The towering walls had a narrow gap – wide enough for a crab or lobster boat – which led out to the North Sea and churned up the water like a wave machine. The harbour was full of wetsuited kids, storming in to attack the swells on SUPs. When they were done, they rinsed their sandy toes in the tidal pool. It was a glorified foot bath.

It's hard to tell water depth in an image online, I've since got quite good at it but only the embarrassment of sliding along the plastic-lined pool on my stomach to see if I could swim in Portknockie pool has made me so observant. When I decided that we'd humiliated ourselves in front of Portknockie's parenting cohort thoroughly enough, we admitted defeat and swam in the harbour where seaweed and flecks of wood surrounded us like dregs in a sink. Among the children was a woman being rocked by the waves as she stared up at the colourless sky. Her wetsuit was so thick it looked as though it were keeping her afloat. She upturned herself to smile at us, then nodded towards two boys as if to express some kind of ownership. They were repeatedly climbing the harbour ladder and jumping into the waves. *That looks fun*, I said. *Doesn't it*, she agreed. *You local?* she asked and I guessed she hadn't seen us acting like newts in the paddling pool. Her story fell out of her so quickly I guessed she hadn't spoken to anyone for a while and her accent told me she wasn't from there either. She was a lawyer from Geneva and her husband's uncle had just died with no partner or children. There was no one else to leave his land in Portknockie to so they were talking about moving in to run the farm. *For the boys*, she said. I watched the youngest hang from the ladder like a pirate, swinging his free arm into the air before hurling himself towards his brother in the water. I hadn't asked her name. *For the boys*, I thought.

The work Miri did calculating routes between tidal pools along the east coast of Scotland was pure trigonometry. I enjoyed our village detours where I picked up a local newspaper that had an article on the new books in the library and a story about a pigeon getting caught in the Londis. Near Bow Fiddle Rock we passed a young woman with her garage door open, selling candles. I was a magpie for the joy of everyday moments like that. Miri and I always enjoyed collecting them for the nest that was our friendship, full of anecdotal treasures and trinkets. If not for this trip, how else would we have found ourselves in charming Portknockie, a former fishing village with no fishing in Moray Firth?

Moray Firth is a triangular inlet on the North Sea on what is known as the Dolphin Coast. It's the most northerly colony in the world and a great place to see bottlenose dolphins. The number of healthy salmon in the water means that the feeding grounds are rich and these dolphins are some of the biggest in the world. We'd entertained the idea of a dolphin-spotting trip, but the boats left early and our schedule was tight, with long drives and the tide to consider. It was therefore sad that our first dolphin sighting was of a rotting carcass on the rocks. We left it in its salt-lashed grave and carried on walking. We were searching for Portsoy Open Air Pool but instead found an abandoned cement structure nestled among quartzites. It was filled with sand, broken glass and puddles of water. Beside the pool was an Aberdeenshire Council sign, 'The Pool is Closed: This Area Can be Dangerous. Swimming is

Not Permitted'. Someone had scratched out letters on the metal sign so that it said, 'The Structure is unsafe'. The pool was originally opened in 1936 but in 2001 the valve had been forced shut so it no longer filled with seawater. There was controversy about its closure due to failing to comply with local health-and-safety legislation. Beyond the structure the waves are rough so – without the tidal pool – this whole stretch of coastline is unswimmable for those who live there. I thought about Eileen and how she said swimming had saved her, and felt sorrowful for the people of Portsoy.

Emerging from Castle Pool

Chapter Twenty-Two

Castle Pool: 56.34192° N, 2.78927° W

Not far from St Andrews, Miri indicated to turn past a town with a pet cemetery. I thought about Annie's dogs and chewed my lip. A conversation I'd had with Flip a few weeks ago kept playing in my head. *It's a loss like any other.* His words gave me the same unbuckling feeling as when I'd read Annie's email.

Before Scotland, Flip and I had been to the theatre twice, which meant we'd spent a lot of time sitting together in silence, our bodies humming beside one another. Arms not touching, but close enough that they could. Flip liked to meet on weekends and called Monday to Thursday 'school-nights', which made me feel that he was much older – and much more sensible – than I was. Both, of course, were true.

It was a Friday in July when he cooked me dinner for the first time. When I'd travelled to Crystal Palace it was as though the bus ran out of breath lurching up the hill. Someone had left tangerine peel on the bus floor so the top deck smelled like sweat and hot citrus fruits.

He greeted me with a tea towel over his shoulder and said he had something cooking, which gave me a few minutes to snoop around. The hallway had a floor-to-ceiling bookcase filled with DVDs. There were a lot of horror films and I was surprised that anyone in 2021 still owned Blu-Rays. A blue typewriter was on the table. I pressed down a key and it made a satisfying clack.

He had art on the wall. I tried to not have such low standards that I was impressed by this. There was something about the process of choosing a print, finding a frame of the appropriate dimensions and hanging it that screamed capability to me. Flip's art was good too. Well, it wasn't bad. There was a skateboard painted in Basquiat style, a poster from his own play at the Royal Court and – in the kitchen above a bar cart full of vodka, Campari and some fancy bourbon – a poster from *Soul of a Nation: Art in the Age of Black Power* from Tate Modern. It featured a painting of a black female nude stood next to four men in white suits and hats. She had a distant look in her eyes and a slight tan on her bottom from a bikini. I thought she looked powerful and gorgeous. When I got home I Googled: *black female nude men in white hats, white trilbies and black nude, black nude suits painting tate* and couldn't find it until I reverse-image searched a photo of it from the exhibition page. The painting's titled *What's Going On* by Barkley L. Hendricks and was painted three years after the Marvin Gaye album. I clicked through the painter's other portraits and read an article on the *Atlantic* about his protest art and the commodification of black culture in the 1970s. I don't know why I hadn't just asked Flip what the painting was called.

I'm cooking crab and seaweed pasta. You eat seafood, right? he asked. *I eat everything. It smells great,* I replied. *Tell me about this book you're working on.* I explained that I'd written two drafts but it wasn't working and I was taking some time to accept it as a learning before I started something new. Flip moved the pan on the hob and it sizzled as he said: *Only twenty-five per cent of writing is actually writing. I wish someone had told me that earlier.*

What's the rest? I asked. *Reading, talking, thinking, eating,* he brought over a dish of olives, *and being committed to knowing you'll explore a lot of things that'll end up being nothing. But they're not nothing.* He told me about a film he worked on that ran out of money a few years ago. *There's a grief when a film project ends . . .*

I interrupted him, *I'm not sure that's quite grief.* I used my teeth to strip an olive of its flesh and popped another in my mouth. Flip pushed on, *it is grief. Just a different kind. It's a loss like any other.* Pursing my lips, I placed the two olive stones back in the dish then sipped my wine so I didn't have to speak.

Have I upset you? he asked. I shook my head. *Do you want another drink?* I shook my head again. *Are you lying a little bit about both those things?* I nodded, and he topped up my glass. He talked about his Saturday routine at Dulwich fish market and Waitrose, then catching a film at Everyman or maybe even just MUBI at home with a bottle of refillable organic red wine from the deli by the station. I sat at the table, in the Hovmand Olsen chairs from my building, and we continued our tradition of laughing in them.

My first time in St Andrews was like stepping into a university brochure. It was all autumn leaves and attractive young people holding books, filling their wicker bike-baskets and contemplatively nibbling their pencils in cafes. Then past all that preppy magic in town, there was a beach. Just right there. I wondered why everyone wasn't talking about moving out of London more, then remembered they were, but I always dismissed the suggestion.

Castle Pool sits below the walls of St Andrews Castle, which has been a palace for bishops since the early twelfth century. It's famous for its bottle dungeon, a pit below one tower that was dug twenty-two feet down. It could only be accessed by a trapdoor and prisoners were lowered, or even dropped, into the dank pit and then forgotten. The ruins sit up high on a rocky outcrop over the North Sea. It wasn't early when we visited but the sand was untouched, rows and rows of ripples across it, these curvy crests still visible from their night-time dancing underwater. Black jagged rocks pointed towards the shore like a witch's fingers. The rocks made a boundary towards the right and two concrete walls – one on the left and one the furthest stretch away – had been constructed to create a pool.

As soon as we were done swimming in Castle Pool, it was time to tick another off our list. We walked around St Andrews with our towels wrapped around our waists while using a combination of Google Maps and old TripAdvisor posts to arrive at where we thought Step Rock tidal pool should be. Instead, we found a rather sad-looking aquarium where the concrete walls had been turned into an enclosure. There was one harbour seal moving through the water.

Thinking it would be nice to ask some questions about how long it hadn't been used for swimming, we wandered inside to ask. An assistant with a polo shirt and Cadillac-blue acrylic nails looked up at us. She shrugged, not her problem, and waved us through. In the aquarium cafe families were eating jacket potatoes off dinner trays next to a gift shop that sold penguin cuddly toys. Above a condiment station strewn with spilled sugar sachets were three black-and-white photographs of the old pool in its former glory.

Step Rock was a natural pool below the sandstone cliffs of St Andrews. It was also known as Witch Lake, as women accused of witchcraft were tried by water there in the sixteenth and seventeenth centuries. Suspected witches had their right thumb tied to their left big toe and were thrown into the pool. If they drowned, they were innocent. If they floated, they were prosecuted and taken to the nearby hills to be burned at the stake.

Trialling 'witches' happened for centuries in Britain. I looked at the blue-black water and thought about the transformation of water as a method for harming women and now for freeing them. Most of the swimmers we'd met in Scotland had been women and, in general, I found this was true everywhere I swam. It made me feel welcome to be part of a community full of women reclaiming their long-objectified bodies.

Swimming had been a way for me to rediscover my body as a place of power, play and movement. For so long I'd viewed my body as made up of too-wobbly thighs, too-crooked nose, too-flat chest. All these parts that need fixing. Swimming showed me I had one body, and that body could do something as extraordinary as swim.

Chapter Twenty-Three

St Monans Tidal Pool: 56.20624° N, 2.75519° W

St Monans Tidal Pool reminded me of something
from a T. S. Eliot poem. The pool is a long rectangle
of clay-coloured water with a tier of stone steps
bordered by cement-filled sandbags like an air-raid
shelter. It sits in the penumbra of a windmill that once
belonged to St Monans salt works, which would've
traded mostly to fish curers. Fuel slag and winkle shells
crunched beneath my shoes. Scotland's largest exports
in the 1790s had been wool, fish and salt, so it wasn't
uncommon for Miri and me to find ourselves stepping
on archaeological sites when we searched for tidal
pools.

It was five o'clock on our third day in Scotland and
the early evening light bathed the stone-built salt-pan
houses in the gold gleam of an old Dutch painting.
Everything was crumbling. The coastal cliff fell away,
fraying at the edges like cotton to reveal layers of red
soil, scorched by the heat of the salt pans. The wall

sloped into itself. Even the stone steps seemed unsure of their own sturdiness. It all succumbed to the sea.

When we arrived, there was a wispy-haired woman swimming lengths. Perhaps from the way I flinched at the chill she guessed that we were from down south. *We used to live in Wimbledon.* The husband watched us from the steps. He was sitting wide-legged on the stone but leaning forwards on his walking stick as though it were a third leg. She told us about their life there and paused in odd places while she caught her breath.

I breaststroked my way around a large red rock. In February, it was cleared for the first time in forty years. A community clear-up rid the pool of slippery stones, broken glass and rusty metal that'd once been part of the pool wall. I'd seen posts on the St Monans Pool Facebook page that showed a group removing a rusted stopper from the wall and it foaming seawater like a popped champagne bottle. There were photos of women in waterproof waders proudly wielding spades or pushing wheelbarrows full of stones. It wasn't clear whether they'd got permission to do this, but our swim that evening felt like proof enough that they'd done the right thing. Permission was funny.

There were still rocks in the tidal pool, and I wouldn't have braved it without my sea shoes – though what real protection the three millimetres of neoprene gave me, I'm not sure – but they felt part of the place. The large boulders that we swam around were reminders that swimming was a communion with nature. An immersion rather than a rejection of its sharper edges. At the return of each lap, we became lizards more than swimmers as our stomachs skimmed the rocky seabed at the shallow end. I swam beside the woman for a while and our arms made slow circles through the water. The hinges of my hips creaked and I noticed how uncomfortable it was to move that gradually, that quietly.

He doesn't swim, she nodded towards her husband, *but he comes to watch anyway*, she said as if concluding something. Miri and I dressed in silence, wind whistling through the long grass, the light still defused like a Rembrandt. I took a photo, but the colours weren't quite right: the brown of the water, rusted white of the mill, sandy shade of the tall grass and expansive nothingness of the grey sea beyond. I put my phone away and took a last look instead.

It would be nice wouldn't it, Miri said and I knew that she was thinking of the woman and her husband. A companion to move through life with. Someone who would sit for a while at the pool edge, for no reason other than to keep you company, to share a part of your day with you. Even when the days have been years and they feel less special than they once were.

Maybe that makes them more special, I wasn't sure. I could see from the way Miri headed towards the car, distracted and playing with the keys, that she wasn't sure either.

Miri often said that relationships should only ever be the cherry on top, and I nodded my head then felt like a bad feminist for thinking they were the whole sundae. I thought that grief was the wrong side of love, and love was where I wanted to be. I hoped there I'd feel unstuck. Miri said if you had good friends and a life rich with passions and pursuits, then a romantic relationship need only be an added extra. *It has to be wonderful, for it to be worth it. A shining red cherry on top or not at all.* I sensed she was telling herself something with the 'not at all' part, perhaps a validation of her past breakup. I wanted to believe like she did. I certainly had passions and pursuits and good friends, but I allowed myself hope – sometimes far too much – and didn't mind admitting that I was mad about the idea of love. Love like lightning, thunderstorms, unexpected rain in July.

As we walked to the car, I thought of the husband watching his wife and of swimming with Jem. On the back of his bathroom door there are goggles and a pair of trunks. He described himself as an occasional dipper.

Jem said swimming was a good place to be angry and he liked to scream underwater. *You should try it*, he said. He swam mostly in Hackney's West Reservoir, but a few weekends ago we'd walked to Hampstead Heath together. The mixed pond was closed so we'd separated to go to the Ladies and Men's ponds then reunited at the dirt track, where I watched a whippet with a bandage on his front paw hop to keep up with his owner. I saw Jem walk towards me, shaking his wet curls out. His trousers were muddy at the ankles. I was still shivering from the water when a separate thrill moved through my body, a contentment that I was walking towards Jem, who was waiting for me.

He pulled me in close, and the world went quiet. Trees held their breath. The fullness and softness of his body pressed into me as we kissed by the gate. His growing hardness was against my hips, still streaked with slime from the pond. My lust for him – which had at first been frantic and unrestrained – was moving towards gratitude for patience. Patience was a sign that there was time for us.

We're not in a rush, was something Jem said often. I'd spent four years being in a rush. Rush to live, rush to work, rush to fuck, rush to drink. Always aware that time was not something to be taken for granted. I'd seen it stolen from someone I loved. Now I was trying to trust that, even if time did run out, living it slow would be better. I couldn't rush forever, or however long I had.

We took our wet towels and ate croissants as we walked through Hampstead, Highgate Woods and then Muswell Hill. Without thinking about it, my feet had walked me to Sami's bench. When we approached Alexandra Park I started pointing towards the trees in the distance, indicating that I had a destination in mind. I couldn't pass this part of London without feeling its gravitational pull. There had been days when it had dragged me all the way from Camberwell. This was one of those days.

Jem and I hadn't spoken about Tom much. I'd been actively avoiding it, which didn't feel very 'active' as it was what I'd been doing for years anyway. We were getting closer all the time and yet there was this brother-shaped space between us. Jem must've seen the photos in my flat, but he didn't comment on them. Probably because he thought I didn't want to talk about it, which was a fair assumption. I felt trapped in the long tunnel of a telescope. I wanted him to look closer.

When we arrived at the bench Jem read the dedication, then moved his body towards mine until the backs of our hands touched. *Was she your friend?* I shook my head, still staring at it. *She's my friend's sister. I met Rohanna after Tom died.* His name occupied the canopy of my throat. I had to stop speaking in case I stopped breathing.

Jem leaned his head on top of mine. I wanted to shrug him off, but instead I moved my face into his shoulder and inhaled. He smelled of sweat and coffee and pond. I was challenging myself to love through the hurt. I tried to pull him in rather than push him away. Just to see what would happen. He held me there for a moment and didn't move until I did.

I like to come here sometimes, I started picking at the dirt underneath my nails. *I've been thinking I'd like a bench. It could be somewhere to be and think about Tom.* Jem sat down, *you have this bench too. And that one over there*, he pointed far away, *and the ones in Brockwell Park.* My stomach tightened, *I know, but this is Sami's bench. I need a Tom bench.*

You can make any bench a Tom bench, don't you think? I closed my eyes and tried to think where to begin in answering that question. I thought about rushing, I tried not to rush.

Chapter Twenty-Four

Pittenweem Tidal Pool: 56.21025° N, 2.73789° W

Just five minutes down the coast from St Monans, there's another pool to be found. Pittenweem tidal pool is below the cliffs of a fishing village in Fife. Its name means 'the place of the caves' and the coastline is rocky and jagged, with St Fillan's Cave nestled in the nearby shore. East Neuk is a magical part of Scotland. It is like it sounds, full of nooks and corners. The tidal pool has been there for, as many locals put it, as long as they can remember. There are records of a pool of some sort from 1895, then after the Second World War locals rebuilt and refurbished it to create the pool recognisable today. Eventually the valve broke and the walls leaked. Six years ago, it was a sad empty pool; unswimmable and forgotten. Locals had been applying for funding for years with no luck when they took matters into their own hands before it was closed forever.

There are many things I'd think to do to fundraise for a tidal pool. Miri and I have seen a few:

privatisation, council support, donations per swim, charity events. All work in their own way, but none have been quite as inventive as the West Braes project, which created a crazy golf course to raise money for Pittenweem tidal pool.

To reach the pool, we walked through Pittenweem village, which was full of white houses with Dutch-style crow-stepped gables and red roofs. I realised how far north we were that throughout the village's history boats from Belgium and the Netherlands would've sailed to these ports. The clifftop golf course was the very first thing I saw. A large green field with oblong stretches of AstroTurf made up the holes. Each was sponsored by local businesses or families to cover the upkeep and I heard it was competitive to reserve one each year. I glanced towards hole twelve, which was decorated with a design of large blue-and-white fish: J Doig & Sons the local fishmonger in Anstruther. The pharmacy had a hole too, as did a local oatcake business, and hole seven – which looked particularly tricky – was a memorial to a man named Keith Grant. Perhaps I had it all wrong with a bench and a putting hole for Tom was actually the way to go. Beside the putting green was a pale blue shipping container with a bolted door that opened to collect change for a club and ball.

Beyond there was the sea. All of it big and black and beautiful. That day the sun was so bright that the ocean, and everything besides it, appeared dark and the light reflected on its surface like glinting diamonds. An amphitheatre of sorts had been carved into the cliffs, which was hemmed by concrete steps down to the pool. I didn't swim for long. The light was in my eyes and I fancied lying on the pool wall with my face tilted upwards so the sun could charge me up. I sat there and balanced a line of grey pebbles on my left shin.

Afterwards Miri and I ordered two teas and a Tunnock's teacake while we chatted to the volunteer at the hut. There was a large blackboard promoting a Rockpool Guddle (equipment provided) and show-casing grainy laminated photos of recent dolphin sightings. A little girl pointed to the sea and said, *look Mummy. There's a seal,* but she was shushed away while her mother complained to a friend that someone had promised to bring cakes to the PTA gathering again then turned up empty-handed. *This is the last time I let Sandra get away with it,* she said, then glanced up. *Oh look at that. A seal!* As if it had just occurred to her. I followed their eyeline to see a faint speck that emerged and dived then reappeared quite near. The little girl scrunched up her face and kicked the blackboard. She ran away to join her friends playing by the water.

We'd travelled over two hundred miles since Wick, and every pool had been touched by people who truly cared. The world that so many people talk about want-ing already exists in these small places. It exists in communities that build tidal pools. I wished I could bottle that kindness and joy, take it to the places that are hurting and show them that this is possible.

Cellardyke was our third of four swims that Sunday. We moved quickly from one to the next with Miri driving fast to chase the low tides. To get in the pool we had to shimmy across a wall with a rusted railing that skirted a playground. There were hooks hammered into the brick in every colour of the rainbow. I hung my towel on the orange one.

Cellardyke was thriving that day. A mum bundled her children into the shallow end while she struggled with an overstuffed Sports Direct bag. A little boy was on all fours barking like a dog at his siblings. A woman rested on a float while shouting instructions at her young granddaughter to teach her to swim. Both were wearing shorties and remained in the water after we'd packed up and left.

I tried to remember being taught how to swim. I had no memories of spending time with my parents or grandparents in the water, only the smell of chlorine from the pool where we earned metre badges that Mum sewed onto our towels. There must've been many afternoons spent in the water as a family as all of us became confident swimmers. I thought about how many moments Mum was with me that I don't remember and what a singular possession a memory with your child must be. Giving love and encouragement, knowing they might not remember.

There'd been a lot of multi-generational family-watching in Scotland. It wasn't something I saw a huge amount of in London: families made up of children, parents and grandparents enjoying the outdoors together. Teaching each other things. Memories with my family were a finite resource, but I often struggled to conjure them. I suspected this was a consequence of losing Tom. Most of the time I didn't think the stages of grief related to me so much as the stages of PTSD. Emergency, numbing, rescue. I didn't deny Tom's death, but I didn't accept it either. I simply chose not to acknowledge it. It didn't surprise me that the years surrounding his illness were a mist but I hadn't expected my childhood to feel foggy too. There were happy family memories, but recalling them hurt as much as recalling the hospital: the plastic chairs hammered into the floor, vending-machine tea, doctors' shoes on linoleum, Mum's Tupperware of pills.

I tried to remember, but remembering was bruising. Deep blue and painful. I'd read that humans spend more time anticipating and remembering moments than living them. I thought about this trip to swim in every tidal pool in a year and how much of it I spent experiencing the swims as something I'd look back on. I watched the woman and her granddaughter, then closed my eyes and tried to open my mind. I tried to remember a day with Tom in a pool like this and when I couldn't I tried to imagine. Maybe that was just as good. Still an exercise in love.

A cloud shifted over us, and Miri began pulling on her coat. *Are you ready?* I shook my head; I wasn't ready for all of this. Miri sat back down. *No, sorry. I'm ready to leave. Let's go.*

Chapter Twenty-Five

North Berwick Law: 56.05223° N, 2.71743° W

Miri and I were staying far out of North Berwick, which was a shame as we quickly fell in love with the unspoiled harbour town. The coast was lined with volcanic islands that glowed golden in shafts of light. One of them was Fidra, which had inspired Robert Louis Stevenson's *Treasure Island*. We took a zigzagging path up a volcanic hill where a whale's jawbone stood boldly on the peak, then returned to the town for battered cod from North Berwick Fry. I dragged Miri to a gelato parlour Emma had recommended to me and ate a two-scoop cup of Italian Cherry Amarena with an Irn-Bru. Afterwards I felt quite sick but didn't admit it to Miri because overeating was my favourite holiday hobby. Next it was Miri's turn to drag me into the local supermarkets, where she inspected the chilled aisle. Her eyes scanned the milk shelves and she took a few photographs of the product merchandising. *Interesting*, Miri said. *Very interesting*. The pubs and roasteries in North Berwick were Scottish-meets-Scandi with bare bulb lights and scaffolding tables. It was all very *hygge*. We'd only been walking around for half an hour and I'd seen four houses, three men and two jackets that I wanted.

We passed an antique shop with a selection of knick-knacks decorating the pavement. It was on a busy road and when cars sped by the stacks of blue and white Spode china rattled on the table. I pressed down the keys of a typewriter and thought about Flip. He'd been interested in our trip to Scotland and said if I could up and leave town with just a typewriter and my swimsuit then I was born to write. I liked the idea of being a travelling storyteller. Flip continued to call me 'Poet' and every time felt like less of a hoax. He read my work and picked out lines to read back to me. *I don't mean to gass you up but your prose is awesome*, he said and a part of me started to think he might be right.

I enjoyed being around Flip's things. The annotated script left open on the table, cup of red pens on the desk, travel-size bottles of cologne and SPF in the bathroom cabinet, coffee machine in shining armour silver that shook the kitchen appliances when he pressed the espresso button. Everything had a place, and I began to have a place there too.

He was working hard, but losing sleep from the pressure. *I just want to start a conversation; people have to talk about this film*. He was serious about things and I liked that. It was something that had been used against me in the past. Having things I wanted to do and places I wanted to go required too much of those around me and I got the impression men just wanted a golden retriever with breasts who they could take for walks and wouldn't question too much. *You take yourself too seriously*, they'd say like that was a bad thing. Flip let me be serious about everything. We shared fantasies that we'd be too ashamed to tell anyone else in case they thought us arrogant or overly ambitious. In his dream he was at a Q&A panel at the Venice Film Festival. In mine I was at the Jersey literary festival. *You'll get there*, he'd say. *I believe it*, he'd say.

The sex was serious too, which was unusual for me, as I always felt I had to be playful to avoid both parties acknowledging that sex with a woman with small breasts is probably quite underwhelming. He acted like I whelmed him. *Poet*, he said into my neck. *Poet*.

When I left in the morning, he let me take books. Ted Hughes poems, Caryl Churchill plays and *The Fisher King and the Handless Maiden*. It explored the origins of masculine and feminine wounds in a mix of psychology and folklore. Flip gave it to me as a storyteller's handbook, but I received it as a feelers' guide and reread the same passage about a lack of terminology being directly related to a lack of consciousness. Other cultures have extensive vocabulary for discussing matters of the heart. Sanskrit has ninety-six words. We have just one. It read, 'Eskimos have thirty words for snow, because it is a life-and-death matter to them to have exact information about the element they live with so intimately. An Eskimo probably would die of clumsiness if he had only one word for snow; we are close to dying of loneliness because we have only one word for love.' I thought about the way Flip gave me love and the way Jem did. I thought about the pure, uncomplicated love that Miri gave me and wondered why that wasn't enough. Why I wanted more.

The book-borrowing punctuated the time between our meetings. *I'll return it to the shelf when I see you next.* There was always enough time between our meetings to finish a book. Weeknights continued to be a thing for him. I asked him how he had time for a social life with that rule and he said, *right now I don't have one. I just see you, Freya.* It made me feel powerful to be the connection between his film and the outside world. There was always the promise of after the edit, after the film. I'd been reading about Orkney and we'd talked about spending a week there together. Just the two of us in a house on the cliffs, to share separate sides of a desk and write. We'd take it in turns to face the window and watch the sea.

While we walked through North Berwick, I told all this to Miri and she said Flip seemed a passionate person. *What's Jem passionate about?* I thought about my conversation with him about his ambition to have more time. I was embarrassed to say I was sleeping with someone who was passionate about life in case that meant I was one step away from having a 'Live, Laugh, Love' poster. Jem's WhatsApp Status read: 'I feel glad'. That summed him up quite well, but felt hard to explain. *You'll have to meet him soon and you can ask him.* I tried to turn things onto Miri. *Was your ex passionate?* She sighed. *Constantly. It was a nightmare. Total enthusiasm for new things before he abandoned them. Our basement was a graveyard to his failed hobbies. It was a shame because he was so good at everything he tried. And every time I hoped it would be different.*

It's good to hope. She tugged at her earlobes where her gold earrings usually were, *maybe. I like it when people can stick at things.* Miri glanced at the traffic lights before crossing the road. *We'll stick at this.* We passed a church called Our Lady Star of the Sea. I thought of it as a good omen.

The Trinkie

Chapter Twenty-Six

North Berwick Tidal Pool: 56.06061° N, 2.71620° W

To get into the old burgh from The Crown Guest House we had to call a taxi, which proved more diffi-cult than we'd expected as everyone said we were too far away. Eventually, we found Mika's Private Hire, who picked us up in ten minutes and told us his life story in just fifteen. Mika was one of those drivers who spends the entire journey looking at you via the rear-view mirror. I began the journey gripping the car door but quickly forgot about anything other than Mika as he told us how he had come to live in North Berwick. He was one of only of dozens of Kosovar refugees who'd been flown to Prestwick in 1999 to escape the conflict. When he arrived he weighed just six stone, a devastating physical sign of the torture he'd suffered for ninety-seven days. The flight was split into groups, travelling to Glasgow, Renfrew and North Berwick. Mika was brought to a large house that had once belonged to a passenger of the *Titanic* and been left to the city after he never returned. Mika told us that North Berwick would be his home forever because the people had looked after him with such kindness. He also said it was getting too busy with tourists and although that was good for his business, he didn't like it. We asked him to collect us again after dinner. *Say you're my friends and they'll look after you in there. Everyone knows me, everyone knows Mika.* After our meal we found him at the bar with a cup of coffee chatting to the barman. *Time to get you home ladies*, he said and drove us back to East Linton.

The next day we walked through town while waiting for the tidal pool to appear. We pointed at Bass Rock. It normally appears white due to the sheer plumage of seabirds covering the volcanic island, but looked whitish grey because of the sheer coverage of bird shit. We peered inside the Scottish Seabird Centre and decided today wouldn't be the day we became interested in birds. Puffins could've got me excited enough to do a boat trip, but it wasn't happening for a colony of gannets.

It was our last day and the sun had come out for us, as if Scotland hadn't wanted us to fall in love with it only for the good weather but didn't mind showing off before we left. North Berwick tidal pool is more of a children's paddling area than a pool, but the sand was so fine and so blonde that I didn't mind swimming with my belly brushing the bottom. We sat on the concrete wall, moving occasionally for three children who were determinedly striding the pool perimeter like guards. Nearby a father and son built a sandcastle with adjacent dam and waterway. The Scottish, much like the English, clearly enjoy building complex civil engineering projects as a way to relax on the beach.

Once there had been a lido in North Berwick, but it was closed by East Lothian Council in 1995. A lamp-post was stapled with a sign that said Bring Back Our Outdoor Pool. I looked up the petition, which was full of archive photos of past gala days. Many of the photos were donated by the final Pool Mistress Shona MacDonald, who started as an assistant back in the '80s. She said, 'my first day in charge I arrived to find a young lad fishing with his grandad's sea rod in the pool. He had told me he caught two the day before and I didn't believe him till we drained for the start of the new season and saw several fish flapping around in the mud.' I searched Shona's name and read her tales from the old lido. In one she said the former Pool Master who'd trained her had left to become a lobster fisherman. On his return from sea he'd throw crabs into the pool, which helped her clear the lido quickly at the end of the day.

The morning sun had burned out and we basked in the cinders. I was still thinking about Mika. I thought about what home meant and wondered if he had a person who made it home here or if there was someone he'd left behind; I hadn't asked. I thought about never seeing Emma again and how lost that would make me. Then I thought about never seeing Tom again and if that was any better or different. Maybe if I knew that somewhere he was safe, I could learn to find comfort. I had felt that Tom was safe in the hospital but not that he was free from pain. Comparing Mika's suffering to my own, I grew concerned that I might be a bad person, but I told myself it was an attempt to connect with others. The answer was never better or worse, just different. I was trying to be less angry about the idea that some might have it better and less comforted that people had it worse. It was all just different.

While we waited for our gate to appear on the departures board, I walked around the airport souvenir shop looking at the tartan scarves and reading what clans the colours represented. My friend Lauren worried about marrying her boyfriend because his family's tartan were such ugly colours, and her flowers would have to be yellow and purple to match. I looked up his surname and decided that she was right, it was the ugliest – or at least in the worst three – from the selection there.

I found a tin of shortbread with two Scotties wearing tartan tam o'shanter caps on the lid. Their expressions were coquettish like they were listening to a joke and were tilting their heads to hear the punchline better. I couldn't tell if it was illustrated or a photograph, but I hoped it was real because I liked the idea of a photographer holding treats behind a camera to make the dogs look down the lens without knocking off their hats. It made me laugh and I thought Jem would find it funny too. Momentarily, I picked up a second tin for Flip, then placed it down. He was busy this week and I didn't think he'd appreciate animals in human clothing the same way I did. I bought a notebook, also tartan, and decided I would write recollections of Tom when they came to me. An inventory of family memories that I could reread.

Seven months later, I found the notebook again, untouched, and threw it away.

As soon as I returned from Scotland, I went to see Jem. My bag was weighed down by my wet swimsuit – evidence of one last swim before the flight – but I felt light knowing I'd be with him soon. I wanted to tell him about Pittenweem, Eileen, Mika, the dolphin and all the things we'd seen. I wanted to hear about Sweden, too. I was unsure what he'd been doing there and with whom but was relieved his trip hadn't turned into weeks away. He'd returned with gifts: a red and yellow can of *surströmming* – which he told me was fermented herring – and a postcard from Fotografiska Stockholm. It was a monochrome photograph by Lovisa Ringborg of a woman's torso with her hands laid out on the table. One was cut off. It reminded me of the Handless Maiden. Something bumped about inside me as the world I'd created with Flip momentarily knocked against my world with Jem. On the reverse the postcard said:

> *Freya,*
> *I want to put both my hands inside your brain.*
> *J x*

Somewhere in the night Jem and I built a dreamworld together. In the day, he was unclear to me or, more, it was unclear to me how he felt. It was like I was staring at him through a mist that wouldn't clear. Then in sex, something came into focus. Our relationship made sense to me in a way that my brain couldn't put into words. Somehow my body understood him, before my head did, and I didn't need to wonder what he was thinking or feeling; it was there. He seemed to sense it too. Jem played with words and ideas in ways we didn't outside the bedroom. *My pussy,* he said. Implying an ownership that we hadn't discussed before. *I've missed fucking you,* he said. Expressing that I'd occupied his thoughts in my absence. *Did you miss fucking me?*

It was the place Jem felt most comfortable to say that I was beautiful, and the only place I was present enough that I stopped to hear it. In those nights and mornings and afternoons, we built something together. This dreamworld. And it made me want to continue. Keep building, keep building, keep building.

Chapter Twenty-Seven

Shoalstone Pool: 50.40130° N, 3.49880° W

Before we travelled to Brixham, I read a lot about a man named Mark Portwood. I'm sure he's used to being known as the man who saved Shoalstone tidal pool and I think that must be quite nice. Brixham is a fishing village full of pastel-painted houses in the southern end of Torbay. In Victorian times there was a natural rockpool, then in 1896 walls were built to transform it into a tidal pool. Thirty years later, it was shaped into its current design with shallow and deep ends. In 2012 a storm smashed concrete into the pool building and bogged it with debris. At that time, Mark had recently left the Navy and was working at Shoalstone as a lifeguard. The council said they couldn't afford the repairs, so Mark took on the work himself and made it his mission to get the pool open again for the summer season. The council continued to say that the pool couldn't – and shouldn't – reopen. They claimed they couldn't afford the £15,000 for the pool's lifeguard despite the car park alone bringing in that income and rumours that the mayor had spent an equivalent sum on a palm tree.

Despite his hard work, Mark's one-man campaign made him the council's 'public enemy number one'. They put up nearly impenetrable fencing, which he had to jump over to make the repairs. With the summer opening fast approaching, Mark worked around the tide to empty, clean and repaint the pool, including restoring a near-ancient cast iron valve. With no cash for the restoration, he relied on the kindness of local builders and engineers who volunteered their time and supplies to make the necessary fixes, including donating Alpine Blue paint.

On a Saturday in August, Miri and I swam a few laps across the east-facing tidal pool and looked out across Torbay. In the distance, I could see the rusted hulk of a freighter. I wondered where it was going and what it was carrying. I noticed the Alpine Blue paint on the pool perimeter. It's noticeable everywhere. The place is touched by Mark's effort and probably by the hands of many others too. Someone told me that the wooden ladder we climbed into the pool on was restored by Mark's father, who was sadly dead by the time we visited. The pool has since been cared for by Friends of Shoalstone Pool. Together, they look after this place and keep its spirit alive.

I'd started this adventure because I was searching. So far, I hadn't found what I was looking for. I still missed Tom, but I'd found other people who were searching. Eileen, Mika, Shona, Mark and so many more. Searching for time away from their life, time to be near others, time to exercise, time to make a community. And in searching, they found it right on their doorsteps. I was beginning to realise that, more than anything, people are searching for a place to call their own. A place that will make them feel like the moment in time they're living in means something and that they have an ability to create some of that meaning.

After a few laps, we returned to the changing rooms with wooden doors that swung on their hinges like in an old Western. I stood outside Miri's changing room and saw her legs, still beaded with seawater. Turning back towards the pool, I watched a woman swimming a careful breaststroke. She turned onto her back and I noticed she was pregnant; her head, stomach and toes were islands emerging from the water. She had the loveliest blonde hair, tinted almost green. I wondered if her baby would be blonde too. Tom had hair like that. Golden. Curled. I was always dark, but the twins had a lightness about them as children. *Angelic*, people used to say. They were the kind of children people stopped to coo over in their pram. Nothing is lovelier than a double pram of twins.

I often had the same recurring dream that I was round as a beach ball and people rubbed my belly like it was a genie's lamp. *What are you having,* they'd say. In the dream, I knew it was a boy and I knew it was Tom. Not Tom, but always Tom. Same hair, same curls, same eyes, same spirit. Then, when he was born, I had to stare down at this bouncing round child and push my swollen nipples into his pink gummy lips and feed him and grow him and worry if he'd leave me again.

I'd always wanted children, but since my brother's death, I had became scared of having a baby boy who looked like him. I was scared of having a mirror of my grief to stare at every day. I was scared of wanting to look away when I couldn't cope, but not being able to because the baby needed feeding. I was scared of everyone expecting me to be happy when I was with child. Everyone would want me to be complete, and I wouldn't be able to argue that I was still broken. Were women with babies allowed to be heartbroken for lost brothers still?

I was scared of feeling all the love that my mother felt and having no container for it. I was scared of what it would feel like to look into her eyes after that, to really see her for the first time and understand the strength of her devotion for us. I was scared to feel pity for her. No child should pity their parent, but who couldn't pity a woman who nursed and loved a child then had him taken away?

I dreamed of the beach ball a lot. Sometimes I dreamed I was pregnant with Flip's child. A beautiful baby I could bounce on my lap with Flip's gentle cooing over my shoulder. There'd be a shiny new look of adoration from him, *look what we made!* That child would look different, not like Tom at all. That scared me more than anything.

Chapter Twenty-Eight

Jem's Skylight: 51.56091° N, 0.05526° W

Sundays became a night for me and Jem to have dinner in East London, then watch a movie. We were at a stage where I felt less apprehensive about making plans; we were becoming each other's default. I'd rehearsed conversations in my mind about how our exclusivity chat would go, and Jem leaning over to touch the soft hollow of my stomach and asking if we could fuck without a condom wasn't how I'd imagined it. We hadn't spoken about contraception or babies or exes or lovers yet. Then that afternoon I'd bled on the rug of his bedroom. He'd presented his fingers to me, speckled with pink, and said *you must've started your period, are you ok?* I'd replied, *I'm on the pill. It must be break-through bleeding.* Jem was playing dot to dot, and I didn't like the way the picture was coming together. I felt robbed of a romantic conversation that I'd been preparing for. I'd wanted him to say that he thought about me all the time and only wanted to be with me. I was often doing this. Having a dialogue with myself, rather than another person, and being frustrated when they didn't act out the part I'd written for them. I put Jem off for time to think. He pulled a shiny plasticky-smelling condom over himself until he was dressed like a deli-counter meat and later I went home to rewrite lines in our imaginary conversation.

Then, late on a muggy night in August, when the air felt static and like there might be thunder, the conversation happened again. *I'm not sleeping with other people and I've been tested. What do you think?* My insides crumpled, and I tried to connect those words to his intentions beyond having unprotected sex. *Those are facts, tell me how you feel about us.* Jem lay on his back facing the ceiling. His arm was around me. Suddenly, I noticed how quiet it was and the absence of cars and neighbours and birds outside sounded deafening. My head was resting on his chest and his heartbeat echoed while his pauses widened. Jem told me he'd been upfront with other girls from the start – that it was casual and he wasn't looking for a relationship – but he'd been avoiding this conversation, because it didn't feel the same with us.

He said kind things, but I forgot them as soon as they left his lips. I remember him touching my chest to symbolise my heart and my temples for my brain. He wanted to show me that, although I was naked beside him, I was many more things to him than my body.

I really like you, but I'm not sure what I want. Not sure, I heard. Not sure. Not sure. At the beginning of the year, he'd got out of a relationship with a friend who he'd fallen in love with. *It was only five months, but it left me tired and it was a bad time.* He kept his arm around me the whole time. We were both too scared to look at one another, but it felt good to touch as I felt his life connect to mine a little deeper. He repeated that he wasn't sure what he wanted and I told him I had this idea that when people met it would be like lightning and they would both instantly know. If he wasn't sure about me, perhaps it wasn't right and we didn't have true feelings for one another. *I am sure about you. I'm not sure about me,* he said finally. I took shelter in the hollow of his armpit.

He was so honest with me, and yet I lay there lying. I held on to my secret that I was sleeping with, and emotionally invested in, another man. I could feel the lie, breathing and beating, a dark red blood pumping through it. *A relationship that left you tired,* I thought. *I'll make you tired.* I wanted him to love me so hard and deep that I drained everything from him. I was a siren calling out from the depths of the ocean, and I wouldn't settle for anything other than immersion. I was jealous of this woman who'd left him a little emptier. All the space she'd taken up. What would I have to do to be that all-consuming? I was always the one left empty. I was jealous of how she was there with us, in the bedroom. I wondered if she thought about this late at night, another woman being told about her.

Really, I was the same as Jem. I was sure about him but not about me. I just wasn't courageous enough to say it like he was. Aloud, I said: *I'm scared of feeling like I've misunderstood.* The moon slipped into the bedroom. Jem moved my fringe from around my face. *You're not misunderstanding. I like you very much.* He seemed to sense there was something I wasn't saying but, true to his fair and patient nature, only asked, *if you could have a wish, what would it be?* I stared at the hair on this chest where it joined and made a riptide of curls. I wasn't sure I had it in me to make a wish. Jem waited a while then said, *mine would be that we'd keep talking like this.* Finally, I said mine was that we would just keep going, which was a steady intention that had underlined the last few years of my life without Tom.

Soon, I would have more wishes. They would be big and bold and full of laughter and love, but right now I needed cautious wishes I could keep close to my chest. *Keep going.* Jem held me and said that was a good one. I spoke the words into his neck, although I was saying them to myself.

I left the next day with a sick feeling that wouldn't go away. Jem called to ask if I was ok and I said I was fine, just tired. He said, *I love figuring this stuff out with you.* Somehow, I was doing worse at being open and honest with Jem than when we'd started. We'd agreed that we were *taking it slow* and in the moment that felt like a good idea. Being alone at home again, I realised I had no idea what that meant. Were we a couple? Did this change how often we saw each other? Were we seeing other people? I was seeing other people. One very particular 'other people'. Yet I knew I was beginning to feel sure that I would give up anything for Jem. The realisation that he might not feel the same was devastating.

I told myself I would stop seeing one of them as soon as someone made a confident gesture towards me. And anyway, it wouldn't be long before one of them let me down. There was no need yet. I wanted to believe men could be good, but I was still waiting for one to prove me right.

I wondered if Jem had asked me to be in a relation-ship with him, whether I would've acted differently and stopped seeing Flip. I thought about the last time I saw Tom and the promise I made to him. The prom-ise I'd never kept.

Chapter Twenty-Nine

Broken Radiator: 51.47478° N, 0.10552° W

Not long after I called her, Miri came over with a bottle of wine. We hadn't swum since our trip to Brixham, but when I shared that I was feeling down about Jem she said she'd be straight over. *I have some work to finish but I'll see you soon,* she said, then muttered something under her breath about recyclable Activia cup containers and hung up.

Before Miri was even through the door, she was telling me about a *Desert Island Discs* episode I should listen to. From what I could gather, it involved the deaths of two parents, an inheritance spent on alcohol and a chef who punched an Alsatian. I went into the kitchen and poured the bottle into two glasses, then leaned over to sip the top so I could carry both without spilling them. Miri pulled a tatty-looking book from her bag and handed it to me. *I saw this and thought of you.* It was a second-hand Pete Doherty biography. I clutched it to my chest. Miri knew trashy ghost-written biographies of pop stars were my guilty pleasure. The only thing I loved more was indulging in the Personal Life section of Wikipedia, then texting Miri saying, *if it wasn't true you wouldn't believe it.* I told myself that when I'd written enough novels I'd write a Paula Yates biopic screenplay one day.

We sat on the sofa, our feet both under the same cushion, and watched *Sex and the City.* It was the one where Berger breaks up with Carrie on a Post-it note. We'd both seen it before, but I needed the comfort of feeling everything just becomes an anecdote. Miri had been dating a guy from the plant-based products department at work and she was getting whiplash from the back and forth of their unclear arrangements. Last week he'd said he wasn't sure he had the bandwidth to meet more than once a week. We were both feeling more like Charlotte, looking for love.

Miri pulled me in for a hug and my legs pretzelled up against my body. I stayed still and let her hold me. I wanted to ask her if I could know Jem was falling in love with me by the way he held me. Flip was good at praise and promises. Jem, on the other hand, was all about touch. I thought of the way Jem held my face in his hands and pulled me to his chest. It felt so real. Could sex be more real than words? Surely the attentiveness with which Jem touched me couldn't mean nothing?

What does it mean? I said finally and Miri replied, *I don't think we can ever be sure that anything means something.* I thought about opening another bottle of wine. *You know what I'm going to say next,* she smoothed the blanket on her lap, *but you should really communicate to him how you're feeling. Imagine if you waste the start of something really exciting with someone really special feeling anxious when you could get some clarity and throw yourself into it.* I ignored this comment and looked past her to the television. Carrie was gesticulating wildly with a cigarette in her hands.

Want to know the thing I find most frustrating? Miri sighed. I nodded and snaffled a handful of Maltesers into my mouth. *Everyone says being single is fun, and I always feel it's a personal failure when it's not. This stuff is really bruising.* She touched my knee.

It's shitty, isn't it. How are things with your fella? I asked. *He is so far from being my fella. He told me he doesn't wear a bike helmet because he thinks the cars look out for him more that way. I need to send a thanks but no thanks text.* The credits started rolling. *I guess we just keep going.*

That weekend my distraction, or perhaps it was just my clumsiness, caused me to drop my keys down the back of the radiator. I knew I'd have to phone Mum if I ever wanted to retrieve them, as she is the most capable human I've ever known. I'd been thinking a lot about Miri's comment on communicating. I'd made a mess of communicating with Jem, but perhaps asking Mum for help would give me hope I could be better. She answered on the second ring. We wasted some time talking about how I'd done something as stupid as drop my keys down the back of the radiator, then she asked, *how's this guy then?* I assembled the few tools I had: a rusting hammer and an old IKEA Allen key. *Is he your boyfriend yet?* I rubbed my forehead; *it doesn't work like that Mum.*

Tell me how it works then? I ignored the question so she pushed on, *you have fun with him though, don't you?* I nodded, then remembered she couldn't see me. *Yes, I do.* She paused, then said, *that's important. Me and your dad have fun, you know.* I knew.

Not a lot of couples survive this. We've done ok. The Allen key in my hand felt sticky. I doubted she was wrong. Mum went to a lot of bereavement events and had told me many times that most couples with dead children get divorced in the end. There are few survivors. Mum added, *and sex. Having good sex helps. Does he . . .*

I moved us onto planning a strategy for the retrieval of my keys. As she explained how to unscrew the bracket from the wall, I imagined her expression of determined concentration, her tongue resting on her lower lip while she worked. It was that imagined

familiarity, the closeness of it, that gave me the courage to talk about a bench. Our conversation didn't go
as well as it had with Emma, who raised no objections
other than pointing out that, wherever it was, the
bench would be a long way to go for someone. Emma
in Birmingham, me in London and our parents in
Wales. *What do you think about a bench?* I asked as I
twisted the valve as taut as it would go. *Don't talk in
riddles*, she replied sternly, Bake Off *is on in twenty.*

*I went to Sami's anniversary. They have a bench, and
everyone left flowers.* Mum remained focused on the
task, *get a towel for when you drain it . . .*

I think it's nice they have somewhere to go, I continued
once I'd grabbed a towel from the laundry pile.
Otherwise you'll warp the floorboards.

Maryam said that every— Mum interrupted me,
Maryam was there? She shifted her tone of voice from
instructional to alert. The bereaved parenting community was a close and competitive one and she'd met
Rohanna and Sami's mum before. I made a noise that
sounded like a nod. *Let's talk about it later. When your
dad's around.* There was a pause and I feared she might
ask me something further about Rohanna that might
lead her to asking me about Tom. *Aha*, I exclaimed.
Here they are! I said, which was a lie as I hadn't salvaged
my keys yet. We said our goodbyes and hung up.

Chapter Thirty

BFI Southbank: 51.50724° N, 0.11474° W

Because I'd dreamed about him and the beach ball, I called Flip. He'd been invited to a party, but wanted to stay in and order a pizza. I said we should go; it would be nice to meet some of his friends. *These are film people. They're not my friends*, he replied, then told me to wait on the street and he'd pick me up in his black Mini Cooper because he wasn't drinking. He was measured in that way, never wanting to be out of control around new people. I wore a dress with tiny spaghetti straps that Flip played with when we stopped at a set of traffic lights.

It was the kind of party where there were so many trays of white and red wine circulating that guests quickly abandoned them and the space was dotted with glasses at varying levels of completeness. People are wasteful when things feel limitless. I was high on the rush of being stood next to Flip while he made people laugh. I had to tilt my head to look at him while he talked. I thought about him saying, *you're the only one I see, Freya.*

Glancing at a woman in her late thirties wearing a velvet jacket with frog knot buttons, I whispered into Flip's shoulder, *she wrote that HBO show I'm obsessed with.* She looked over and waved at us. *You know her?* He rubbed his head, *yeah we worked on this thing a few years back.* They talked about someone they both knew who'd mysteriously left a production mid-shoot. She kept trying to pull Flip into gossiping, but he just repeated, *I didn't hear about that,* which she appeared to find tiresome. They continued like that for a while, then she seemed to realise I was there. Flip introduced me . . . *and this is Freya. She's a writer, but I'm trying to persuade her that poetry is her thing. I think you two'll get on.* He was right, we did.

We spoke about our favourite female comedians, television algorithms and if we were reaching the end of human patience, then swimming came up and she said it was a real bore that all the *Guardian* ever wrote about was wild swimming. *We used to just call it swimming in my day,* she swiftly picked up a white wine from a passing tray. I looked at the lines around her eyes and wondered what she was referring to as 'my day' as she couldn't have been more than ten years older than me. *Not 'wild swimming' like the dry-robe brigade calls it,* she made quotes with her fingers while clutching the glass. I felt a tug inside me and wanted to point out that I didn't have a dry-robe, but resisted the urge to be pulled into a divide that didn't exist. Swimming made me happy. It kept me healthy; it kept me outside. What did it matter to anyone else? Her joy clearly came from gossiping and synthetic kimonos. I'd rather be a wild swimmer than someone who complained about how other people found their happiness.

Anyway, she continued once she'd emptied the glass and had the use of both hands for wildly gesturing again, *that could be good for you, throw yourself into that world. Put yourself at the centre of it so you have a right to tell the story. Nowadays you can get a Channel 4 pilot from an Edinburgh show or a poxy blog. Even a viral tweet is enough to get you a film deal for fuck's sake. You're a talker, start a podcast or something.* I expressed my reluctance; *everyone has a podcast.* I moved my weight to the other foot. *So why not you?* Why not me, I thought.

I wondered what everyone in the room saw when they looked at me with Flip. She clearly thought I was someone who had something to say. The thought turned me on so I put my hand on the small of Flip's back and said, *nothing good ever happens past midnight. Let's go to bed.*

When we got back to mine, Flip neatly folded his clothes over the side of my sofa. I thought they looked good there. *I like being out with you. You make me feel like I can do anything.* He laughed, *what you doing with that feeling?* I said, *I have an idea for a story. It's about swimming.* He nodded; *I look forward to reading it.* Flip took off his socks and put them inside his trainers. *For what it's worth, I don't believe that you don't know you're talented without me.* Now it was my turn to laugh.

Seriously Freya, is there anything you've ever wanted to do that you haven't made happen? We got into bed, and he rested his head on his hands, elbows outstretched like two diamonds. *I get it. I stayed small for way too long. You've always known you can do anything, right? It's just scary deciding when you're going to start, really start doing things no one else could do. I don't think you'll waste as much time as I did.* I smiled. His belief in me was electric. *Then, when you're famous, we'll work on our screenplay for a sexy siren tidal pool horror together.* He rubbed my shoulders like he'd done in the car. Flip's words sent a sharp prick through me, then the long pull of thread like he was trying to use my body as a needle. I realised how much I'd been yearning to hear a future plan that involved me. Some sign of commitment, which I'd been unable to secure from Jem.

Soon Flip's body was above mine and I gripped both his arms. He moved in and out of me, which was enjoyable, but didn't compare to the sensation of holding his arms, which I knew would be around me all night. I was overwhelmed by feeling both safe and adrift. I tried to move my arm between us, working my spitted-on hand towards my wetness where I could make some kind of rough magic. Something flashed across his face. We moved again, trying to make this jigsaw puzzle fit. My shins pressed against his chest. His body behind mine. But there was a new, distracted look on his face. The soft mystery of my clitoris felt subordinate to his masculinity. I gave up on the hope of an orgasm and removed my hand. We continued moving our bodies together a while more. When the sex was over – and it was over when he'd climaxed – we held each other. There was a position we defaulted to where I rested my head on his shoulder and my knees against his side, but the rest of my body curved away like the shore of a bay. I didn't feel unsatisfied because this was the default interaction I'd been taught. In those hours, we read poems to each other in bed and I accepted the nourishment from him where I could get it.

When Flip left, it was quiet again. I went to my bed and stripped the sheets, wrapping them into a heap of white. They glowed in a shaft of morning light. I buried my face in them and smelled musk, sweat, sex, sleep.

Whenever I change my sheets, I think of the time I walked past Mum changing Tom's sheets for the first time after his death. I remember the mourning care she did it with. It must've been painful to know it would be the last time his breath would be tangled up in the cotton. The patina of living from the dead. I was surprised she did it and watched her strip his bed, place the sheets in the basket, watch them swirl in the machine, carry them from the dryer and fold them. Her main act of motherhood these days was grieving and I could see why she needed more. Something domestic, present and hopeful.

I wasn't sure what act I tried to perform when I changed my sheets after Flip left. A spiritual washing, an acknowledgement of guilt, a cleansing perhaps. Really, I knew they were the same sheets, just a spin cycle apart. I inhaled again: musk, sweat, sex, sleep. Then studied the pillowcase for strands of hair, commas on a blank page. I put the washing machine on eco setting, and the steady drone kept me company for a few hours, filling the silence.

Chapter Thirty-One

Rio Cinema: 51.54963° N, 0.07535° W

Somehow, a year had passed since my first trip to Cornwall, and I was back on the Great Western Railway to Truro. There was a churned-up uneasy feeling in my stomach that September often causes. A non-specific blankness and anticipation that change is coming. I could smell it in the air as much as I sensed it in my body. New pencils, ripening berry bushes, unopened books, leaves exhaling as they fell to the ground. It was, therefore, an appropriate time to take a holiday and think about it all. Whatever 'it' was. Miri and I travelled separately, because she'd got stuck at a food packaging conference. It sounded like she'd done enough boring icebreakers with boring people to last a lifetime. *Everyone here is so vanilla*, she texted, *and not like vanilla bean, just the one in a Neapolitan that only exists to provide contrast to the other flavours.*

This gave me time on the journey to look out the window while I drank weak cups of Tetley from the tea trolley with two fingers of shortbread. There's a spot on the journey I particularly love between Exeter St Davids and Newton Abbot, where the two views on either side of the carriage are different. On one side, there's the harbour with its small boats resting on the shore, masts pointed towards the heavens like tiny violin bows, ready to conduct an orchestra to accompany a five-and-a-half-hour train journey. Then, on the other side, there's a woodland area where you can spot deer with the creamiest mottled fur and large waxy antlers.

The first time I travelled to Cornwall was for the swimming holiday where I met Miri. From the train, I'd seen a flock of cormorants near Dawlish station. They were perched on red rocks that looked like totems. I'd never seen the oily seabirds before and told Miri – who I'd known for less than a day – that I didn't know there were penguins in Britain, but I'd seen some from the train. She narrowed her eyes. Months later, when we were swimming in Wales, I saw one. *There, that's what I saw.* Miri laughed so hard her mascara ran.

I went past the same spot and the cormorants were there again. Their backs as black as mourning jackets. I thought of Tom's funeral and all the young men in their suits stood outside like a huddle of wild birds without a migration path for winter, directionless. Funerals are never not awful, but there's something particularly grim about a funeral for a young person. I remembered the school gave everyone the day off. They were all invited to pay their respects and celebrate his life. I sat at the front beside Emma and only looked back once. The doors at the back of the crematorium were open and people had spilled out into the hallway and street. So many people. Those outside couldn't see the service, but they stayed and bowed their heads.

I still think about the young men putting their suits on that morning. I wondered if they'd asked their mothers for help with the tie or borrowed their father's cufflinks. Their suits had probably only been worn to football dinners, leavers' balls or the occasional family wedding. I supposed some would've had to buy suits just for the funeral. Regardless, it would always be the suit they wore to Tom's funeral now. It was four years since the funeral. One year exactly since I saw the cormorants and met Miri. That was a milestone I wanted to remember.

The train journey this time involved a lot of struggling to remove things from my overstuffed backpack. My bag said it was sixty-five litres, which was the equivalent weight of one towel, two books, four swimsuits and not nearly enough clothes. I finished a poem about cormorants and wrestled my notepad back into the side pocket. As I retrieved *Year of the Monkey* by Patti Smith – which I'd packed, unpacked and repacked while preparing for this trip – Jem called me. He was in Portugal chasing the last of the summer sun with his friends. I missed him and tried to pretend to myself that I didn't. I was still unsure what taking it slow meant. We were getting closer all the time, then I'd remember him saying he was unsure, and I'd retreat into myself. Going to Cornwall for seven days seemed to come at a good time.

Jem was walking on the seafront and had stopped at a bench to read me the dedication. It said: *Sit. Feast on Your Life.* I was collecting them, still hoping I could find a place for my grief. He asked if there were any updates on Tom's bench. I said I was working on it.

Hello? I asked, checking if he was still there. *Hello,* I heard him smile through the phone. Jem always let our pauses run on, and I could never tolerate the silence. I always rushed to fill it. *I guess I'm nervous to talk about Tom with them,* I said. *Of course you are. That stuff is scary. You'll feel better when you do. Enjoy the quiet,* he said and left me to the journey.

Not long ago, Jem and I had been walking back from the Rio Cinema. I pointed out a nail salon called

Lady Glitter and we carried on down Kingsland High Street. We passed a chicken shop with a gap between the ground and door. I read the graffiti above it, *beware the limbo dancer*. Jem laughed then rubbed my shoulder and said, *Freya says things aloud that she notices*.

Sorry, my face went red in the dark. *Don't be sorry*. He put his hand back in his pocket. *We can walk in silence if you like*. I hadn't meant them to but the words came out sounding passive aggressive. *Do you want to?* Jem asked and I shrugged although I knew walking in silence was a particular kind of torture to me. *What do you want?* I asked and he laughed again.

Sorry, have I done something wrong? I said. Jem moved his arm around me and pulled me in so I had to slow my pace to walk beside him. *No, it's just interesting to see your mind work. I feel like*, Jem looked up and down the road before we crossed, *sometimes you point things out to stop being a bit thoughtful or sad when you're with me. You don't have to do that*.

If I don't speak, we probably wouldn't talk half the time. My voice came out harder than intended. I licked my lips. *What would be wrong with just being in silence together?* We both sidestepped to avoid a man running to catch a bus. *You can be sad with me Freya, that's all I'm saying*. As I resisted the temptation to pull my body away, I felt Jem tighten his grip.

I'm not sad right now, I said in a voice that sounded like the most unconvincing portrayal of a happy woman I'd ever heard, *and I can't just walk around moping all the time.* Jem asked why not, and I thought about it. What was the real answer? I thought it was so easy for men. If they were silent they were considered intro-spective and thoughtful; if I did the same I'd be sulking.

Finally I said: *I don't want to be a moody London literary lady writing poor Plath-imitation poetry.* I nudged into Jem, *that's where you tell me my poetry isn't poor.* A pigeon flew across the street and he replied, *you don't need me to tell you that.*

Skinny dipping on the Cornish coast

Chapter Thirty-Two

Treyarnon Bay: 50.52795° N, 5.02504° W

The train had taken us as far as Truro and from there Miri and I were picking up a Volkswagen T6 campervan to drive around the coast – and twelve tidal pools – over a week. We collected the van from a guy called Harry, who was wearing a baseball cap and Carhartt trousers with pockets down the leg. Harry hadn't had a haircut in a while and looked like he was into rock climbing. He talked at us about the van so fast that a bit of spit came from his mouth and landed on Miri's cheek. She flinched enough that I knew she'd noticed, but didn't move to wipe it until he'd turned away. I couldn't work out if Harry was especially proud of the van or if he hadn't talked to anyone in a while and was just excited to be chatting. I think it was a combination of the two.

What orange would you call this, I asked Miri. Before she could answer, Harry replied it was Lamborghini

Orange and his other van was California Blue. I could see it parked down the lane and thought it definitely wasn't California Blue, but Mint Green. *I'd say this van is the same colour as a Terry's Chocolate Orange*, I said, to which Harry reiterated that it was Lamborghini Orange. He wasn't much fun.

I didn't talk while Miri was still getting the hang of the gearstick. It was funny watching her with the driver's seat as far forward as it would go, like a perspective trick where she was actually very far away and the large car was in the foreground. I scratched a spot on the car door where the orange paint was chipped. My parents both used to work at Terry's, which, apparently, used to sell confectionery other than just chocolate oranges. I'm quite certain that when they met, Dad was Mum's boss's boss, but I've never got her to admit this.

My mother is a beautifully complicated and private woman. Perhaps the leaving of her father and any stigma that came from that had made her this way. She's a mystery. A powerful force of nature, a forest full of undiscovered wild creatures, a desert with mirages and its own folklore. It's never been clear to me which things are secret and which are not or why. The story of how my parents became a couple has been mythologised. I once learned from my godmother that Mum had been married before she met Dad and both my mother's weddings were *on the same roll of film,* as she put it. I hadn't yet learned what this meant for my two relationships existing in one snapshot.

～〜

Harry had gone to great lengths to equip the van. He'd even packed a picnic basket for us with plastic plates, cups and all kinds of utensils. There was a solar-powered torch too. It was sweet, and I felt bad for being put off by his spittle. *Maybe all we can ask for is a guy like Harry,* I said to Miri, *the kind who thinks to pack a picnic basket.* She pulled a face. *God help us. No offence to Harry but he forgot the bottle opener. We don't share the same priorities.*

～〜

Our first day in Cornwall was full of driving down tight country lanes, realising we'd gone the wrong way, then having to reverse back up them. Perhaps the universe was trying to tell us something about being cautious of moving forward too quickly. When we arrived at Trevone Bay, we walked down a sandy road and saw nearly a hundred white-lipped snails the size of five-pence pieces dotting the grasslands. I told Miri that the collective noun for snails was 'a walk', something Dad had told me once while leaving slug-kill on his plantain lilies. I second guessed myself and typed *a walk of snails* into Google. Apparently, you can also say an escargatoire of snails. *Why does everything sound better in French?* Miri said. *Except tidal pool,* I replied, *bassin de marée just sounds like someone put Mary in the sink.*

Trevone is also known as Rocky Beach for its sloping stone formations. As we walked across it, bending our knees to stop us from slipping on the wet slabs, I thought of Hecuba's tomb laid across a rocky outcrop. It felt Homeric beneath my feet, like a story that had been told before and that would be told again. It was dusk when we arrived. A glorious dusk that reminded me of the waning days. Seasons were changing. The sky tipped into a soft champagne-yellow at the corners.

Past the rocks, the sea was thrashing and crashing. Then the tidal pool was still and calm, a saucer of milk. Miri rushed ahead and kicked off her shoes by the edge. Trevone tidal pool was both earthliness and unearthliness. Surely there could be nothing more concrete than the bedrock of this sea wall, but also, nothing could be more heavenly.

From Trevone Bay, it was a short drive to Treyarnon. The cliffs were covered in a thorny wilderness and it was hard to see a clear path ahead through the thicket of brambles, bracken and nettles. All reached higher than our hips, so we held our arms out of reach.

Twisting and turning around the Cornish stone, it reminded me of Tristan and Iseult, illicit lovers enamoured by a love potion on a sea voyage from Ireland to Cornwall. A briar so thick grew from Tristan's grave that it formed a bower rooted to Iseult's grave, protecting it with shade. The king cut the branches three times, but nothing could stop them growing back and being together. I liked the idea of something sprouting from death providing shade and comfort.

What we found at Treyarnon Bay was not a tidal pool at all, but a series of rockpools by the sea. We paced back and forth for a while before realising that the tide had covered the tidal pool, which was further into the sea. The dewy night was falling from the sky. It was almost evening, getting late.

We decided that swimming in the same waters would count and chose the largest rockpool to swim in. No one was around, so we took off our shoes and placed them on a ledge in the rocks. We stripped off our clothes, stripped off the day, stripped off any worry. I took the sea between my legs. We were silver shadows, barely catchable in the water, only just sewn to reality, by the thinnest of threads. Maybe our shadows could forget us and we could leave them behind. I dug my fingernails into the rock and clung on, floating like that for a while, imagining I was a siren watching the horizon for sailors coming home. Closing my eyes and exhaling, I felt my body drop to the temperature of the water. I noticed the sensations outside my body and the sensations inside. I tried to feel where the water ended and I began. I felt the edges of my body.

~ ~

I was more familiar with the shores of my body than I had been in a long time. Sex was more meditative. Jem knew that I was distractible and, in one of his many acts of love towards me, made it his mission to help me escape my mind by inhabiting my body. I began to feel the edges of my body. I began to feel the edges of his body.

Before Jem, I thought pleasure was offering pleasure to someone else, and seeing it in their face. That's not to say I didn't enjoy sex. I enjoyed it all, because I liked making other people feel good. Nothing turned me on more than feeling I was wanted.

I was an observer of myself. I looked into a man's eyes and saw myself through him. When I was on my back, I held my breasts so they didn't disappear and leave me flat-chested. When I was upright, I tilted my chin so my nose didn't look too crooked. I made noises to imitate woman experiencing pleasure that I'd collected from pornography. I rearranged my face into an expression that I hoped looked like ecstasy, not concentration, which is difficult when you're thinking about not opening your mouth to stop anyone seeing the metal bar behind your bottom teeth. Coming was clenching my eyes with mouth shut like I was looking into the sun.

Then I met Jem and he looked at me like I was the sun. A solar planet full of light that shone only on him. He made me feel powerful, but never that the power was something he gave me. That it had been in me the whole time. It had simply been sleeping, dormant, hibernating, and this ancient power as old as the mountains and the sea had awoken, roused by his touch and taste. I closed my eyes with him inside me and meditated on the boundaries of our bodies blending together.

The music of sex changed too. It was wetter, louder and there was laughing. I hadn't known there could be laughing. Coming was a mountain-moving shudder I let rumble from my chest, then Jem pulled his fingers from me and smeared the luminescent liquid across my mouth. I acquired a new lust for the sounds and scents of it. Occasionally, I smelled the sheets afterwards and enjoyed the metallic tang to them like ripe, sour fruit.

I felt his edges. I felt my edges. They didn't seem so far. I learned to be nowhere but my body. It felt like nowhere. And everywhere. Just the two of us, floating through time and space.

Chapter Thirty-Three

Chapel Rock: 50.12246° N, 5.47554° W

Wild camping – including parking campervans overnight – isn't allowed in most of Cornwall. Friends said
we'd get away with it for a few nights, but the 'No
Overnight Camping' signs put us off. Instead, Miri
and I stayed in a field near Padstow owned by a tarot-
card reader. She lived in a shed on the corner of the
campsite. As she greeted us she waved a foldable fan
that she'd written DREAM on in Sharpie. She introduced us to the chickens and ducks as *my sweet sweet
children*.

Dinner was a picnic from Padstow Farm Shop:
cheese, crackers, onion marmalade, potted duck,
Chablis, vine tomatoes and rubbery cavolo nero that I
stripped from its stalks and massaged with a lemon. We
ate in the van headlights and watched moths flickering
through the hedgerow. Once we'd finished eating, we
switched off the lights to look up at the moon like
light from the bottom of a well. Living in London I'd

forgotten how much I missed seeing stars. I breathed in and exhaled a lot of trouble I'd been holding on to.

In the morning, I emerged from the van with sour breath and tried to find my shoes so I could step outside onto the dewy grass. A white duck appeared by the van and gave me a fright. Miri was already up, alternating between blowing on and sipping a boiling cup of tea she'd made on our camping stove. Her forehead glistened with sweat. Despite the warm weather, she'd never skip her morning Yorkshire Gold. Miri is a creature of habit.

Our first tidal pool that day was in Perranporth, a seaside town in North Cornwall that gets its name from Saint Piran, the patron saint of Cornwall. I didn't know Cornwall had patron saints. In fact, I wasn't really sure what a patron saint was except for someone people put on coins and necklaces. Miri said they were the original influencers. *Endless merch.* I read about Saint Piran and liked his stories. Legend says that his first disciples were a badger, a fox and a bear, which sounded like the kind of rumour Jem would start about himself. Most of Saint Piran's tales were tin-related, but my favourite was that someone had tied him to a millstone and rolled it off a cliff into the sea. Rather miraculously, he floated on the waves and landed on the beach in Perranzabuloe. He built an oratory nearby that was buried under sand for centuries and only unearthed in 1835. I knew what it felt like to be buried in sand, waiting for someone to unearth me.

Chapel Rock can be found in the centre of the beach in Perranporth. It's a fifty-foot-tall rock with a tidal pool in it and has a black-and-white crossed flag poking proudly from the middle. The flag of Piran, the tin-miner saint. *This can't be it*, Miri said when we arrived. *It's so*, she scratched her arm, *scummy*. Scummy was certainly the right word. The pool was covered in a foam the colour of muddy foot-printed snow. Although it looked grubby, it was a sign that there was an active marine environment. The weather had changed, and winds whipped up a settled area underwater where the tide wasn't strong and created a scum that washed up on shore. It was a mixture of dead algae, plankton, fats and proteins. Maybe pollutants too. I offered Miri a rebrand from 'scum' to 'algal bloom' but we weren't sold on swimming in it.

Miri brought her hand to her forehead to look out to sea. *We haven't come all this way not to swim.* She hiked down from the tidal pool and strode towards the shore. I stayed on the beach and held her things. The tide was out. She was miles away. I watched the life-guard patrol the beach for a while and spent some time filling my pockets with rubbish from the tidal pool: a lump of blue plastic, Nik Naks packet and a ring pull.

It looked a little better, but still frothed like someone had poured a Guinness in it.

Later, I saw an aerial photograph of the tidal pool and felt robbed. It looked scenic, magical. If I'd seen the picture before, I would've had Chapel Rock at the top of my list for the most gorgeous tidal pool in Britain. Yet when we visited, it was a tub of scum and kelp, carved into the rocks near a sandy car park and fudge shop. It was a reminder that we weren't on an adventure to visit every tidal pool and catalogue an exact description of them. We were gaining experiences. Some days were sunny, some were not. Some days were sad, some days were happy. Some days the sea was violent, dangerous, scummy. Some days the sea was calm. We couldn't talk about these pools like they were places we could tell people to visit and they'd have a great time because of this or that. They were moments in time, unique to just me and Miri.

Once the tide dropped, we'd found Porthtowan tidal pool, or 'mermaid pool', as locals call it, on a long sandy cove at the edges of St Agnes heritage coast. I swam surrounded by sunstruck spray. There was just space to dive and underwater glide. When it was time to leave, I gripped the ancient cliff above the pool wall. My reflection lifted a leg from the silver-blue water, as if getting out of bed from the longest sleep. I was taken aback by the woman I saw. She had strong thighs and hair beaded with saltwater. She was a woman who set out on an adventure with courage and curiosity. She had many miles to go. She looked like someone I might like to know. Might like to be.

I wondered if I'd ever reach her – the woman who I was supposed to become – or if I'd forever be separate, peering through clear water, unable to cross the relentless trawl of a riptide, that relentless grief.

The grass across Smugglers Cove blinked fire-exit green in the wind. We were hiking towards the west side of Portreath beach to spot Lady Basset's baths. Created in the early 1780s, these pools were cut into the rocks for Lady Basset by her father, who believed in the healing powers of cold seawater. There are six baths across the beach so that one would always be accessible, whatever the tide. We weren't sure if these odd bathtub-shaped pools were technically tidal pools, but we went to see them anyway. While researching our trip, I'd found an article that said, 'lidos are to swimming pools what lingerie is to underwear', so we joked that Basset's Cove was the equivalent of a skimpy thong in the topsy-turvy world of *Cornwall Live* journalism. I decided our dear Brockwell Lido was a comfortable cotton pant, but Miri said the Art Deco was sexy. *It's suspenders, no doubt about it.*

As we looped our legs around grey stones, the path became increasingly hazardous. Miri slipped on the wet rocks and a frilled razor-sharp edge with as many layers as a mille-feuille sliced through the flesh of her knee. She brought her hand to the wound and as she clutched it, vermillion blood oozed out. It looked deep. It looked like it might need stitches.

We spent the afternoon in a small community-hospital waiting room with a boy who had broken his arm and an elderly woman with a flask of broccoli soup that smelled like Dad's garden shed.

That night, Miri didn't sleep because she was busy worrying about not swimming and I didn't sleep because I was worried about Miri worrying. She hadn't needed stitches, but her knee was bandaged up and they'd instructed her to avoid water for a few days. The tidal pools would have to wait.

Cairns on the St Ives coast

Chapter Thirty-Four

There was no tidal pool in St Ives, but we'd wanted to pay homage to the sculptor Barbara Hepworth and, of course, find something to do that didn't involve swimming. She was a pioneer of modernism and, I found, there was a Hepworth quote for nearly everything. On love, life and even on getting shit done: *I found one had to do some work every day, even at midnight, because either you're professional or you're not.* It's rumoured that towards the end of her life, she made a habit of taking a sleeping pill then smoking one last cigarette in bed to help her fall asleep. In 1975 she died in a house-fire. After her death, the Trewyn studio where she had lived and worked was placed in the care of the Tate. It remains like it was when she was creating there. Tools still on the bench, an unfinished sculpture waiting on the table, potted cacti lovingly watered in the greenhouse, a linen apron still on a hook behind the door. The sculpture garden has an earthly silence about it. There are places to sit and just be by the sculptures. I chose a low wall by a bed of white anemones and watched the sunlight shift over the hedge, casting a glow on a statue that turned it from bronze to a waning blue.

Hepworth's work reminded me of tidal pools. The coming together of the architectural and the natural. One of my favourites is inspired by St Ives Bay, where two stretches of land are embraced on either side by the sea. The sculpture is made of wood and there are strings pulled over the dark oak that Hepworth said express *the tension between myself and the sea, the wind or the hills*. I thought about the tension in my body and the directions I was pulled in. I lived between my desk in London and the coast. I kept tabs open on my laptop for the next tidal pool so I could escape in daydreams to these places. At the sea, I wondered why I returned to London at all. What did the city give me, except constant distraction? I wondered what form my body would take if I released that tension.

Through the large-leaved foliage and flower beds of the garden there was a marble sculpture, stood nobly like a lone walker in a field. Miri was bending over to inspect a stone orb. I heard birdsong. It seesawed between two notes, then gave a closing shimmer. I sat and thought about Jem saying reflection could be found in quiet. I tried to notice things.

Deciding it was too hot to go back to the stuffy van, we walked around St Ives searching for the views that had inspired Hepworth while in a heatwave ennui. I sensed Miri was itching for a swim by the way she looked longingly at the water. It wasn't clear if we'd be able to finish the tidal pools in Cornwall on this trip, but I silently doubted it. We passed two blackbirds washing in a puddle by the marina car park, then stopped at a harbour-side cafe.

No one has had a better year than the QR code. Miri scanned the menu on her phone. I laughed, but because I was reading a message from Jem. Miri drummed her fingers on the table and said to herself, *a bottle would be nice, but I've got to drive later so guess I'll just have a small glass.* I was still typing. She stretched out her bandaged leg below the table and put her phone face down to signal she was giving me her undivided attention. Still typing. Miri cleared her throat.

Sorry, I put my phone in my bag and looked behind me. I pointed at the waitress, who was squirting surface cleaner on her glasses then wiping them with her shirt. *Isn't life funny when you stop to notice,* I rested my chin on my palm, *Jem said it's good to take time to slow down and sit with your feelings. You know, notice things. Sometimes I feel like he knows what I need more than I do.* The waitress seemed happy with the new clarity of her spectacles and pushed them onto her nose. *You're a writer. You notice things.* I pondered. *Really? I never feel like I'm looking.* Miri licked her finger and rubbed at a stain on the table. It squeaked.

Have you noticed how you do that? After a beat, Miri looked up at me. I hadn't realised she was waiting for an answer. The waitress arrived with a chalkboard, but Miri said no thank you without looking at the specials. When we were alone again, I half-heartedly shook my head. *You use men as a means to deliver learnings to you.* I sucked in my cheeks as Miri added, *is it ok if I say this?* I wafted my hand as if to say go ahead, but did it instinctively to be polite and wasn't sure if it was ok with me at all.

Miri began counting on her fingers, *Flip is teaching you how to be a writer. Jem is teaching you how to be grounded. Marlowe was teaching you about techno and Japanese literature, or whatever that was,* I winced, *did it ever occur to you that these . . . men,* Miri paused like the word had an unpleasant taste, *can't teach you anything you don't know yourself? And maybe it's all a distraction from thinking about . . .*

I think . . . I pressed my lips together and realised I didn't know what I wanted to say. *I think that you're probably right, but not in the way you think you are. I know exactly what I'm doing. This isn't a revelation. You haven't figured out anything new.* Miri's eyes twitched.

I continued; *I'm enjoying my relationships right now. It's better for me to be preoccupied in this way.* I pushed my plate away then added, *I know what I'm doing. I am very much in control.* The last six words came out of my mouth with such confidence and conviction they shocked me.

Enjoying? Miri pushed. *Yes. Enjoying.* It was the first time it occurred to me I might be a good liar. *I don't think you're enjoying it at all. I think you enjoy Jem, and you should tell him how you feel and that you want to be with him.*

I played with my napkin. *If I tell him how I feel and he says he's not looking for a relationship, then that's it. I'm not ready to not see him again. I need more time.* The napkin lay shredded on my lap like sad confetti.

I get that. I really do. Look, he seems to really like you and is investing a lot of care into your time together. Don't you think you should meet that with openness and tell him how you feel? Tucking in my upper lip, I replied, *so it's all on me to start these conversations?*

Quelle surprise! That's just how it is. I wondered where the bill was. *I don't want to embarrass myself initiating something he's made no indication that he wants. Flip has actually promised me things. At least he makes plans for the future with me.* There was a noise by the entrance. A man caught his coat on the umbrella stand and knocked it over. Miri watched him return the stand to upright,

222

then looked back at me. *When people say they'll do something, their brain releases the same chemicals as if they've actually done it. Flip says you'll go on a writing retreat then he says you'll write a film together. I have no doubt it feels good when he says that. But what has he actually done for you?*

More than Jem, I said pointedly. Miri rolled her eyes. *Seriously Freya? What did Jem write you in that card?* I imagined the postcard. *That he wants to put his hands inside my brain.* I felt a pang of embarrassment saying it aloud.

The only promise Jem made is to get to know you. Really know you. So far, he's delivered on that promise. Maybe it's not the promise you wanted, but it might be the promise you need. Miri changed the tone in her voice and looked like she wanted to reach towards me, *the thing is, Freya, thinking about something longer rarely changes the answer. I don't want you to forget—*

I interrupted her abruptly: *I won't forget you.* The waitress approached with the bill but took a look at our thundery expressions and turned on her heel. Miri tapped her fingers against her empty wine glass, *I don't mean you'll forget me, maybe a little. I meant I don't want you to forget yourself.*

I was suddenly exhausted. No one else had a clue, not even Miri. I took a breath, but rather than calm me down it drew my awareness to how fast my heart was beating. *I'm sorry if me dating is making you feel excluded.* Miri opened her mouth, then closed her eyes and abandoned whatever she was going to say. I'd gone there and it didn't feel good. It was an unwritten code of being women, forged by shared singledom, that we should never imply jealousy over each other. We were all jealous. None of us wanted to admit it. No one needed to. Now I was accusing her of being single and a bad friend. A woman not fulfilling either of her roles. I got up and in the process the aluminium chair made a metallic sound against the concrete and my napkin feathered to the floor. Anyone who hadn't been alert to us arguing was then. I walked away, because I couldn't think what else to do with myself.

I arrived at an ice cream shop and bought two waffle cones. Strawberry and clotted cream for me and rum and raisin for Miri. I'd never seen her eat that, but it felt right in the moment. I waited on the harbour and eventually she found me when hers had half melted down my hand. It was not a peace-offering, because Miri didn't have as much of a sweet tooth as me, but more a gesture that I was willing to sit and be upset together for a while.

The coast was covered in cairns and a couple were building one close to where the water lapped against the shore. Within the hour, the tide would wash them away, but they carried on building. I watched them for a while, working silently to build their tower of wave-smoothed pebbles. They didn't speak, but held up stones for one another and nodded to place them down or shook their heads and kept looking for the right size. The way they communicated without words hypnotised me. I wondered how many days it took to see one other so clearly.

~⌒~

Miri was still unsure of swimming, so I entered the waters of Porthmeor beach alone that evening. The waves were enormous, nearly taller than me, and a few surfers were still out on the water, hoping to catch the last swells of the day. Each time the waves receded, they trailed rocks back with them. The low, grating roar of tidal drag. I ran into the water after a pattern of three waves and tried to swim past the break. Once I was there I tipped my head back and let the waves rock me.

After a while, I decided I'd had enough and started swimming to shore but was repeatedly pulled back into the foam. Going from swimming to standing, I tried to run but was going nowhere. I turned around to see how much time I had before the next wave. A wall of green appeared before me. I dived beneath it, attempting to make my way through the looking glass. Flailing my arms, I tried to swim, but the weight of

225

the water kept me down. I couldn't sense which way was up, which way was out. White noise drowned out all thoughts. The water had no direction but against me.

Finally, it relented and my body arrived at the surface. I gasped as deep as I could, saltwater spilling into my throat. Miri rushed towards me. *You were a bit tumble-dried there. Are you ok?* I nodded and knew that I still needed the safety of tidal pools.

Chapter Thirty-Five

Priest's Cove: 50.12547° N, 5.70670° W

We met the mist – thick and fuzzy as terrycloth – at the National Trust car park in Cape Cornwall. Poking my head out of the car window, I opened my mouth to try to swallow a cloud. *It's magic isn't it*, Miri rolled down her window too, then wiggled her nose and looked towards the back of the car. *What's not magic is the smell of this van.* Damp weather meant our towels weren't drying and everything smelled like the ocean: salt and rotten fishing nets.

It was a short enough walk to the water that I went in just my swimming costume, anorak and sea shoes. We walked downhill into the harbour, moving our feet in small steps to stop ourselves from falling on the shingle slipway. Miri had made a contraption for her knee involving a plastic bag and some surgical tape. It crinkled like a turkey wrapped in tinfoil and the more she fiddled with it, the less watertight it looked. *Forget it.* She abandoned the sheeting, stuffed it into her bag, then strode into the pool with just her bandage on.

The tidal pool is called Priest's Cove. It's surrounded by the Tin Coast hills, where you must stick to the paths because tunnels leading deep underground can still be found. High on the cliffs is a tall chimney stack. The mist was timeless that day. I could nearly imagine we were there when the mining town was thriving. There was little that revealed technology had moved on. I could picture furls of smoke from the chimneys, the clang of coal being moved.

On a winding path, there's a stone carved with the distinctive outline of a can of tomato soup. It's inscribed: 'Cape Cornwall. Purchased for the Nation By H J Heinz Co LTD to Mark Their Centenary Year. Presented to The National Trust March 1987.' The sign says this area is England's only cape, though I wasn't entirely sure what a cape was. Just that it's mystic and beautiful, a rugged rocky beach by a fisherman's shed overgrown with wildflowers.

There were two small boats on the water's edge piled with buoys and a coil of slimy rope. The colours against the mist were bold and primary: green cliffs, orange buoys, blue rope, yellow and red boats. I posted a photograph on Instagram with the caption *Hot Buoy Summer* and checked it immediately to see if Jem had viewed it. We were messaging every day, but I couldn't get enough. I worried my appetite for him was insatiable.

I distracted myself with a swim in bruise-blue water held by a roughly hewn pool in the rocks. Beyond, the headland reached out into the ocean where the Atlantic currents divide. The tide battered the beach, but I felt safe there. Miri and I lay on our backs and placed our heels on the tidal pool wall, using only our hands to keep us afloat. My ears slipped below the surface. I heard the thud-thud of my heart against the mysterious blankness of the water. The sound of the womb. When in utero, twins are known to touch toes or even press their noses together. Bending my knees, I laid my feet flat on the pool wall and pressed my toes down. Someone had carefully pressed pebbles into the wall to spell out '2000', as it had been repaired at the turn of the millennium. I practised lifting and landing each toe. I thought of Emma. The twinless twin. My heart broke for her all over again.

Miri's movement in the water jolted me upright. Someone had joined us in the pool. A woman in a navy swimsuit and waterproof boots asked if she could join us. We spoke about swimming groups and she told us some gossip from her local meet-up. Apparently, Tanya was furious that Marg kept bringing her Labrador to the swims because she always tied him up and he barked the whole time they were in the water. *I'm done with all that drama*, she said and explained she'd driven from North Devon to check this place out. There are no dogs allowed here because it's still a working slipway for fishermen. Miri asked if she swam in Bude Seal Pool and Tunnels Beach while I drifted about to distract myself from the chill. Miri noticed my fidgeting and said we had to be going, we didn't want to get cold. This sparked a conversation about my brush with hypothermia in Scotland and delayed us a further five minutes, but when we finally left the woman said, *let me get a picture of you*, and took a very wonky photograph of us grinning in the mist of Priest's Cove.

As we approached the refreshments hut in the car park, Miri rubbed my shoulders through my coat. I knew then that we'd made up. The man behind the counter put his hand up to silence me when I said hello and poised his pencil over a nearly completed crossword. *Donna Tartt novel, nine letters. Any ideas?* I shook my head. He huffed, folded the paper and put it down. I asked for two hot chocolates and he made them while shaking his head and handed them over with a thick air of begrudging that reminded me of London. Our drinks came in royal memorabilia mugs. I let Miri have the Princess Diana one. I turned back towards the man. *Have you tried goldfinch?* He lifted his pencil and a light came on behind his eyes. *Ah! Goldfinch, of course.*

The week before I came to Cornwall, I'd been walking with Jem in Brockwell Park after a swim. It felt strange to go to the lido without Miri, but also exciting to invite Jem into the routines of my life and see how eagerly he wanted to share them with me. He put his goggles on and held his breath to watch my bottom as I breaststroked up and down the pool. We left the lido with his arms around me, my bag weighed down by our wet swimsuits tangled up together in a towel. Sliding through the turnstile, I held the gate open for a woman with a pram. I wondered what she saw. A happy young couple. Were we a couple? What was the name for what we were doing? I wanted to ask, *what are we?* But that felt stupid and childish, so instead I continued meeting up with Jem to walk and eat and have sex, then went home and worried about the million alternate paths our relationship could follow.

That day we found a bench in Brockwell's community garden and sat to watch volunteers making a new planter. It looked like hard work. *We don't deserve Londoners*, I mused. Jem was that kind of Londoner. He volunteered at Hackney Foodbank and watered neighbours' plants when they were away, then carried their boxes when they moved. He was a kind soul who thought about his community and how he could nourish it.

Jem collected some birdseed from the feeder and sat with his palm outstretched. He told me that his dad had taught a robin to feed from his hands. *Patience is all it takes.* Jem propped up his elbow and made his body a crane, holding steady in the hope a bird would be curious. There was a bird in the trees, its big billowing chirrups lit up the blossom. I loved watching Jem's curiosity for the outdoors, his gentle respect for it. He was full of admiration and never tried to squash or rule over nature.

Giving up on the birdseed, he straddled the bench and tugged at my shoulder, until I was lying with the wood pressed against my spine and Jem's knees near to my ears. I thought about Tom's balsa wood bones, learning to walk again after an operation, his crutches. I swallowed and asked Jem what he wanted to do for lunch. He looked around as I started listing options nearby. *Let's just listen for a bit.* He placed both hands on my shoulders.

I closed my eyes, not entirely enjoying the sensation of him being sat up while I was lying down. I listened and tried to surrender my body to my surroundings as Jem guided me through the sounds in the garden. *There's wind through the trees, footsteps in the garden, bees in the hives, earth moving as they repot plants, the sound of the saw.* We paused like that for an eternity. Time seemed to move differently for the two of us. My mind wasn't one for surrendering. Saw, wood, balsa wood, spine, pain, pain, pain.

I fidgeted, sure I was getting a splinter on the strip of exposed skin on my back. *I'm uncomfortable.* I shifted my body till my cheek rested on Jem's thigh. He stroked my forehead, and I thought of that final scene in *Notting Hill* where Julia Roberts is lying on the bench, Hugh Grant's floppy hair, haircuts from Mum in the kitchen, sharp scissors, doctor, open-back hospital robe, Tom's long legs, daddy long legs, cobweb, attic, plastic boxes labelled 'Tom's School Books'.

Jem's voice broke through again. *Can you hear that? It's a goldfinch.* I listened to its fast tinkling verse and tried to imagine it moving along a tree trunk. Jem rested his chin in the open fold of his palm. I could feel his hot breath on my forehead while he spoke. *There's something asking to come out, and it's quite loud right now. Maybe if you let it out, it won't be so scary or so angry or so big. I've always found sadness only feels so bad when it's deep.* I opened my eyes just to close them again, blinking away a tear that changed the bench from ash to hazelnut brown. The goldfinch flew from the tree and left us in silence. Jem wiped the tear from my face and said: *everything passes by.*

Slowly, I sat up to look into the green-grey of his eyes. The mystery of them angered me. He was being so open and transparent, yet there were things between us that seemed opaque. *You don't know that,* I said, *you can't know that.* He shrugged. *What else are you going to believe?*

Crimson flickered through me. Everyone was always telling me to be more sad, to process Tom's death. Whatever 'processing' meant. I wasn't sure that they were right. If I took time to really think about it, how would I keep going? I didn't think it was possible to exist in two worlds. One was the reality where young people get ill for no reason and the patient gowns look like cloaks on their tiny bodies. Then I had to exist in a world where people muted the television when the Macmillan Cancer advert came on and my inbox pinged with emails about Editorial Strategy so I took a break to order a coffee in a throwaway cup and friends texted: *my flatmate's a bitch she used all my John Frieda shampoo again* or *shall we go to XOYO or Corsica Studios tonight* like any of it mattered. My two worlds didn't match. So I tried to forget about one, in order to cope with the other. I tried to forget about the promise I'd made Tom the last time I saw him.

Jem was talking about sadness he didn't know. *Anyway,* he said, *what do I know?*

Chapter Thirty-Six

Guildford Hospital: 51.24163° N, 0.61102° W

I made a promise to Tom once. When I woke up on that grey Saturday, I knew that it was the day he would die. I leaned out of bed to check the time and had twenty-six missed calls and text messages saying: *Lawrence is on the way to get you* then *Freya pick up the phone* and *we're at the hospital now.*

The night before, I'd been on a date and the man – a radio producer with a Daffy Duck tattoo – was still in my bed. Sex was a distraction method I adopted back then and have remained committed to ever since. I don't remember what I said to make him leave, but I remember it was fast because just ten minutes later I was dressed and stood in the To Go aisle of the super-market. I stared at all the food: yellow mango fingers, green apple slices, a little tub of coconut chunks for £1.60. My stomach felt empty. I bought some diced watermelon – which I later threw up in the hospital sharps disposal bin – and stood on the corner of my road to wait for Lawrence. I don't remember the car journey or how long it took. I remember Lawrence fiddling with change for the hospital car park ticket machine and swearing a lot. I stood there with my tub of melon and said nothing.

Emma was at university. There'd been a lot of discussion about what to do as no one wanted to tell her on the phone and no one wanted her to get the train on her own. My aunt set off early that morning to collect her from halls. There are small, strange acts of kindness when someone is dying. It had taken a while for my aunt to wake Emma up; she'd been out drinking. Thinking about that later, I realised we were both using the same coping mechanisms. Both running in the same direction. I wished I'd spoken to her about that more and given her the advice that drinking wasn't the answer, even if I hadn't believed it myself. The doctors kept Tom going until Emma arrived. They wouldn't let him leave the world without the person he'd entered it with.

We took it in turns to say goodbye. I didn't want to, but Dad said that if I didn't, I might regret it. The room was large. There were machines beeping, and I didn't know what any of them did. I touched Tom's hand and was surprised that it was warm. I held Tom's hand. It was limp. I tried to bend his fingers around mine. I wondered when the last time

I'd really held his hand was and wished we'd been the kind of siblings who touched more. I was so angry that we wouldn't grow past being young adults embarrassed to be intimate with one another. I wished I could remember times we'd held each other so I wouldn't just be left with the memory of trying to meld his fingers around mine on his deathbed. I released his hand, and nothing resisted. In some ways, that made it easier to let go. I knew then that his body was still going, only just, but that didn't mean he was living anymore.

I didn't believe that he could hear me, but I wanted to say something. There were hundreds of things I wanted to say. Goodbye wasn't one of them. I thought about what Emma would say and the thought of her coming into this room full of tubes and beeps – and in the centre of it all, Tom's warm hands – was the saddest I'd ever known. I couldn't bear to think of her living with such pain. That a nineteen-year-old girl should have to live with the agony of saying goodbye to her twin brother. I was so far from being able to feel anything about Tom. None of that felt real, and I couldn't intellectualise the reality of losing him or what dying might feel like. I could only feel how incredibly sad I was for my sister.

I promise to look after Emma for you, I said, *I'm so sorry you won't be here to do that yourself. No one will ever be able to love her like you did. But I promise I will try. I promise I will look after her.*

After we all had said goodbye, we were invited to go back in as the doctors turned off the machines. The others went in. I sat in the waiting room on my own. I didn't want to acknowledge the hospital as an end to his life. Perhaps there was something symbolic and safe about it ending where it had started, but I wasn't interested in that then. Later, Emma said that it had been very quiet when he ended.

Every time I look at Emma, I think about my promise and have no idea how to keep it. Beginning any attempt feels impossible.

Lunch above Mousehole pool

Chapter Thirty-Seven

Mousehole Tidal Pool: 50.08458° N, 5.53545° W

The mist stayed behind in Cape Cornwall and it was all gold-bannered skies once we'd ventured east to the fishing village of Mousehole. We wound around streets of painted houses with thatched roofs. I peeked inside forget-me-not-blue shutters at the lives other people were living. The sea was visible through the alleyways. Miri was animated, happy that she could swim again. She told me about a children's book called *The Mousehole Cat* that she used to read with her brother. *It's about a very brave fisherman called Tom and his cat Mowzer.* Every December there's a festival to celebrate the legendary fisherman who went out fishing in a storm because his catch provided a feast for the starving village. Locals eat stargazy pie, made with egg, potato and baked pilchards – their heads poking through the crust as if gazing at the stars. Instead of stargazy pie, we had crab sandwiches at the Rock Pool Cafe while looking over the very square Mousehole tidal pool.

After lunch we climbed into the water and swam for a while. A little girl tugged at her father's t-shirt and asked, *why are those ladies swimming?* She was right to be suspicious, as the pool was very shallow. Barely swimmable, really, and it was overpacked for comfort with two little boys rock-pooling and a man with his dog that was paddling enthusiastically then shaking near us. I gave the man a look, but he didn't seem to notice and continued throwing a tennis ball into the water for it to retrieve. I had a new appreciation for Priest's Cove and their No Dog slipway.

I felt sad that our time in Cornwall was coming to an end. *Only for now*, Miri said, *we'll be back*. We walked slowly through town, both nursing a reluctance to return to London. I peered into an Oxfam to see what the people there had given up. A brown brocade armchair with a piece of paper sellotaped to it: *Definitely not haunted*. Two women had their jumpers outstretched to collect the plums they were picking from a tree. Beside them blood-red hollyhocks leaned over a wire fence and onto a concrete garage. We passed a second-hand bookshop and Miri pointed out a Mermaid Handbook in the window. I'd never been a little girl who liked mermaids, but somehow I'd become an adult who believed I was one. I was comfortable in the odd contradictions of being a woman who loved the sea but hated sand and who loved the rigidity of my colour-coded calendar but also the wilderness of the tide, who could be uncompromising then play like a child. I was myself in the water.

I followed the musty smell inside to look for a book about identifying bird calls. Miri expressed her concern at this level of *old-biddyness,* as she called it. Wildflower-spotting was très chic, in her eyes, but bird-spotting was too close to fishing and I already knew her thoughts on that. In truth, I wasn't interested in whether we saw guillemots or razorbills, but the process of looking for them and listening was one of the few ways I could slow down. Existing with my grief was too much, but I was open to trying to listen to the music of the birds.

Miri pointed to a laminated sign that read: *Don't take pictures of my books then buy them online. It destroys my business!!* On the opposite shelf another read: *Please don't steal my books unless you want me to close down and sell to another pasty shop!* I felt the fiery glare of the shop owner assessing us as potential customers, thieves or timewasters. I waved. Among the Natural History section, I found the RSPB Field Guide to Birdsong and took it to the till, where the owner's frown remained.

Back on the cobbled high street, I flicked through and discovered the book had once come with a CD, which was missing from its plastic wallet. I didn't know how much help it would be, but I was pleased I'd had the intention. The page about gannets said: *as pairs squabble with neighbours, they give a repeated brrró-brrró-brrró . . . deep and guttural with a strong rolling of the 'r's.* Yep, there was absolutely no way I was going to have any luck with this book without the CD.

Miri was still laughing about the effort the shop-keeper must've gone to to laminate her signs. *How can anyone be that grumpy when they live here?* I asked. *People find a way, wherever they are.* I flicked through the book. *If that's true, do you think it's possible to be happy wherever you are?* Miri took a picture of me with my new book, *trying can never be a bad thing.* I thought I was happy then. I was happy in Cornwall. And trying to feel more of that would only do me good.

The weight of the book in my jacket pocket was pleas-ing. It fit snugly like it was meant to be there. The last time I'd seen Flip he'd told me to close my eyes and placed a book in my hands. *Feel the weight of that?* I nodded. *When you write your first book, whatever happens, no one can ever take that away from you. The physical weight of the thing you created.* I thought about everything that had been taken from me up to this point. Chewing my bottom lip, I tried to meditate on what an incredibly solid and real thing a book is. How it would last forever.

I blinked and looked into Flip. His shelf of Blu-Rays suddenly made more sense to me. What had been taken from him that he felt the need to create art that would outlive him? Maybe we didn't know each other very well. He removed the book from my hands before I'd had a chance to study its cover and slipped it back into the shelf. I knew that, in the same way no one could take my book away from me, no one could give it to me either. I'd wanted Flip to help me write my life exciting, but only I could do that. Only I would do that.

Flip was already flicking through MUBI, choosing a film. Over an armchair was a yellow blanket knitted with aspect ratios. With his eyes still on the television, Flip tapped the leather sofa beside him. *Come here my little Booker Prize winner.* Once, an epithet like that would've delighted me, but in that moment I felt like a show pony. I told myself not to be so fickle. I couldn't want something one minute and not the next. Then I decided that I'd been that way all my life, and probably wasn't changing. I'd wanted Flip to take me seriously, so I might feel entitled to feel that way about myself. Now the reason I felt so strongly for Jem was because he freed me from that behaviour. He was serious about not taking himself too seriously. My heart wanted something my head hadn't known to ask for.

In Cornwall, Miri and I had hiked the South West Coast Path, swum in secret coves, filled our pockets with sea glass and driven for miles across clifftop roads to find tidal pools. I'd tried to find Tom in each one. I'd looked hard for him.

One of the many strange things about someone you love dying is that they're both everywhere and nowhere. Was Tom in the sunset? Probably not. I hadn't found him in the water at Trevone Bay or in the sky at Mousehole or the wind that whistled through the grass at Priest's Cove. But in each place I'd thought about him. I would keep looking. For the moment, he was in the search and the search was taking me to tidal pools.

What mattered in life was the joy of the journey. When Tom first got ill, there'd been talk of taking him out of school to go on holiday and do things ill people do in movies like hot-air balloon rides and swimming with dolphins. In these movies, the ill people are usually old and we realised that Tom's bucket list looked different. It involved going to school, passing his driving test, going to the pub, getting a girlfriend. All the small joyous moments of becoming a young adult that most of us take for granted. To live a life long enough that your bucket list isn't going to school is a privilege I'd never considered before.

On the day Tom was diagnosed we saw a consultant who said Tom had a year, at best. After that, we only saw specialists who worked with young people regularly and none ever mentioned a timeframe. I think they knew that with teenagers what keeps them going is a hope for the ordinary milestones in life. Because of that, there's no point in giving an estimate of a year here or three months there to book a safari or a jet-ski experience. As a family, we followed the example of the oncologists and never acknowledged what the first consultant said. Then we passed one year and we passed two and we reached three. Tom was still fighting, and I wondered if I'd imagined what that doctor had said. Just like Emma had said, no one mentioned that he was dying.

We pretended like life would go on for Tom. Like it would go on for us all. Mum even took him to university open days. I remember walking around Southampton University campus looking at Fish Fridays in the cafeteria and thinking we were living the oddest little lie. As the different paths the twins followed became more distant, it got harder to pretend. In 2016, Emma went to university and Tom stayed behind, still receiving radiotherapy. Just a few months later, Tom died. I think the only thing that was different was the fading of hope.

Chapter Thirty-Eight

Madingley Hall: 52.22463° N, 0.03754° E

In one of my many searches for true happiness, I thought a Master's might do it. Applying for a writing programme, rather than writing, became a new distraction that produced several short stories. I was even proud enough of one to read it aloud and imagine I was at a slam poetry night. Then one day when I'd just clicked on an article about the climate emergency, a ping radiated from my laptop. An email with the subject line, 'MSt creative writing: offer'. The informality of the lowercase punctuation sent a jolt down my spine. The article was behind a paywall so I assumed everything was ok, closed the tab and read the email instead. The place was mine, starting in just a few weeks.

I knew that I'd developed a habit of starting things in the hope they'd fix me. If I do the Master's, I won't feel sad. If I get a boyfriend, I won't feel sad. If I swim in every tidal pool in mainland Britain, I won't feel sad. But surely, just one more thing would do it?

On my desk was an upturned oyster shell filled with sea glass that I'd collected with Miri. She called it Mermaid Money, and we calculated our own currency based on the rarity of the shades. Olive green or emerald were our penny equivalent, the sea-foam green our pounds and the cornflower or cobalt blue more prized still. I had a small chunk of light lavender glass from Scotland, which was my most valued treasure. When we'd been beachcombing, Miri had presented me with the tiny amethyst fleck and said, *we're rich*! The collection reminded me how rich my life truly was, despite all the loss. Now it was time for me to spend some of my riches. I had a job and savings, which I'd always been told I should spend on sensible, concrete things like a mortgage or a dish-washer. I wanted to prove to myself that I was worth investing in.

I accepted my place on the course and acknowledged, to myself, that I still hoped writing would finally be the way I could coexist with Tom.

The course was part-time and involved four days of studying in Cambridge, four times a year. I travelled on the train, biting my nails, with a bag full of books on my lap. I'd been using a postcard from Miri as a bookmark:

Dearest Freya

Congratulations on your course. So excited for everything you're going to learn (and teach them too). What an inspiration you are!

With much love, my aquaphile pal

Miri x

My friendship with Miri was the pinnacle of romance in my life. I tried to treasure these gestures from her, rather than use them as fuel for my frustration that men weren't as romantic. I was disappointed that a similar letter hadn't arrived from Jem. Flip, on the other hand, had been exceptionally encouraging and brought it up frequently. Last week, we'd had dinner at a wine bar in Dulwich and he'd told the waitress we were celebrating. He raised a glass, *to the poet*. My cheeks flushed and I enjoyed the sensation of praise. He was filming in a new location soon and would be away for a few weeks. He assured me we could chat on the phone and continued to tell me I should pitch a horror film with a modern twist on the siren myth set in tidal pools. *It's commercially very viable.* I sipped my wine. That wasn't the story I wanted to tell.

Occasionally, Flip and I fell out of messaging and into exchanging emails instead. I sensed a yawn through his lengthy, unspellchecked paragraphs. He adopted a formal tone that suggested he was amidst replying to work matters late at night. Once he'd signed off *Best, Felipe.*

That week we went to the Harold Pinter to see *Blithe Spirit* and had planned to have a pre-show dinner, but Flip got caught working on his script so I had an egg and cress sandwich by a commercial bin on Oxendon Street while I watched a young man try to steal a bike. That didn't quite kill enough time, so I drank two glasses of wine alone at the theatre bar. *I was thinking,* he reached out to brush a crisp crumb from my lap, *when I'm done shooting we should go on a trip. Make up for lost time. Maybe Yorkshire or Devon, a writer's retreat of our own.* I thought of his hands on *The Hawk in the Rain* when we first met. *And if you ever want to come and meet me on set, you're welcome.* He pulled some Juicy Fruit from his pocket and popped a piece of gum in his mouth. The yellow and red packet lined with fish-hook silver paper looked nostalgic, almost childish, in the enormity of his hands. We watched the play, laughing together when we needed to, as I meditated on the smell of chewing gum on his breath.

We agreed on the idea of our writing retreat, but there would be weeks of distance before then. Weeks where he'd gain experience that would take him further from the Flip I knew and separation that would disable me from having the patience to catch up. I decided I would sit with that for a bit. The evening was a goodbye of sorts. A goodbye, for now. I kissed him and wondered if our time together was burning out.

～ ～

It would've been easy for Cambridge to be a disappointment. The libraries, sand-coloured colleges and students on bicycles but, rather magically, everything delighted me. During my undergrad at Durham, there'd been a competitive atmosphere I hadn't enjoyed. Seminars had felt like arguments and I didn't have the confidence for the combative debate. Classmates asked where I'd schooled, and I didn't understand the wider context of the question. My friends studied Anthropology, Classics and English Literature, then I watched them shelve their interests for law conversions or jobs in recruitment. I'd hoped after graduating I'd write the leaflets and object labels for exhibitions in antiquity museums, but when I discovered I'd need a PhD for that kind of job, the thought of more education with more of these people was suffocating.

It took me a while to stop expecting aggressive competition on the Master's. I learned to raise my hand when I didn't know, because often I didn't. One of my tutors said, *have a talent for your talent,* and I hoped whatever my 'talent' was would soon become clear to me. Every morning I looked in the mirror and practised introducing myself as a writer.

The course was held outside the city in Madingley Hall, a grand manor house with a garden full of rain-soaked roses and cobwebbed topiary. We had our lectures in a double-height room with patterned carpets. When it rained, dust and chimney-stuff fell down from the fireplace. The portrait directly oppos-ite me stayed wonky the whole week. It was a good place to stare mindlessly when I got stuck.

It was a strange and wonderful cohort of students. A ghost-writer of political memoirs, a flame-haired young man who'd just left a Zen temple in New Mexico and a playwright who'd taken a break from being a bird researcher in Montana. He said that in movies when you hear a bald eagle, it's actually a red-tailed hawk, then performed the bird call for us so we could hear the difference. He wore these brown cowboy boots stitched with blonde swirls and a block heel that clicked through the corridors, even with his tuxedo and gown for his matriculation dinner at Wolfson College. When a lecturer asked the room if anyone would like to read the poem we were studying, he often raised his hand, then cleared his throat to read. I envied the space he took up.

Like always, the women found a way to each other.

Natalie and I sat together on our first day. She wore round gold glasses and had a big American laugh. Natalie had left her friends, family and a media job in New York to study, and I thought that made her very courageous. It was easy to just do a little of the reading list, turn up for the classes, then submit the assignments. Whereas Natalie had committed herself to writing full-time. She was lodging with an older couple in Cambridge and living out of a large grey suitcase that she said was full of books and knitwear – or *sweaters*, as she called them. I remembered my dish full of sea glass and decided Natalie was one of the richest women I knew.

Chapter Thirty-Nine

Grantchester Meadows: 52.1810° N, 0.0932° E

I woke up that Thursday in a single bed in Madingley Hall. My insides ached. There was a lump in my throat like a knot in wood and a tension in my temples hinted I needed to cry, but I knew if I started, I wouldn't be able to stop. Some days grief was like that.

I took two steps to the window and stared at the hedgerows. I tried to think of the birds that might be outside: blue tit, sparrow, greenfinch, Tom. I took three steps to the bathroom and washed my face. The tap made a juddering sound when it started and the water smelled ancient.

For four days I'd been staring at the page, writing poems and working. I'd lift my pen and the letters to form his name would appear. T – O – M. As a little boy, Tom struggled to master writing his name and wrote it backwards. We called him Motty. I used to draw dots on his page so he could join them together.

It was all so painful; I couldn't write anything past his name. I wanted to try in case it was the answer, so I got back into bed, put my laptop on my chest and opened Word. I hovered over the T button, which was waiting right beneath my index finger. The cursor blinked at me. I hit 'Exit and Discard Changes', although there were none to 'Save'.

I thought about Miri; I missed her. I wondered what she'd say right now. Probably, *go have a swim*. Recently it'd felt like there was lots she'd told me I couldn't do, but maybe I could try this one. I typed 'Swim Cambridge' into the search bar. Jesus Green Lido wasn't far, but it didn't open till 7 a.m. and the booking app looked like it was made on Microsoft Publisher 1997. I booked an Uber to Grantchester Meadows, which involved reassuring the driver that *just here is fine please,* despite his reservations about why a girl wanted to be dropped off by the river so early.

I walked to a bend in the River Cam and found a wooden ladder. It was simple. It was quiet. It was perfect. There was an orange fire in the sky, dawn had arrived. I undressed quickly. A ruffling in the marshes signalled I'd disturbed a brown hare enjoying its morning by the water. The flamed sky was mirrored on the still pool of water and the meadow blazed with wildflowers. Knapweed, ox-eye daisies, field scabious and meadow buttercups still in bloom. I slipped into the brown water and my heart beat fast, a radiating thud-thud. I heard it in my ears and remembered that I was alive, which often felt like an accidental detail. Blood was being pumped around my body at four miles an hour. I would keep going.

A cloud of white floated onto the river. I stayed still, treading water, wondering if I should fear the swan. Her wings were folded by her sides, but I knew if she lifted them her strength could overpower me. She made the slightest movement of her beak, almost curious, which I took to mean she was content sharing the river.

I inhaled deeply, then placed my head under the water and screamed. Bubbles escaped my mouth like I'd boiled the water with my anger. Jem was right, it helped the rage. I sensed the beat of wings as a trio of birds fled the reeds. My entire face felt frozen, jaw stuck.

Standing by a cluster of yellow fieldcap mushrooms, I peeled my sodden underwear from my body. I was ill-equipped for emerging from the swim and only had a white towel from Madingley Hall that was streaked with brown mud once I'd dried myself. I took a moment to just be, then, as the mist cleared, I walked away from the river.

Somehow I made it back in time for the first session of the day and without anyone seeing me return to my room with a brown towel, wet knickers and squelching trainers. I was so embarrassed by the state of the towel that I packed it in my weekend bag and hoped they wouldn't charge me for it. I sat in the classroom smelling of wet earth and river. When I curled my toes in my shoes, I could feel the soft friction of silt and was sure if I lifted my shirt there'd be traces of mud on my skin.

I wanted to tell Natalie I'd just been swimming. She'd been talking about 'Grantchester Meadows' by Pink Floyd; she'd like to know. I worried the words would fall out of my mouth in a Tom-shaped disguise. There was a small twig tangled in my hair, which I freed and placed in my pocket.

The rest of the day went well. We had a poetry class and I wrote about watching the swan at dawn. One of the tutors said, *no one reads a poem to get to the last line. That's the difference between poetry and prose.* I wondered what conclusions or endings I had to offer. I felt questions most of the time. My poem about a swan ended up being about Jem. The way he lived felt like the closest thing to truth I knew. He lived life like it was a poem, no meaning hinged on the last line. Sometimes the poems I wrote were of the birds, then the questions again. *Everything passes by*, I thought.

Punting in Cambridge

Chapter Forty

Jolene: 51.55130° N, 0.08467° W

I was emboldened on my return. I wanted to build something with Jem and worried what our foundations were if he didn't want to join me on the new adventures in my life. I wanted us to share things. Cambridge felt shareable. *Let's go for dinner to toast my first week at Cambridge,* I texted and tried not to be embarrassed by how grotesque that sentence sounded. He replied straight away, *great idea* and a thumbs up emoji, then followed up that afternoon with: *Angel Station 8 p.m.*

We met at the tube and walked through Newington Green to a restaurant called Jolene, which was painted the same colour as Umbrian tiles. Its logo was scribbled in a wobbly mix of upper and lower cases. *You might think that looks like it's drawn by a child,* Jem said, *and that's because it was. Apparently the designer's six-year-old did it to reflect the,* he did air quotes, *simplicity the food expresses.* He put his hands in his back pockets, *I quite like it.* I thought about Jem's handwriting on the post-card. *I want to put both my hands inside your brain.*

I was already falling in love. It was easy when we went to places like this. Unpainted plaster walls, candlelit, natural wines, dried sage hanging from the bar, piles of homemade garlicky focaccia that Jem tore at with his fingers and placed directly in my mouth as he rubbed olive oil over my lips. It was only when I was steadily through my second glass of wine that I felt bold enough to say it disappointed me that he hadn't said more about my studies.

Do you really think I don't celebrate you? The chinks of green glass in his eyes flashed and the tone of his voice made me feel guilty. *It's not that. I'm just really proud. It's a big adventure and if we're starting something here,* I laid my fingers flat against the base of my wine glass, *then I want to know you'll share this stuff with me.* I was a demanding person. Surely it was better to show that now, rather than it be a surprise later? Maybe I was being spoilt? I thought of Miri's post-card. I thought of what I felt I deserved and tried to put that first.

You haven't even read my writing, I prodded. *I didn't realise you needed me to read it straight away,* he blinked. It'd been a few weeks since I'd emailed him. I quietly considered if I thought he'd ever get around to it. I wasn't sure.

What was I hoping for? That he'd arrive with a bouquet and a card, then I'd read it and think, *ah I know how much he adores me now.* I hadn't paused long enough to think about it. In truth, I wasn't sure that the flowers would even do it. The waitress appeared between us and refilled our tumblers. She was wearing a completely colourless mood ring.

I don't want to invalidate any of what you've said, because I always want to celebrate you. Maybe I just, he scratched behind his ear and I was suddenly aware of how bony my bottom felt on the wooden stool, *I don't care about that kind of stuff.* I raised my eyebrows and he rushed to add, *obviously I'm happy that you're happy and you're learning, that's great. But it's not like I'd like you any more because of it. I like you because of you.* I didn't know what to say. Because of me? I didn't know what 'me' was if it wasn't Cambridge and the rest of it.

I felt the heat rising from my neck and up into my face. Jem brought his mouth to my ear, beside my now-hot temples, and whispered, *I like you because of you. You kind, joyous, maddening, wonderful woman.* Closing my eyes, I tried to hear the words and store them safely for later.

I replayed Flip calling me Poet. It felt like I ascended a new level of appreciation from him with every accomplishment. What was at the top? A pedestal of success. I thought about his typewriter, De'Longhi coffee machine, Juicy Fruit gum. He was concrete and absolute. He acquired and he created. I'd been attempting to do the same. I was dripping myself in gold like an Egyptian queen preparing for a funeral – shining Master's, shimmering job, sparkling poems – then asking Jem to celebrate my adornments and getting frustrated that he wanted me to shake them all off. He wanted who I was beneath it all.

Balanced on our two stools, Jem and I ate cuttlefish with capers and tagliatelle with girolles and creme fraiche. I imagined saying, *I could do this with you forever.* In my fantasy, he'd say, *do what?* And I'd reply, *eat food and figure things out together.* Instead, I said *the plum pudding is very good,* then he placed his hand on my shoulder and agreed.

Once my heart had decided I was in love with Jem, it was difficult not to think about it. The following week, we went to the Roxy for the Eddie Chacon gig. Every reflection of a low purple stage light in Jem's eyes, the tilt of his face, the smell of his sweat as he lifted his arm around my shoulder intoxicated me. I welcomed the wet slick of the beer bottle in my hand and pressed it against my forehead. Jem had my blood running hot, and I enjoyed how love made me aware of how it felt to live in my body. Flip became something to deal with later, a conundrum future-me would solve along with unravelling why exactly I'd been unable to end things with him straight away.

That weekend, Jem and I were going to stay in Wales while my parents were away. I'd planned to say it there with the backdrop of the mountains, but my heart had been swelling all evening and when he pulled my body closer to his in bed, I couldn't contain it any longer. *I love you*, I said. And Jem thanked me. I felt like my heart had been placed on the rope of a slingshot and pitched out the skylight towards the moon. *I care about you a lot, but I need more time.* The bedsheets moved around me as I curved my shoulders inwards. I wanted to make my body as small as I could.

We talked for a while, but I wasn't listening once I knew nothing that left his mouth would be those three words. I left early the next morning and the journey back south was filled with a lovesick composed of embarrassment and rejection. It was my own fault for breaking the rules of 'taking it slow'.

My empty duffle bag was on the kitchen table. I'd planned to pack for Wales that day, but was suddenly overwhelmed with uncertainty. Looking at it made my stomach churn. The night before, my bag had represented excitement for the weekend ahead and the memories we'd make on a time that would forever signpost the beginning of our relationship – what I'd interpreted as us falling in love. Now, the bag reminded me of what a fool I was. Jem called me and I couldn't pick up. The bag stayed empty.

Chapter Forty-One

Sugar Loaf: 51.85715° N, 3.06175° W

The next day, Jem arrived at my flat. *You didn't answer your phone*, he looked past me to the empty bag on the table. I explained my uncertainty, rejection and paranoia. He shook his head, *you're a funny fish. Go and pack your bag. We'll leave in ten.*

Wales was sloping through September faster than London and we used the weather as an excuse to begin our transition into autumn: cold walks with my hand in his pocket, nut roasts and apple cider, thick jumpers under anoraks and kissing with our cold noses pressed together in front of an open fire. I took Jem to the moorland ridge of the Blorenge. The mountain's name comes from the old Saxon word *blore*, meaning wind. The land is blistered with signs of mining: black mounds of slag heap, disused bell pits and quarries to the northwest. We traversed the bruise-purple heathland, searching for hobbies, a type of falcon with long pointed wings that can often be seen hunting large insect prey in this stretch of the Brecon Beacons.

Passing the Foxhunter car park, we returned to where we'd started, Keeper's Pond, where I swam with Mum on Boxing Day. It's a small pool in the mountains, filled with water the colour of a two-pence coin. We zipped our coats up, hoods on. Just a small sliver of my face exposed to the wind. Jem pulled his hands from his pockets to place them against my cheeks. They were warm. He pushed the hood of my coat behind my ears and cupped them so I could listen to the wind. We stayed like that for a while, heeding to the wild wailing of a gale tearing through the mountains. The forceful torrents brought us to our hands and knees until we had to scramble near the summit. Crouched low like that, I could smell the boggy footpath, ripe with the stench of peat. Jem collected stones to build a cairn. The wind was so loud that we didn't speak, but moved our hands in anticipation of one another. I thought about the couple I'd seen in St Ives; how they'd silently constructed some-thing beautiful together. My life was mirroring the wishes I'd held inside and I couldn't help but feel it was a gift the search for tidal pools had given me.

That evening, Jem cooked dinner while I researched the Concord Pools in Essex, where I was going the following weekend. It was an unusual delight to see him moving pans on Mum's AGA. Just seven months ago, I'd been there hoping my life would change. I hadn't thought to hope for this. I watched Jem move his eyes over the shrine Mum had built Tom. Ceramic angel ornaments, photographs, toy cars. Jem looked at them and said nothing. I said nothing and wished one of us had said even the smallest of somethings, but tried to trust that Jem was acknowledging it in his own quiet way.

The wind knocked on the windows, so we built a fire that raged for the whole evening and made love in front of it. We found my mother's riding crop and he spanked me with it, then added more logs to the open flaming mouth until the room was filled with the scent of sparked matches and pine. Despite the fire, the bedroom was cold. Jem's body was a kiln that warmed me all night.

My parents had been on an orienteering course and said they kept getting lost so came back early. Jem said he'd like to meet them. I knew they'd like Jem, and would comment that it was good I'd found someone who enjoyed cooking, as I could barely boil an egg. I thought that would sustain us for the first hour of conversation, then we could fill the rest of the time listening to Dad talk about his decision to watch Sky News because the BBC was 'too biased now'.

I chatted to Mum while preparing dinner. We looked at our hands peeling potatoes and not at each other. *You're so lucky to have a man who cooks. Why can all men cook these days?* Mum watched Jem with an air of suspicion as he diced olives for a tapenade. *My next husband will be able to cook,* she said loudly, but Dad was in the other room watching *Coronation Street* and didn't hear.

The bench is being installed on the twentieth, she studied the Maris Piper in her grip. I froze. Since I'd suggested it, we'd had a few discussions about the bench. The family had agreed on the parkland behind our old school and we'd looked at a list of woods: teak, oak, roble, pine. As far as I was aware, nothing had been agreed. Suddenly, holding a potato peeler felt danger-ous. *What do you mean?* I asked. *In two weeks. The bench is being installed. What more is there to mean? If they're that big, cut them in half twice—*

I thought we were organising it together? I interrupted, but Mum only continued, *otherwise they don't roast like the others,* and sliced a large knife through the potato I'd just peeled.

Well, that's when they could do it. And I've already told Tom's friends. So the boys have . . . I laid the peeler down. *The boys are going to be there?* She nodded and added

268

that Nicole, Tom's girlfriend, would be there too. Mum was good at organising things for Tom's friends. She felt a duty to gather them each year and support the young grieving men. I knew it was the right thing to do, but being around their skinny jeans and Paco Rabanne cologne was a sensory punch in the gut. Hearing about their jobs and girlfriends and cars was too much of a reminder that they were growing older, and Tom was not.

So you'll get the train and meet us there? Mum confirmed more than she asked as she filled a pan with water. *I don't know if I'm free.* My swim with Miri was on my mind. I could easily reschedule, but I wanted the excuse. I left a brown spot on a potato and plopped it in the pan.

I can never get hold of you, you're always busy then don't return my calls. You can't miss it, Mum said. I knew she was right, but I also knew myself well enough to know I'd find a way out. She sighed, *Emma thought you might do this.* Although the saucepan was now full of bobbing bald potatoes, we continued peeling and I knew we'd have more leftovers than usual.

At the dinner table, I nestled into Jem as if he could protect me from learned dynamics that had been forged over my entire childhood. *You're very tactile with each other,* Mum skewered a potato onto her fork. *It's not very easy having a child who doesn't like to be hugged.*

Freya can be quite frigid, she repeated the myth I'd been told about myself for so long that it became true for a while. Dad said nothing and continued tightening his sunglasses with a screwdriver I recognised from last year's Christmas crackers. I was momentarily angry at her, then the waves of my frustration subsided into a gentle lapping of guilt that she felt I didn't touch her enough. The thought of hugging her felt impossible. Jem tapped my knee under the table, *Freya's a very affectionate person.* Something undid itself inside me and I let go of a truth that I'd been holding tight for too long. I decided I could rewrite my life.

The next day, Jem and I woke up at 4:40 a.m. to climb Sugar Loaf for sunrise. I worried we wouldn't reach the top in time because Jem kept stopping to feed the wild horses grass, but we made it to the summit and opened our flask just as the rosy-fingered dawn appeared. When we'd descended, it was still morning, so we went into Crickhowell for sugar doughnuts and coffee, then climbed Skirrid. A path led us through the shelter of Pant Skirrid Wood and up onto the ridge. Jem raced me to the top. Following him with the wind in my hair, his body smaller in the distance, I was overcome with a memory of following Tom up Scafell Pike. I stopped. Jem turned back towards me, and reached out his hand, though he didn't let me beat him.

At the peak, we could see the Black Mountains in the west, Usk Valley in the south and Malverns in the north. Jem pointed to the mountains and gave them new names: Togbasket, Cobbler's Crag, Colin Gobbles and Jessop's Fist Fight. While we walked, we talked a lot. The outdoors had become a safe space for us as a couple. Jem was often reserved, but on walks we talked with our hands in our pockets while we looked at our boots striking the path. He told me he found it hard to express how he felt with words. *I'll try harder*, he said. He also said he worried I didn't truly hear him sometimes. *I'll try harder*, I said. I truly meant it. I'd wanted a lot of assurances and commitment from Jem. Maybe what I wanted and needed were not the same thing. And what could anyone need more than being one of two people who were continually committed to trying?

When I'd said 'I love you' to Jem, I wasn't sure if I was telling him or trying to incite a reaction. Had I said it at that moment because I'd known that this would be his answer and a reason to run away? A reason not to pack my bag. I wondered if, in some ways, I felt I deserved his rejection.

Whenever I'm in Wales, I sleep in Tom's bed. It's a queen-size cloud. White and firm. My mum bought it hoping the orthopaedic mattress, with eight hundred pocket springs, would support his balsa-wood bones. I lay with my face pressed into the mattress and exhaled. My breath was hot against the cotton. My arms down by my sides and the backs of my palms cushioned against the sheets. I saw just black and blinked my eyelashes, then thought about butterfly kisses. I let my body sink into feeling like I was connected to Tom through this bed that he'd had a hundred dreams – and a hundred nightmares – in.

Autumn

Chapter Forty-Two

Bus Depot: 51.46565° N, 0.01392° W

October was a month I wished I could banish from the calendar. It was just a month like any other, but it always felt different. It was the anniversary of Tom's death; a day I'd rather forget, but my body was a clock that struck when it approached. *It's been five years*, it rang, *five years*.

In previous years, we'd attempted to create a ritual around it. A walk at Leith Hill, then a pint followed by sausages and mash at The Abinger Hatch. Extra lashings of gravy in memory of Tom. Now, members of our family were disbanding. Lawrence had moved to Toronto. I was ready to be next.

This year, I didn't want to be with anyone. I didn't want to acknowledge it. I didn't want to be sad. I wanted to go for a swim, then get back into bed. I wanted to drink a bottle of wine, and for no one to tell me I shouldn't. I hoped it would be a day of private shame and grief. Cambridge was a convenient excuse.

I had a full-time job and coursework too. Phoning Mum to tell her I wouldn't be there for Tom's bench was a painful betrayal that felt like the only way to avoid more pain.

I swam with an urgency that week. Clinging to my slot at the lido like a life raft. I went every day because I knew if I missed one, then it would be easy to make an excuse to miss the next. Swimming got me out of bed and kept me moving. Swimming kept me afloat. Swimming kept me aware of my body and that I was alive.

Jem was away surfing before winter truly set in. He called me while he was at the beach and I imagined his hair still wet. There was a noise down the line, like an animal moving quickly through leaves in a forest, and I heard a woman's voice: *it's not that cold. Are you coming back in?*

I can't remember what we'd been talking about, but I know we'd been laughing as the sensation of my smiling cheeks collapsing into a look of disbelief was how I imagine falling down a lift shaft would feel. I listened to their muffled conversation for a while. Pressing my fingers against my mouth, I held my breath. I can't explain why, but I didn't end the call. I couldn't.

I concluded that there were two viable options for what was happening. Either he thought he'd hung up or he was talking to her with his phone hidden under the towel, not wanting to reveal he'd been on the phone to a girl back in London.

If it was the latter, there'd probably be sand in the headphone port and it'd overheat soon. Was the beach sand or stones? It was going to be my next question, but I hadn't had the chance to ask. *Pebbles are my favourite*, I'd have said, *I enjoy rearranging them into a pillow under my towel while I sunbathe.* I thought we were lovers who shared inconsequential preferences like that. I'd been so open and curious by collecting details about him to cherish. We had such magic between us. He'd just met my parents. I'd said I loved him.

Hearing the woman's voice say: *nectarine*, I had to put my hand on the table to steady myself. I imagined them eating soft fruit on the beach together. I wondered if she'd lick the juice from his fingers. Imagining her wet, soft mouth, my heart tugged like a jolted seatbelt. I braced for impact. Then the line went dead.

Jem's name flashed up on my phone again. I answered. *Sorry*, he said, *we got disconnected.* The clouds in my heart started raining and I knew then why storms are given human names.

That evening I went to a gig in South London. When the show was over and the lights came on, I wasn't ready to go home. The thought of being alone in my flat made my insides knot. I said, *next round on me,* to my friends and left for the bar next door before anyone could protest. There was a simplicity to drinking as the answer to grief. I was full of rage and sadness so having all that darkness swirl around inside me with liquor felt right. I tried to talk about Jem, but people seemed uninterested, so I quipped that I'd chased him away anyway. I pointed to my chest and said, *this is where men pit-stop before they decide they deserve better.* Everyone laughed. They thought I was joking.

Not done talking about Jem, I told an anecdote about him spanking me with my mother's riding crop and the mood shifted. I felt embarrassed, so I left without saying goodbye and went to a pub where there was a band playing Bon Jovi covers. Everyone seemed to be ignoring the music, and I pitied the singer who was wearing a fedora and looked chronically uncool, despite his very obvious attempts. I spoke to a woman who said she had a cockatiel in her car if I wanted to see. I said it seemed quite sad to have a bird trapped in a car, and she said it seemed sad to be my age and drinking alone. Eventually, I ran out of bars to go where I could hide. I hated London for being a city that shut its doors on you so early.

Jem and the woman and the nectarines crossed my mind again and I felt sick. I thought about Tom's anniversary and felt even worse. Clicking my phone to check the time, I was reminded I had another missed call from Flip. I pressed his name then cancelled it on the second ring. I was disgusted with myself. What was I trying to prove? It was too late for a train, so I boarded a bus and tried to stay awake as it shuffled through the city. More and more passengers left until it was just me drifting off to sleep. Drifting, drifting, drifting.

A noise, perhaps a scream or a fox, woke me up on the top deck of the bus. My cheek was pressed against the scratchy moquette of the seat. I sat up and the world spun. It was dark, and I almost didn't recognise the bus without the fluorescent lights and passengers. Panicking that I was trapped, I rushed down the steps, nearly tripping, to see the driver with the caddy door open. He looked surprised to see me, but I started running through the bus depot before he could say anything. If he was there, then it would still be open. Did these places ever close?

I walked down a street with chicken bones on the pavement. The road was empty, dark. I zipped up my leather jacket to cover the thin moon-white sliver of skin exposed between my top and jeans. Unsteady and quick, the sound of my footsteps filled the night. Then I heard a second pair of footsteps, more certain. Also quick. Someone was following me. I wanted to look behind me, but was scared that the time it'd take me to turn around would give them a chance to catch up. From the volume of the steps, they weren't far away.

Hey! a man's voice shouted. *I have something to show you!* I couldn't think of anything to say that wouldn't cause a retaliation. Unsure if it was a bad idea, I started running. The sound of pumping blood filled my ears, but not enough to mask the sound of footsteps accelerating. I was being chased.

I looked up the high street. Where was I? There were no shops open. I could bang on a door. No lights on. No one home. If I got an Uber, I'd have to get out my phone. That would slow me down. Then it would be minutes away. I could call the police. Same problem. I couldn't decide, couldn't think. I stopped trying to escape and just focused on my feet. My previously foggy brain was suddenly sharp with adrenaline, but my body was still clumsy and I nearly tripped on the pavement. He came close enough that I was sure he'd tried to reach out and grab my hair. Maybe it was just the night air against the back of my head. This couldn't be how I died.

I wasn't scared of dying, I just wasn't ready to give up on living yet. I'd always hoped I'd have a pain-free and perfect death like my paternal grandma. She was having her hair done then said, *I don't feel very well,* and slid off the chair. It was such a good way to go. I fantasised about having a death that good.

We'd been in a Center Parcs waterpark when my dad got the call. It was strange seeing him cry. Mostly because he was wearing tight swimming trunks and it made the whole thing seem quite indecent. The air was muggy with chlorine. Perhaps that was why his eyes were watering. We decided there wasn't much we could do, so we went on a few more rides. It's hard to enjoy a rubber ring slide when you're thinking about your dead grandmother.

Once I asked Emma if she ever thought about dying. She hopes death is like when Mum used to carry her to bed if she fell asleep in Tom's room. The half-awake hearing of people talking while you drift off. *That sounds nice,* I said.

So no, I'm not scared of dying. I just worry about the admin. I always leave my flat tidy in case my parents have to clear it out when they end my tenancy. It's Mum who I worry about. I remember her phoning to cancel Tom's gym membership. They said he'd have to come in to cancel it himself and she had to explain, again, that he couldn't come in because he was dead.

It clicked onto the hold music and I watched her inhale, preparing to explain to another stranger that her son had died.

I don't know when the footsteps behind me stopped, but it was so sudden and yet so gradual that I doubted there'd ever been someone there at all. Arriving home, I struggled with my keys in the lock, which made me feel like a drunk person in a movie. I checked my phone.

3:47 a.m.

Soon I'd have to get up to go swimming. I got in the shower then worried I'd slip, so I sat down and let the water run over my body, cleansing me, until it ran cold. I put on my swimsuit, then my clothes, so I'd be ready tomorrow, and fell asleep on top of the covers in the whiskey dark. I slept so still I could've convinced myself I was dead.

Chapter Forty-Three

Canvey Island Beach: 51.51242° N, 0.60131° E

Both Miri and I had taken a Friday off work to visit Concord Tidal Pool. My insides felt fragile and I thought I'd split open at the gentlest touch of sound. Getting to Canvey Island took us from Fenchurch Street to Benfleet in Essex. We realised too late that we'd gone past the Pay-As-You-Go zone and needed to buy tickets at the other end, which caused an irksome conversation with a ticket attendant who was clearly having a bad day.

I slowed down at the bus stop to let a woman pushing a pug in a pram overtake me. It was possible that I'd be sick in the bin. Swaying slightly, I stared at it and used all my brainpower to assess the situation. It had an ashtray on top and opening on the side. The practicalities of it were not ideal. Something swelled inside me. I swallowed. It tasted of vinegar and stomach acid.

You alright? Miri asked. *Yeah fine, think I just have a tummy bug.* I was too embarrassed to admit I was hungover in case she asked who I'd been out with last night. I put my sunglasses on as we boarded a bus from the station to Concord Beach via the suburban villages of Canvey Island.

Once we'd arrived, we climbed up onto the concrete boardwalk beside the Thames Estuary. The sea wall was painted with truly disastrous murals, mostly of the Second World War. The faces looked like melted candles but on closer inspection it was hard to point out what exactly was off in the proportions. Miri thought it was the foreheads, I thought the eyes were too far apart. Towards the tidal pool, there was another mural. A baby-blue collage of sea creatures painted by the primary school: limpets, green crabs, whelks, cockles and razorfish. I particularly enjoyed the seal, which had a line-drawn smile and CBeebies bonhomie about it. I was so fragile that I had to stop looking at the children's paintings or I thought I might cry.

Concord Tidal Pool itself is an expanse of water contained by silver railings. That bright but sharp Friday in October, they glinted in the sun. The pool is simple and has been there in a similar form since the 1930s, when it was a popular seaside holiday destination for swimming, amusement arcades and Billy Wells' pony rides on the seafront. There's a town website with a summarised history of Canvey Island and a page where people can share old family photos and get help identifying the place, year or people. *Anyone know who the boy leading the donkey is,* one uploader asked. I enjoyed the 'Tourism' section, which featured old postcards from the 1930s to 1970s. Some had excerpts of the writing, 'tonight we have been watching a clown disco' and 'this is a very scruffy place. I don't think much of jellied eels.' I printed a particularly tacky one that read: 'At Canvey Island the breeze is soft and balmy, and so are some of the men!' I'd been meaning to post it to Miri. It was on my list of Random Acts of Kindness that'd recently been neglected in favour of waking up and going to work. I congratulated myself for making it on this daytrip.

Along the boardwalk there are benches at five-metre intervals and a concrete ramp down onto blonde sand that looked recently litter-picked. That day, an elderly couple, a family eating fish and chips and a mother and child joined us. The mother was wearing a puffer jacket and looking at her phone while the little boy filled and emptied a yellow bucket.

A few steps into the sea there was a ridge that Miri and I both stumbled on. This sudden drop made it easier to get in as we were unexpectedly up to our chests. I held my nose and submerged myself in the water. I had yet to find a better hangover cure. When I resurfaced, I watched Miri move her arms and look at her body through the water. *It's so clean.*

Miri and I were the only swimmers on the beach. A man on a bike slowed down and shouted, *aren't you cold*. Miri gave a wave and laughed. *Crazy*, he said, then carried on cycling. I looked towards the elderly couple and wondered if the bench was their special place or just where they'd sat that day. I'd asked for a special place. Now I had one and I didn't want to go. I'd wanted somewhere that Emma and I could go together to grieve. Tomorrow, she'd be at the somewhere and I'd be nowhere. When I'd confirmed with Mum that I wouldn't be going we'd argued then I'd said sorry, then she'd said sorry then we'd started arguing again and had carried on like that for a few days. I told myself by not going I was demonstrating self-care. I told myself my actions were ok.

Placing my swimming socks on the bench, I watched them drip onto the pavement. Suddenly the fragrant smell of chip-shop vinegar was nauseating. I felt faint. No, I felt sick. I grabbed my swimming bag and vomited into it. Then I inhaled a gulp of air and retched again, this time until my stomach muscles were taut.

Are you going to be sick again, Miri rubbed my back. I shook my head. With her thumb and forefinger she pincered my phone and rinsed it with her water bottle. Miri peered into the bag at my towel, swimming costume and hat, which were covered in a stringy acidic vomit, and decided nothing else was saveable so zipped it up and put it over her shoulder. *Let's get you something to eat.*

We walked to a greasy spoon beneath Fantasy Island Arcades that had a sign outside: 'Sue's Cafe: All Day Breakfast' in blue and yellow. Miri ordered two sausage-and-egg sandwiches with runny yolks that Emma would call a 'jammy' egg. She returned with two teas. I always appreciated it when tea was served in a decent-sized mug. *Are you ok?* Miri asked and I wondered where to start. Arguing with Mum, avoiding Emma, heartbroken by Jem, screening Flip's calls, homework at Cambridge, forgetting last night's near escape. I shrugged.

As I took my first sip Miri said, *got yours with a bit of sugar. Always good for a hangover.* I clearly hadn't convinced her of my 'tummy bug'.

I looked out the smudged window, *at the hospital the nurses always put sugar in my tea. I only ever said milk, but I guess they knew I needed it.* Both my hands were wrapped around the mug and it was burning my hands, but I didn't move them. I carried on, *lots of people hate hospitals, but I liked being there. It felt good to be around people who understood. I don't feel like many people understand. They don't understand what I feel like inside,* I shifted in the plastic seat but it was nailed to the floor, *and I'm not saying that to upset you or say you don't understand me. It's not that, I just miss being in a place where people know what I need, because I have no idea.*

Miri nodded slowly, *that doesn't upset me. I don't understand, I can't. But I can bring you tea and we can swim and chat. We can chat about Tom more if you like.* She said it like a statement more than a question, which I was grateful for because the thought of producing more words made my throat tight. Talking about Tom was both what I wanted and what I knew would ruin me. I took another gulp of tea then put my sunglasses back on. There was a man eating a full English on the next table. He was buttering a slice of bread without paying much attention to the edges. He could probably tell from my perspex Ace & Tate sunglasses that we were from London.

What can I do to help you? There was a clock on the wall that had knives and forks for hands. *Have you seen that clock*, I pointed towards it. Miri turned her neck and laughed. I wanted to laugh too, but found that I couldn't. She swivelled back and said softly, *don't avoid me.* I thought about the bag of sick fizzing with phlegm under the table. I'd not had a chance to test how waterproof the bag was before, but I couldn't smell the stench of vomit, so it must've been as airtight as advertised. *You're doing so well.* Miri held my hand and we finished our sandwiches. Outside the cafe was an old ice-cream tub of water that someone had written *Dogs Only No Seagulls* on with marker.

Chapter Forty-Four

Brockwell Lido: 51.45298° N, 0.10614° W

The day of Tom's anniversary arrived. I told myself the only thing I'd do was swim. If I could wake up, get out of bed and cycle to the lido, then I could survive. I reminded myself it was only a matter of weeks, maybe even days, before the water would get colder. Soon we'd be counting backwards in degrees till April. Soon I'd be counting backwards till the next anniversary. I could hold on a little longer and it would all reset. It was only degrees. It was only time.

Swimming hadn't always been available to me as a coping mechanism. I'd tried other things first. There was a time when I tried to lean into all the grief stuff. So much so that I attended a bereavement weekend. The sessions happened in a draughty room that smelled of old school gymnasiums with bowed wooden rafters in the ceiling, heaving like a whale's ribcage. We sat in a makeshift circle of fold-out chairs and took it in turns to say our names like Alcoholics Anonymous meetings in movies. I said my brother was called Tom and he'd died three years ago. Everyone told me it was soon. *That's very recent*, they'd say and I thought it'd been the longest, most painful three years of my life. *It gets easier*, they said. That felt impossible then, but when I reached five years I finally knew they were right. I hated it. Feeling better made me feel so far from him.

I wasn't sure what I'd expected from the bereavement weekend, but it wasn't how it was. Perhaps something more clinical, more forced, more awkward. In the morning, we'd made an assembly line to clean up the dishes from breakfast. The woman next to me had henna-red hair. I couldn't remember her name but learned that her older sister had sledged into a barbed wire fence at the bottom of Newlands Corner during the snowstorm of 2010 and choked to death. Most of us there had stories like that to tell, and I felt almost guilty that after the first two or three, I felt my shock and emotion diminish, like my tolerance for tragedy had increased. I'd developed antibodies. Immunity.

The general gist was that when people die before their time, it's very awful. It's awful when anyone dies, but there's something particularly cruel about how fate can steal so much in the blink of an eye. The deaths were all different, but the themes were the same. Loss, guilt and grief. I was surprised how much admin was involved. One man described at length the emotional ordeal of arranging for his brother's body to be flown back from Patagonia. And, of course, the horrible sense of irony in someone travelling on an adventure that would catapult them into adulthood, only for them to die during it. I became confident that after that weekend, I'd never go paragliding or caving and might even find it difficult to enjoy a walk again after hearing about someone who tripped on their shoelace and cracked their skull on the pavement. But what was I to do, never leave the house? Death was clearly cunning and had a twisted sense of humour.

Getting in the lido felt like a punishment, which something inside me needed. Getting out felt like a rebirth, which everything inside me needed. I took short, sharp breaths as the water burned my ankles, thighs, stomach, then chest. Crying happens on an inhale, and swimming gives me that same breathless sensation. I swam three laps, then at the deep end screamed underwater. When I emerged, I couldn't stop crying.

Witnessing someone having a breakdown in a public pool must be a good way to see British manners in action. The lifeguard tentatively approached and hovered nearby, unsure if my tears were a genuine safety concern, while the other swimmers made their laps shallower to avoid the crying girl in the deep end. Miri rubbed my shoulder while treading water and ushered me to the steps. Somehow I climbed out of the pool, but my legs were so numb I tripped on the last step, slid off the metal ladder and landed on my knees. The tears poured out of me. She put her arm around me and our two bodies thawed each other out.

Miri sat me down on the changing room bench where I stared at my bright red legs. There was grit from the pool's edge embedded in my knee. When Miri realised I wasn't moving, she rubbed me a few times with the towel then started dressing me. I watched her – squatting on the changing room floor, which was slick with hair and leaves – as she put my socks on and realised that I truly loved her.

When I left the lido I saw a message to our family WhatsApp group about the bench. They'd placed a bag of Tom's ashes in the ground before they installed it. We'd never spoken about Tom's ashes. I took a shaky breath and swayed slightly. I couldn't believe someone had done this. Even the decision to split them felt big and complicated. What if I'd wanted them to stay together? I looked at the photo of a small black velvet pouch. It looked like it might carry a fine gold necklace coiled like a 14-carat snake. Instead, it contained the dust of a human. I thought about the difference in sound between dropping a bag in a hole and ashes flying to the ground. That, in itself, was a decision I'd not been part of.

I was continually surprised by my obsession with the remnants and relics of the dead. The bereavement retreat was where I'd met Rohanna. When she spoke in the sessions, she moved her silver ring with an amber stone the size of a toffee chunk. I complimented her on it and she told me it was made with some of Sami's ashes. One man was wearing his older brother's leather jacket and a woman had a tattoo on her wrist of her mother's handwriting: *I'm so proud of you.* Someone said she had nothing fashionable to wear from her dead father and the only handwriting she'd be able to find was probably his NatWest details on a Post-it note and that wouldn't make for a good tattoo or any personalised jewellery. I looked down at my ringless fingers and felt jealous I didn't have any grief mementos. Facebook must've known I was bereaved as they kept serving me Co-op Funeralcare adverts or sponsored posts saying, 'Feeling Hopeless? Try These 5 Things'. I complained about my data being used to profit from my vulnerability, but never received a reply, and they continued advertising memorial candles to me.

I looked at WhatsApp again and felt hot and sick and empty. I didn't feel that I had a right to any of the emotions inside me. I didn't deserve to be hurt by this when I'd been the one to distance myself. Emma and Mum posted on Instagram about the bench. I looked at the hashtags. Should I have posted today? If I didn't, did that mean Tom wasn't on my mind? My last post was an Olivia Laing novel and a cinnamon bun. It felt odd to imagine the two posts together. I deleted the app from my phone.

The last time I'd seen Jem he'd been clearing his garden for winter. He had a long bamboo pole that he called his Spider Stick and was using it to clear cobwebs from the metal steps. Coat on, hands in pockets; I sat on the bench and read my book. Being quiet was feeling more possible.

We were reminiscing about our phone calls in North Devon when we'd first started dating. He laughed and said, *I still remember how angry you were about those signs at Bude Sea Pool*. My screwed-up face only made him laugh more. Exhaling sharply, I folded my book on my lap. *It just drives me crazy. The tidal pool is safer than the sea! So having signs there but not on the beach makes absolutely no sense. Plus, they always look hideous. Tidal pools are these gorgeous natural places then there's a sign whacked up telling people to be careful of the nature. So many have been closed because councils deem them unsafe. Then people are left with either no open water or the sea, which is just, well it's the sea . . . it can be fucking dangerous out there.* Leaning back, I opened my book again: *I just worry it's us moving towards being liability-obsessed like America and prevents people from being able to experience nature in their communities.*

Jem nodded as if to say, I get it. He picked at a dead sprig of rosemary. *Ok so the signs have their literal meaning that winds you up. Then there's also a deeper meaning that might not be literal, but resonates as more true in your heart. So the more curious thing to ask might be why they upset you so much on a deeper level?*

Sometimes talking to Jem feels like walking into a therapy session. It's all 'resonates' or 'deeper meaning' and it takes me a minute to adjust because I've spent so long trying to hide from these kinds of revelations. *Well,* I hesitated, *I guess you could say sometimes I'm a little uptight or rigid and when I'm swimming, I'm trying to be free. So someone putting up a sign and giving me rules, maybe feels like what I'm trying to go against within myself.*

I glanced at the fence to see if anyone next door was outside. Jem took his Spider Stick to the back corner of the garden and nodded, *maybe.* I forced a fake laugh, *if you think you know something I don't then maybe you should just tell me?*

Jem tidied his watering can away. *I don't know anything you don't. But do you think maybe it's because your grief is the pool and deep down you want to jump in?* Something sank inside me. He was right that when there was a deeper truth, it resonated.

A squirrel swaggered onto the garden fence, but Jem ignored it. *And what do the signs make you feel?* He walked over and put his hand against the back of my head as I replied: *That there are rules, boundaries. And that I'm not allowed.* He stroked my hair. *You can jump in though. You can jump in with me.*

I didn't want to jump in. It was all so untouched, this dark pool of water. My tear ducts felt as though they were being squeezed. Throttled, even. Jem gestured for me to move up so he could sit on the bench. *When you don't give feelings space they feel really deep. And really scary. But when you do give them space, they won't take over like they used to.*

The shadows in Jem's eyes had confused me for a long time. I used to see myself in them and think they contained a truth about our relationship; a resistance, a reluctance or a secret. Now I appreciated that, much like me, Jem had his own feelings that needed space. His own demons. Not everything was about me. For so long I'd been looking for some kind of clarity about us that I hadn't always seen him. I understood then that truly loving someone might not be about what you say, but about what you see.

Jem placed his crooked index finger under my chin to tilt my head. I pulled away, embarrassed by my blotchy cheeks and wet nose. He tugged again until I was looking up at him. *You can be yourself with me. You can jump in.*

Chapter Forty-Five

John's House: 51.44316° N, 0.01469° W

John wasn't my godfather, but I always told people he was because I didn't have another word to describe the extent of his devotion and dedication to me. He'd been at Oxford University with Dad and they'd bonded over a mutual love of T. Rex and washing their shoulder-length hair with strawberry shampoo. John has a long grey beard and wears his Tottenham Hotspur tees under unbuttoned paisley shirts. Whenever we greet one another, he asks how I travelled and I try not to be impatient while he explains the benefits of the 185 bus versus the Northern Line. He's encyclopaedic about London's transport system, Champions League football, psychedelic rock and mythology. Not necessarily in that order.

For many years John travelled around Greece and India as a writer for the *Rough Guide*. He's lived many lives in the time that most people barely live one. Some of the greatest personal epiphanies I've experienced have been products of conversations with him. I often avoid these revelatory discussions because I'd rather not have an uncomfortable conversation. Life feels uncomfortable enough. I wondered what John would say about that.

That week I needed familiarity without accountability and visited him for tea. I sat on his sofa, which was covered in a shower curtain. It crinkled as I tried to get comfortable. *The cat's not feeling well*, he explained. John's Maine Coon, Aggy, blinked at me. Aggy is named after Agamemnon. She seems indifferent to her name. She rarely responds to it, or anything for that matter, and prefers to stare longingly from the window onto the main-road traffic.

John told me to carry on talking while he got something from the other room so I spoke about my recent swimming trips. *The main thing that surprised me*, I started, *was that the bus timetables were just a suggestion. One started pulling away a whole four minutes before it was due to leave. If we'd missed it, we would've had to wait an hour and a half before the next one.*

John returned with a burned CD of a band called Melted Welly. I never had the heart to tell him I had nothing to play them on and just searched his handwritten track list online instead. *That was what it was like when I was travelling. And when your dad and I were at Oxford.* He presented a selection of teabags. *What did you do if you missed one?* I chose the Redbush. *Always an opportunity for thinking time.* I thought that John and I were very different people. *You'll get better at that with time.*

I looked around the room, which had a collection of Keith Haring memorabilia and a brass Durga statue by the television. On the coffee table there was a book called *The Psychedelic Gospels*. As I turned onto a page about hallucinogens in Christianity, John returned with our teas. I leaned back onto the sofa, which crinkled, again. John dabbed his forehead with a handkerchief then placed it back in his pocket. He looked towards me as if waiting for directions to somewhere so I began by admitting that I was lost. *I asked Mum and Dad if we could have a memorial bench for Tom. It was installed this week and I didn't go.*

Your dad mentioned it. I was grateful he resisted expressing any judgement or telling me I should've gone. *I just . . . I guess I knew it would be too difficult. There's this,* I blew on the tea, *well inside me. Maybe it's more like a pit. I'm so angry and I don't want anyone to be near it.*

If you can't allow yourself to feel the anger, will you feel entitled to the good feelings too? Emotions are a rite of passage. Part of life is experiencing them both. Only love and death can change all things. Do you know who said that? I

300

shook my head. *Kahlil Gibran*, John moved towards the bookcase, *you'll like him. I found this book down the back of a library sofa in York.* He pushed a slim poetry collection across the table, *it was delivered to me when I needed it and now it's yours.* I thanked him and played with the corner of the book.

We were quiet for a while and I tuned into the sound of a clock ticking. Also Keith Haring. *Are you not angry John?* He looked taken aback. I fiddled with my shirtsleeves, embarrassed to bring our conversation to a part of his life that I knew about second-hand from Dad. John was adopted as a baby by a single woman. When he was a young teenager she got ill and died. His aunt came to look after him. Dad described her as *crazy as a box of frogs,* and recalled visiting them outside term-time when she'd put salt in his tea instead of sugar. She'd died shortly after John finished university and other relatives inherited the house. *What do I have to be so angry about?* he asked and I replied, *well everyone left you.*

John took a cleansing breath, *that's one way to look at it. Another would be that I had my mother for a number of years then my aunt for a few after that. I had a lot of love, just crammed into a short space of time. The love is what matters.*

He placed his fingers in a steeple and leaned forward. *What if you imagined that Tom was only ever meant to be nineteen? Perhaps his life wasn't a story cut short, with many blank pages, but a book that was simply shorter. And meant to be that way. That was the story.* The image of Tom's life as a slim, but perfectly complete, volume just like the one John had given me was an image I found calming. I remembered Flip placing a book in my hands and saying, *no one can ever take that away from you.*

~

After Tom's funeral, and every anniversary since, John had emailed me thoughts of remembrance. I never replied, I just filed them into a mailbox folder called Admin along with reminders that my eye test was due and local mayoral elections were upcoming. John still emailed each year.

That afternoon in October, I journeyed home from his flat and tried to lean into nothing but thinking time. John had advised me that the bus was the best way to go, so I sat on the top deck and watched the traffic in Catford. In front of me a woman with Cookie Monster nail art watched *Holby City* on her phone with the subtitles on. A father and son were nearby. The little boy kept tapping his dad's Costa Coffee cup curiously so eventually he let him try it. The boy grimaced at the taste. I searched John's name in the Mail app and found the following:

Greetings,

Just wanted to let you know we are thinking of you today. Hope Tom's remembrance goes well and you all feel his gentle spirit. Talking of spirit, here are three wise observations from different traditions on the subject of death:

1) Never the spirit was born
The spirit shall cease to be never
Never was time it was not
End and beginnings are dreams
Birthless and deathless and changeless
Remains the spirit forever
Bhagavad Gita

2) There is no death, only a change of worlds.
Chief Seattle (Native Indian: 1786–1866)

3) In the Buddhist approach, life and death are seen as one whole, where death is the beginning of another chapter in life. Death is a mirror in which the entire meaning of life is reflected.
Sogyal Rinpoche (Buddhist master: born 1947)

Love,
John xxxxxx

John emailed on a Thursday in 2016, but it had been delivered to me at the moment I was ready to read it.

Sometimes when I couldn't sleep I imagined holding the book of Tom's life in my hands. It had a sky-blue cover and the paper was creamy. As I flicked through, the words blurred into black lines like footpaths. I dreamed of the sound of air as the pages brushed past each other.

Collecting shells

Chapter Forty-Six

Abereiddi Blue Lagoon: 51.93769° N, 5.20986° W

I kicked split conkers down the road while I waited for Miri to collect me from the corner of my street. In the distance, I could hear the metallic clang of scaffolding being unloaded. We were travelling to Bristol and Wales to visit Clevedon Marine Lake, Sugar Loaf Beach pool and Abereiddi's Blue Lagoon over a long weekend. Annie, who has family in Bristol, told me that when she'd walked her dogs she'd seen a sign saying they were cleaning the lake and we'd arrive when it was empty. I didn't feel winded by Annie and her dogs anymore. Her happiness was no longer a gut punch. On her advice, we flipped our itinerary and got the train to Bristol, where we picked up a hire car and drove to Abereiddi.

It felt odd to be travelling over the Prince of Wales Bridge without a plan to see my parents. Miri suggested I write a list of all the things I'd like to say to Mum, then cross out the ones that felt too difficult and see what I was left with. I thought about returning Mum's calls, but I didn't know what I had to offer. I didn't want to take, either. Every swimming trip I added to my hoard of sea glass, but these days it felt like the collection I contributed to most was unanswered voicemails. I wanted to ask Mum if she'd survived the anniversary like I had – barely, but proud to have made it through. There were few people who knew the particular pain of losing Tom. She was one of them. Thinking about that gave me the sensation of discovering a close acquaintance grew up in the same hometown as you. *Huh, what a coincidence,* then realising, despite the serendipity, nothing about your relationship had changed. I wondered how such dark shadows could be cast by an absence of words.

As if I'd conjured her spirit by thinking about her, Mum called. We passed a car with too many passengers for the backseat. I let it ring out. Another one for my collection.

After three hours of driving, we arrived at Abereiddi. We parked on the beach and followed a dusty stretch of Pembrokeshire coast path north until we arrived at the former St Brides Slate Company quarry, which was used until 1910. Dynamite had blasted a narrow channel in the quarry, allowing the sea to flood through and create a turquoise lozenge in the rocks. Now, the Blue Lagoon is a spot for swimming, shore-scrambling and rock-jumping. In summer, it's popular with groups of teenagers coasteering from the cliffs, but that day it was quiet. It was empty, except for us.

From the water, I looked at our cradle. The water wasn't clear, but chalky. Like God had swirled his brush in the pool after painting the sky blue. I opened my mouth to say that to Miri but couldn't form the words.

The rugged rocks were dotted with creases to place hands and feet into. Jumping was the kind of thing Tom would've done. He was always more comfortable in a wetsuit than anything else. When he was little he'd said, *when I grow up I want to be a penguin.* Mum interrogated him about this and he said it was because then he could go on all the water slides at London Zoo. If Tom had been with Miri and me that day, he'd have persuaded me to do it. Probably through tugging and teasing, then after he'd have denied holding my hand.

I stretched out my legs to see if my toes could touch the bottom, but my ears dipped beneath the surface. The depth meant the water was cold, and I knew I didn't have too long before I'd have to climb out and get warm. *Shall we jump?* I asked Miri, already swimming to a platformed wall at the lagoon edge. She agreed, clearly surprised by my suggestion, and followed me to a point where we could scramble out.

I stood up, defiant. Then when I looked out across the water, my stomach lurched. I was paralysed and couldn't peel my feet from the wall. From the water, it hadn't looked that high. We were only on the lowest ledge and, embarrassingly, that felt towering. I contemplated it, aware that every second we stood with the wind against our skin our body temperature was dropping. A sound escaped my lips, a small spasm of fear. *It's ok. We can climb back in*, Miri said.

Tom would do it, I said, *he loved this kind of thing*. When I spoke about Tom it was always in the past tense. I was so tired of him being trapped there. I wanted to do something active and present. A cloud cleared and scattered a beam of light onto the water. Miri gripped my hand and forced her fingers to entwine with mine. Before I had a chance to think, she leapt forward and pulled me with her.

A rush of air. A roar of joy. I emerged euphoric with my face cold and heart fastened. The tide turned, and waves began to lash against the quarry wall as if the leaping sea was applauding us for our bravery.

I'd asked Miri if in between our tidal pool visits we could stay in Tenby, a harbour town in southwest Wales, as it was somewhere we used to go on family holidays. The wardrobe in our hotel room was infested with ladybirds, but the receptionist wasn't much help other than saying she'd send a hoover, so we went out.

We had fish and chips at Fecci & Sons then walked on the beach while the dusk hung there; a crescent in a pink sky, the moon already watching us. The sand was still wet from high tide and felt cold when my feet sank in. Without words, Miri and I began beachcombing. Our bodies zigzagged along the shore searching for shells, sea glass and pebbles. A pinecone had washed up on the beach. It was the size of a Christmas-tree ornament, chocolate-brown and puckered. I felt a slow, sad yearning. The pinecone wasn't at all like the ones Jem and I had found in the woods, covered in lichen. If he'd been with me, he would've filled my pockets with sea treasure. I thought about him everywhere. I saw him in everything. I wanted him with me, always.

What I needed to do suddenly struck me with a thunder-like clarity. The woman's voice on the phone had gone around and around my mind. I'd been ruminating in self-blame, which was a place I'd lived for five years. I was done with feeling anything other than the particular type of home I felt when I was with Jem. The threat of him being with someone else had created a vortex of all of my fears: being abandoned and feeling that I'd opened all my wounds, only to be rejected and back where I'd started.

Hadn't the jump at Abereiddi proved that the things I feared were not there to ruin me? Maybe my fears would be right, but things could also turn out better than I hoped, if only I tried. I decided I would bring Jem a shell back from Tenby and start acting from a place of love and not fear.

Will you help me choose a shell for Jem? I asked Miri. She was crouched on the sand, her knees bent outwards in a diamond. *Of course,* she said and turned over a netted dog whelk with part of its outer broken off, exposing the whorl.

I wanted to express to her that moving closer to Jem would never mean moving further away from her. *There are parts of my relationship with Jem that only you know, Miri.* I wasn't just thinking about my secrecy, insecurities or even Flip, but all the small moments I'd shared with her. The conversations that helped me learn how to love like I needed, not how I wanted. She'd carried so much of the imagined world I'd created when I'd met Jem, and now a new future was possible. *Thank you for sharing that with me,* I said.

She held up a wave-smoothed dark pebble. *How about this?* I shook my head. I liked its simplicity but it wasn't joyous enough. *Too plain.* We turned over topshells, mussels and winkles until, together, we chose a cockle in an unusual shade of grey that reminded me of the stretches of rain between the green in his eyes.

311

Its ridges radiated outwards like his warmth and it was concaved like an open palm, offering. The underside of the shell glowed with a pearly hue. I placed it in my pocket and left the beach.

Chapter Forty-Seven

Clevedon Marine Lake: 51.43594° N, 2.86823° W

We were staying in a Portishead pub called The Poacher. It appeared rather suddenly on a main road, announced only by a sign swinging gently in the autumn breeze. It was painted with great zeal and I enjoyed the charming depiction of an aproned rabbit poaching eggs. The rooms were described as 'unfussy' and that suited us fine. All night I could hear the soft clack, roll and thud of snooker balls being potted in the pub downstairs. When I was young, my older brother Howard and his friends found a snooker table in a skip. He begged my parents to let him have it in his bedroom, but Mum said there wasn't enough room for a bed and a snooker table. Howard said *fine*, got rid of his bed, and put his mattress underneath the snooker table. He slept under it for three years.

While I lay awake listening to the sounds of the pub, I thought how much I missed living with Howard and Lawrence. Seven of us in the house. The ease of it.

Their constant presence. It felt hard now. I wished we talked more and blamed it on boys being bad with their phones, but knew it was also me who wasn't brave enough to call.

Miri and I woke up early for swims in Portishead and Clevedon. There are records of Sugar Loaf Beach Paddling Pool from Victorian times. Once, it was popular for bathing, but over time it fell into disuse and filled with large rocks. The pool is tall and sits raised off the beach like a large stone bathtub. There are even three stone steps that add a touch of elegance. I had hoped our visit would feel like visiting an outdoor spa, but the beach was thick with a salty brown mud. A Google review had warned us that this was often the case. It suggested: *getting on with it* or perhaps even, *turning it into a fun game of crocodiles with the kids*. Walking towards the pool made our shoes filthy. We peered into the pool, which was murky with a few visible large stones, then retreated and ate our sandwiches on a fallen tree, looking towards the Severn Bridge.

A dog-walker arrived and led his beagle up the pool steps where he released it from its lead. It paddled for a while then gave itself a shake and started lapping up the brown water. The dog suddenly took an interest in us and bound over to place its muddy chin on my knee. I gave it a quick pat on the head and glanced at the owner with a tight smile that I hoped conveyed:

please take your dog away. The beagle grinned and dribbled the scummy water that had been brewing inside its mouth all over my leggings, leaving behind a string of saliva so thick it wobbled in the breeze before breaking our connection. The man laughed in a way that suggested he assumed everyone shared his adoration for this dog. *Sorry,* he shouted, *Sabrina loves sandwiches!* I smiled, tighter this time, then put my lunch away, having lost my appetite. Later, I stumbled across bristolbarkers.com, which said that the *small pebble beach is great for dogs, especially when the pool has filled up and they can have a little swim!* I thought of all the dog's tails that had wagged in the pool and it validated my decision not to swim there that day.

Clevedon Marine Lake sits on the North Somerset coast. It's the world's largest seawater infinity pool and a little slice of heaven. The tidal pool fills with seawater from the Bristol Channel every spring tide. These tides occur twice each lunar month at full- and new-moon phases. At the top of high spring tides, the sea overtops the walls and refreshes the water. When the lake overtops it becomes part of the Severn Estuary and both the sea wall and lower promenade disappear under water. There's a strong tidal pull there; in fact, it's one of the largest tidal ranges in the world.

Marlens, the community group that care for the pool, ensure that twice a year it's emptied. We visited after the autumn draindown Annie had mentioned. Strong currents stop silt in the Bristol Channel settling, which is why the water looks brown, especially compared to the estuary we'd visited in Essex. This revelation made me feel bad for judging Portishead's murky waters so harshly. When the water rushes over the wall it brings silt that settles on the lakebed, so without these draindowns the lake would get shallower and shallower. There were still piles of debris on the pool's edge, waiting to be taken away. Seaweed was piled beside the steps; it crackled like bubble wrap as people walked over it.

A woman with her head slicked into a swimming cap placed her bag down beside us as we changed. Her oval face and the shine of her forehead below her cap reminded me of the eggcups Grandma used to serve boiled eggs and soldiers in. *Lovely to be back after a week off, isn't it,* she said while grappling her bosom into her swimsuit. *We're actually from London. Visiting on a special swimming trip.* Miri told her about our adventure. The woman sat on the bench and pulled her feet into swimming boots, which took great effort. *The weeks they drain the pool are always a blessing in disguise. A week without swimming reminds me how much I need this place. We all need this place.*

You're so right, Miri agreed and talked about how the lido had saved her life on more than one occasion. *Everyone has a story,* the woman nodded and looked at me, signalling that it was my turn to share. Miri waited. I waited. *I started swimming after my brother died.* Saying it, I realised the significance of when I had begun swimming. *Most days, I feel like I can't be alone with my thoughts. I'm scared to feel sad or think about him, so I stay busy and it's exhausting. When I'm swimming, I can't think of anything else. The cold takes over. My mind is clear. It's the only break I get.* The woman slapped her hand against my shoulder like a schoolmistress. *Everyone has a story,* she said again and walked towards the water, *everyone has a story.*

Hampstead Heath Ladies' Pond

Chapter Forty-Eight

Hampstead Heath Ladies' Pond: 51.56668° N, 0.16013° W

In childhood, I'd been a keen swimmer. Then I reached adolescence and stopped. Hair began to sprout from my underarms and in between my legs. I started my period. My hips widened and I didn't like the way my thighs looked. I viewed my body as pear-shaped and ordinary. Being asked to put on a bikini and splash around felt like an act of violence. As my body became more womanly, I felt forced to give up the childhood joys of swimming. It didn't feel mine to give so freely to the water. After some time I accepted my body – though I don't know where I'd learned to reject it in the first place – but the memory of swimming was so distant by then, it would never have occurred to me to pack a swimsuit and find the nearest body of water.

My first wild swim in adulthood was on New Year's Day at the Ladies' Pond with Rohanna. In 2019, 1 January fell on a cloudless day that blessed Hampstead Heath with an almost biblical showering of sunshine.

It was the universe's parting gift for a year of awful choices. Rohanna rushed towards me, already apologising for being late. She gave me a moment to take it all in. 'Women Only. Men Not Allowed Beyond This Point', the sign commanded. I'd wanted to start the year bold and brave. This seemed like the place to do it. Closing the gate behind us, we followed a long path until the tree canopy swept away to reveal the pond and changing hut. There was a hubbub of women, shuffling on the concrete pontoon. A few ducks watched from the bank.

As we approached the water, the lifeguard waved to Rohanna and asked me if I'd been before. I shook my head. *Alright, swim from here to there*, she pointed to two silver ladders on either end of the concrete, *so I can see you're safe to swim in winter*. Peering into the murky brown water, I realised I was shivering before I'd even got in. I glanced at the chalkboard leaning against the hut, which said the temperature was five degrees. *Want me to go first?* Rohanna offered and white plumes of air appeared before her lips. She didn't wait for me to answer, but squeezed my shoulder as she turned to face me and began lowering herself down the steps. She paused when it reached her stomach. With her lower body submerged, she turned from the steps to the expanse of water before her and exhaled slowly as she took her first stroke. To my right, a tall skyscraper of a woman stepped over the chain and dived in. The impatient ripple of water she left behind motivated me to start moving. I made it in and closed my eyes, wincing. I didn't let out a scream like I'd heard a few others. It felt like there were teeth marks on my lungs. I wanted to gasp, but Rohanna had instructed me to focus on exhaling. Quietly and calmly, I took deep breaths and moved from one ladder to the other, only focusing on the water in front of me. It kissed me with tiny pinpricks.

Then everything melted away.

The water was silky and thick, my arms visible, but tinged amber like a spyglass. Rohanna followed me out of the water while I hopped from foot to foot. I looked down at my hands, which were crab-shell red, and the hair on my arms stood upright like the white fuzz of a stinging nettle. She rubbed up and down my arms as if starting a fire with sparks between her fingertips. I moved mine apart to check they were still there. The cold was so anaesthetising. *It'll be easier next time*, she promised. I looked towards the pond where women still lowered themselves in or waited on the pontoon, ready to bring quick-dry towels to their friends. Everyone seemed to carry a light inside them, the hope that this year would be the best yet.

In the changing room, women of all shapes, sizes and ages jostled against each other as they rubbed their naked bodies with towels. Rohanna joined them and tugged her swimsuit down towards her ankles. I noticed streaks of mud on her tummy. Her tattoo is hard to miss. It's almost the width of a palm and shows two sisters wearing saris sat atop a waterlily, their hands upturned to the sky. She exchanged hellos and smiles with a few people. A woman wearing nothing but a fuzzy pink bobble hat waved enthusiastically towards her. *Sandra taught me how to knit,* Rohanna whispered then added proudly, *being a regular at the Ladies' Pond is like being in a little club.* We often joked that we were in a club of our own. One that, of course, no one wanted to join. I thought about how odd it was that grief had delivered me something as beautiful as this friendship, and now swimming.

Once we were dressed, we shuffled to a fold-out table laden with food: sausage rolls, shortbread, fruit cake and mince pies. Rohanna unwrapped a loaf from a faded canvas tote and placed it down; her boyfriend is a baker and she always arrives with treats. From somewhere within the crowd, I was handed a paper cup half-filled with mulled wine. Bringing the steaming cup to my lips with a shaking hand, I could see why they didn't fill it further. I felt my body thaw from the inside.

Most people take up swimming in summer, then continue into autumn and through winter, building a tolerance as the temperature drops. I was so hooked after my first swim that I carried on from the first of January. Rohanna helped me keep swimming through those winter months. She'd drop me a text when she was on her way to the ponds and we'd have a quick dip then sit on benches dedicated to women we didn't know, but felt like we did, and eat a packed breakfast. Rohanna brought bulbous grapes from Ally Pally farmers' market, hard stubs of cheddar and her boyfriend's sunflower rye, while I came with a flask of coffee. If it was just the two of us we'd see who could spit their grape seeds furthest over the fence. We swam like it was August. I suppose that's because, when a dark thing happens to you, you choose to live in the light, so we went back to Hampstead Heath where we felt that we were alive, and like it was summer.

Clevedon was gorgeous. A pebble beach and strip of seafront shops selling food from Somerset and Weston-Super-Mare. Swimming always gave me a sweet tooth so we walked through town to Mr T. G. Pullin's Bakery for coffee and lemon macaroons. Despite the autumn breeze, there were more tables outside than in as groups of people in cycling jerseys or dry-robes sat to have lunch. Clevedon has the only Grade 1 listed pier in the country. It was constructed with sections from one of

Brunel's railways. That day, the sky was still, and the pier's cast iron looked naked against it. I squinted beneath my sunglasses. A man watched the waves over the edge, near motionless. The boards creaked beneath our feet like an old wooden desk. We travelled home, and I fingered the shell in my pocket, thinking about what I'd say to Jem when I gave it to him.

Chapter Forty-Nine

Hackney Marshes: 51.55985° N, 0.02626° W

The following night, Jem pulled me through the long grass of Hackney Marshes. With each step his pace quickened and I struggled to keep up. We were chasing the sunset. He pulled a blanket from his bag and laid it down on a slab of concrete in the bushes that bordered the train tracks. *Your seat for this evening,* he said and wiped his hands on his trousers before sitting down, *this is my special place.* The red-rusted sky was like the afterglow of a bonfire. It was one of those just-right gestures from nature that reminded me how glorious winter could be. The days were shorter and I looked forward to having more evening. Cloaked nights for love-making, talking, eating and reading.

The sky tipped from red to orange to rose until only a pool of gold was lagooned behind the telephone pole wires. We were quiet for a while, and I wondered how long it takes the sun to set. It gave me my answer and slipped suddenly below the block of flats beyond the canal. This could've been my moment to ask about the woman's voice on the phone, but I wasn't sure anymore what it had to do with moving forward. I had my secrets, maybe he had his. I hoped we could move into a new dawn of truth. Perhaps to do that, some things should be left unsaid.

I cleared my throat, and a bird flew from the trees above us. I was surprised to see a late migrator. Shouldn't it be leaving? Maybe it was a pigeon. Did they ever leave the city? Leaving made me think of staying. I wanted to stay with Jem.

I pulled the shell from my pocket and put it on his knee. *I think about you*, I swallowed, *wherever I go*. He placed the shell on his palm, then turned it over to admire the other side. *I love you*, he said, *I love you . . .*

Chapter Fifty

Powfoot: 54.97513° N, 3.33382° W

Miri had kept me swimming throughout October and November. In Herne Hill, parents arranged rain covers over their pushchairs and fallen leaves had been swept into piles around the lido. We started swimming in our woolly hats as the weather cooled and the days shortened. Peeling bark fell from the silver birches like half-stripped wallpaper and the sycamore's winged seeds helicoptered to the ground. There was a smell in the air that I forget about, then remember each October. It's damp, mushroomy and rotten. The decaying nectar of autumn.

I missed the smell of my father's bonfire on Sunday afternoons; watching him stand in the glow of burning branches when the early evening light was already snuffed out. When he first met Jem they'd talked about gardening and Dad joked that *the garden is the only place you can escape for some peace and quiet when you have five kids*. We laughed, but I knew his hours outdoors held a deeper value. A long time ago he'd said to me *gardening is exceptional for feeling well. Planting something gives you a reason to stick around.* I think that was the closest I ever got to understanding him, and I try to recreate that connection when I look at the oakleaf hydrangeas in his garden.

My swimming routine with Miri had kept me going through the dark days of Tom's anniversary. Now winter was settling in and soon it would be my birthday. Things were looking up. Someone once told me that grief is not linear. It doesn't just get better and easier; it snakes back and forth throughout your life. *One day*, she'd said, *you might get married or have a baby and those days will be very difficult. You'll have new relationships with your grief at those times and it might hurt or heal in new, unexpected ways. You'll carry it with you all your life.*

That someone was Fiona. She worked at the Rainbow Trust Children's Charity and used to visit me when I was at university, miles from my family. The acknowledgment that I also needed help meant a lot to me then. The first few times we met, I didn't say much. Durham was a small university town and I worried about crying when I recognised the girl waiting tables from my 'Monuments and Memory in the Age of Augustus' module. We had a coffee and sat in silence. Then Fiona said, *lovely to chat. I'll see you in two weeks.* She was the only person who witnessed my silence without assuming I didn't need to talk. The next time, Fiona picked me up and took me to a carvery and soft play out of town. It was good to have someone to answer my questions. I asked her how people died of cancer. She said sometimes it wasn't the cancer, but a cold or pneumonia and their body might not be strong enough to fight it. I don't know what Tom died of in the end. He just stopped one day.

I knew about the charity because I had done work experience folding newsletters when I was at school. It'd never occurred to me that I would be someone who needed their help. I suppose that's what we all think. People say, *I just can't believe it.* Yet newspapers remind us every day. In truth, dying is the most believable thing that can happen.

I didn't understand Fiona's words at the time, then my life kept going and they made sense. A new flat was a home Tom would never see. A new boyfriend was a man he'd never meet. A birthday was a year he wouldn't touch. They became less of a linear progression in age, but represented moving further away from Tom; an estrangement that spanned the years between knowing him and not. I counted my birthdays not in years I'd lived, but years I'd lived without him. I moonwalked in that space.

Miri and I were supposed to visit Powfoot tidal pool in Dumfries that winter, but an uneasy feeling about the lack of information we'd been able to find online caused me to do some last-minute investigating. It's a unique, circular tidal pool made from Victorian timber. I emailed a hotel close to the beach and asked if their staff ever walked that way. They replied:

> Thank you for your email regarding the pool at Powfoot. The pool was built in the 1880s by a local landowner's family; they still have land and properties today such as Hoddam and Kinmount Estates. The family are called the Birbecks. Unfortunately, the pool is a ruin now, full of sand and silt – no swimming I am afraid. Should you still wish to visit the area please get in touch and we can check dates for you. Kind regards.

The word 'ruin' made me sad. Passing the burnt-out carcass of an abandoned building always gave me an empty feeling inside; this somehow seemed worse. The tidal pool had been designed to be for everyone, now it was for no one. Locals I'd been in touch with online said that the beach was still worth visiting as the surrounding water was golden on sun-dappled days and nearby Loch Arthur was as close to paradise as you could get in Scotland. Others said the muddy beach was *a good place to test wellington boots*. I studied the images on a geo-caching site and scrolled through grainy jpegs trying to decide if we should go. Eventually, Miri and I concluded that we weren't up for the eight to nine hours travelling for an unswimmable tidal pool. We crossed it off our list and something close to failure stirred inside me. Why was I giving up so easily? Then again, this was our adventure. Surely we didn't have to do the swims we didn't want to?

I looked at the list pinned to my kitchen corkboard and the shaky pencil line through Dumfries tidal pool. I wondered if some of my hesitation was because I didn't feel lost in London anymore. Before, leaving had been going to a place I hoped I'd hate less. That was when the present felt uninhabitable. Jem had made London feel like home again, or perhaps it was me who had arrived.

Chapter Fifty-One

St Mildred's Bay: 51.38577° N, 1.33816° E

My parents have always been very good birthday-card writers. Mum will fill the left side, Dad the right. It's clearly something that he taught her, as Grandma June will only ever underline the sentiment printed inside and sign, 'Grandma'. Some years there has also been an 'x'. In my family we don't talk much about how we feel, but on birthdays we fill an A5 card with our reflections on another year together. Miri has commented that it's this dependency on words of affirmation that's made me a writer, and she's probably right. I spend eleven months of every year unsure how most people feel about me and then become obsessed with how they'll show their gratitude for our relationship on my birthday. I am very into birthday cards. I am very into birthdays, in general.

That's why for my twenty-seventh, I organised a weekend on the Kent coast, right on the beach beside a tidal pool, with eight of my friends. Becky is my oldest friend from school. She smells of argan oil and we call her Becky with the Good Hair. She has a young son and boundless patience. The thing she says to me most is, *you need to chill out babe.* Lauren and Orla are friends from university and are both accomplished and intellectual in a way that means they have something to offer our alumni organisation. I avoid admitting that I'm not really sure what either of them do other than that it's something impressive. Then there are the three girls from work: Ellen, Nikia and Saz. We met at our office book club and make an effort when we're in larger groups to talk about things other than our colleagues. Miri was there, of course, and Emma.

Before the others arrived, Miri and I visited St Mildred's Bay tidal pool. It's a small, square pool of beer-bottle green. The tide was pulling away and more of the mossed walls appeared by the minute. I swam to the edge where Miri was already wrapped in her towel, searching for something in her bag. Resting my head on my folded arm, I mindlessly ran my wet fingers over my jawline. The previous week I'd found my first chin hair. I was crawling past the time where 'young' prefaced 'woman'. Shopkeepers never asked for my ID anymore and my friends had started talking about loft conversions and buying wine subscriptions. I'd spent so much of my life wishing I was grown up and now I was here I wanted things to slow down.

Miri pulled out a mini prosecco and I cheered. *How are you feeling about it all?* She passed me the bottle. *Good, excited to see the girls.* I tipped my head back and the bubbles fizzed up my nose. *You're doing distant eyes,* she said. I was thinking that today was the youngest I'd ever be. *I feel old for the first time.* Miri took the bottle back and didn't attempt to hide her 'here we go' look.

I want to feel it's a privilege to get older. I know that! But there's also this deep and animalistic instinct inside me saying I'm scared. And that voice is louder than the perspective Tom's death gave me. I took another sip, *do you know what I mean?*

Miri gave an exaggerated sigh. *I think it's very easy to call feelings you don't want to take the blame for instincts.* I grumbled, *I hate the word blame. Don't blame me. It's my birthday!*

Hey, I'm not blaming you, Miri laughed. *Fine then, tell me what I have to look forward to. Get me excited for being older.* She dangled a towel towards me to usher me out. *Knowing yourself. And not letting people persuade you so easily.* I took it and began drying myself. *And coming more. You come more in your thirties because you're not embarrassed to expect an orgasm, so if you can get an extra three years of that then you've won at life.* I liked the sound of that. Maybe twenty-seven would be a good year.

I asked Jem the same question. He said the best thing about being in your thirties is liking yourself. Miri took a swig. *Well, of course he'd say that. He has lots to like. Most of all, being with you.*

Emma put down a bottle of vodka, dropped her weekend bag and hugged me when she arrived at the Airbnb. When I was released from the embrace, she handed me a gift from Mum. It was the waterproof dry bag that Tom had used for sailing. *Mum said she heard you needed a new one of these.* I looked at Miri, but she avoided my eyes. I didn't mind if she'd told Mum that I'd been sick in mine (despite multiple washes, the smell was not reversible), I was just intrigued that they'd been talking at all. I wondered what they spoke about and felt quietly touched that anyone had noticed I might need checking on.

That weekend we ate lobster rolls with lettuce and lemon slices on the beach. Hands freezing. Hats on. We walked along the shore collecting seashells and stored them in our pockets. Becky collected enough that she filled her lambswool beanie with them. I don't excel at spontaneity and as it was my birthday I thought it only fair that I allowed myself to indulge in my greatest guilty pleasure: organised fun. I delighted in assigning everyone a meal to cook and asked them to send me a shopping list ahead of the trip. The itinerary showed the groceries would arrive between four and five o'clock and they arrived at quarter past. The fridge was stocked with fresh fruit, lush green vegetables, fish and wine. Miri was chef on the first night and made a spinach and cheese tart with borlotti bean salad. I'd bought the wrong pastry (filo instead of puff), but she didn't complain and improvised, as if to remind me that she was better at 'going with the flow'.

Becky and Emma made a batch of margaritas and white wine sangria strong enough to knock out a sailor. Most of my friends had met the others at gatherings before. They all did a polite job of pretending they didn't know each other's dramas from me, until we had a drink and everything descended into chaotic gossiping. There was a conversation about whether women could fulfil their potential at work without the advocacy of male leaders and I heard Saz say her wish on her last birthday was to reduce her 'ha's' on WhatsApp and exclamation marks in emails and she was failing miserably at both. Lauren added that she spent her whole life saying, *no worries*, but really meant, *absolutely worries*. We talked about money and whether it was worth it to get laser hair removal (yes), arsehole bleaching (no) and baby botox (maybe). I licked the salt rim of my glass and told Emma it was the year I'd freeze my eggs. She said that's something I only said because I live in London. *Get a cat*, she said, *marry Jem and get a cat. It'll calm you down.* Ellen leaned across Miri to take a bite of cucumber like it was a salami then added, *that's not how you play the game.* Miri took the cucumber back and started chopping it into the salad. *What game?* Emma asked, but Ellen ignored her, *it's your own fault Freya. You said I love you first. Never say I love you first. They don't respect you after that. Not that I respect them, but you know,* she shrugged, *honestly I love Russ, but God knows I don't respect him. They just don't have the bandwidth we do.*

I respect Dan, Emma said, but she might as well have said it to no one. *I like the sound of this Flip guy*, Ellen continued, *he pushes you, he motivates you, that's what you need right now. Twenty-seven is gonna be your year Freya. You need a cheerleader in your corner.*

Who's Flip? Emma asked and, again, no one replied. *You never know. He might say it first*, Ellen pointed a manicured nail towards me. *Never say I love you first*, Nikia repeated with a slow shake of her head. Emma rolled her eyes. If she'd been less drunk, she might've disguised her judgement more from the others, but Emma likes a drink how I like a drink and how Mum likes a drink. *Don't look at me like that*, Ellen raised her hands as if accused, *I know what you're thinking, but it's just the truth. Honestly, I have so many real-ass thoughts I don't say publicly. Like, I should get a fund to continue this work of silencing myself because it is needed,* she sipped, *is there more of this margarita shit because it's the bomb?* Emma was the youngest at my birthday and was fooled by no one.

St Mildred's Bay

Chapter Fifty-Two

St Mildred's Bay: 51.38577° N, 1.33816° E

It's always been a birthday tradition between me and my friends to go around the table and say what we're grateful for – like Americans at Thanksgiving. The best thing for communal self-worth is to celebrate confidence and encourage it in one another. Performing my self-consciousness would only be a burden to all of us who were struggling. The fresh sea air and sisterhood had clearly filled us all with gratitude that night as with each toast our celebratory cheers became louder and louder until we reached a crescendo. *And the birthday girl?*

Well, I started and Orla tapped her fork against a glass to quiet the group, *cheers to having a job I love, with women who inspire me*, I raised my glass towards the work girls. Ellen placed her hand on her chest while Nikia and Saz put their arms around one another. *In fact, I'm grateful for all of my women here, who are so fucking wonderful and I don't know what I'd do without you.*

Lauren faux-dabbed her eye with her napkin. *A toast for the boys. Boys, boys, boys. I do know what I'd do without them. Probably more work.* The table laughed. *In all seriousness, I'm grateful to have always dated men who can cook because who knows what I'd eat otherwise.* Ellen jeered and Orla nodded in polite agreement; she'd bought me a Nigella cookbook for my birthday. Ellen heckled, again, this time to ask if I was going to have one stay-at-home husband or two. Emma shifted in her seat and leaned in to ask Miri something, but she just tapped Emma's knee and shook her head. *And finally . . . I'm grateful for my peachy butt because I think it looks great in Levi's and it's honestly the greatest gift I've been blessed with.* Becky whistled with her fingers, which was something I'd always been jealous she could do at school. I stood up to present my behind to her and she gave it a spank.

As I sank back into my chair, I felt my body deflating. I'd wanted to make everyone laugh so I didn't have to feel vulnerable. I'd collected the people who knew me best then tried to trick them out of seeing me. My smile was taut like I'd stayed in the sun too long. I sipped my drink to give my mouth something to do and caught Emma's eye, watching me. She smiled and I felt even worse. I wished I could've done my list again. Just to say I was grateful for my sister.

We got drunk and danced on the sofa, theatrically shushing one another with our fingers pressed against our lips in case we woke the neighbours. It started with Kate Bush, then Madonna and in between there was a disagreement about playing ABBA. Saz made the mistake of asking Becky to teach us how to twerk so she made us do a seven-minute Booty & Ab workout on the floor while telling us the body holds trauma in the hips, which is why daily stretches are essential. Ellen put a straw in the jug of margarita mix and said we were crazy.

Collapsing into the sofa, I rested my head on Emma's shoulder. *You're sweaty*, she nudged me. The evening had mellowed into chatting and we were all cosied up on the armchairs and beanbags. *Want to look at some videos?* I nodded, then rearranged myself to look at Emma's phone. Her screen lit up her face with a cool blue light. A video of Tom with our cat, Bluebell, was playing. He was laughing while he held her. I inched away from Emma. Suddenly the margaritas I'd drunk churned in my stomach. She remained glued to the video, and I felt an urge to pull away.

Anyone want another drink? I headed to the kitchen where four masticated limes were strewn across the counter beside a nearly empty bottle of tequila with its lid missing. Emma appeared. *You can just say if you don't want to look at any videos of Tom*, she leaned against the open doorway. *I don't want to say. I want to look at them.*

I just . . . my voice trailed off while I searched for the lid. *Do you want a drink? I think there's some wine left.* She shook her head while I placed a mug on the table. We'd used all the glasses.

You know I worry about you, Emma said. I was staring into the fridge and couldn't remember what I'd opened it for. It was cool on my face. *All the jokes your friends are making about this guy. What's going on? I thought you were happy with Jem?* I didn't reply.

Sometimes you say things or do things that I think only a sad person would do. And I don't want you to be sad, I closed the fridge, *I just want you to be happy.* I was mildly insulted by this. Happy? How could anyone want or expect me to be happy? I looked at Emma. She always found a way. Maybe it was unfair to assume she was. I certainly hadn't asked. She always tried, though, and put the time into trying. I wasted so much of mine wanting to be seen as smart and attractive. Both were largely genetic. No one could take credit for a good starting position in life. Choosing to be kind and cheerful was something I'd really have to work at. Cheerfulness demanded continuous effort. Emma made that choice every day, then again the next day and kept going in pursuit of a joyous life. If not for myself, I could try for her.

I know, I said and we stood like that for a while with the empty mug between us. *And you know being happy isn't the same as not being sad, it's just that*— Before she could finish, Becky hurled herself into the kitchen. *Hello bitches, who's coming for another dance?* As quickly as she'd tornadoed in, she left again with the bottle of tequila.

Shall we go for a swim? Emma rounded people up for a skinny dip. We pulled on our wellies and coats, naked underneath, then headed towards the boardwalk, where the tide was already halfway up the steps. The waves were violent and came towards us in lashings. Orla and Miri had come too, but quickly decided the sea was too rough and headed back to the house so that it was just me and Emma. With each wave our bodies were showered with salty needles. They broke over my head, shoulders and breasts, tranquillising me. My body carried so much guilt about not being able to witness Tom's pain when he was dying. Then Emma had had the courage and vulnerability to show me her pain, and I couldn't witness that either. I wanted to be punished for failing to care for Emma, breaking my promise to Tom and being unfaithful to Jem and Flip. I wanted to be punished for being a bad sister, bad daughter, bad woman.

On the third swell, the force knocked us over, until we were on our backs against the boardwalk. I felt a sharp pain and moved my hand to where it hurt; my fingers came back red. I'd fallen onto a barnacled step that had broken my flesh. Emma reached out her hand, *take it easy*, she pulled me past the waves, where we floated for a while.

The current rocked and tipped our bodies, occasionally breaking in our face like a foaming champagne bottle. Emma started laughing and the velvet of her voice made me giggle. Before I knew it, we were howling at the moon like lunar-lust wild dogs. She was so caught up in it she nearly choked on a gulp of seawater and spluttered it out, which took us to new levels of hysteria. I looked at my sister and thought what a rare, gorgeous thing her joy was.

Chapter Fifty-Three

St Mildred's Bay: 51.38577° N, 1.33816° E

On the morning of our departure I cleared out the fridge while Miri sprayed the surfaces. We were both hungover, but equally committed to a five-star guest rating. I put our seashells into an empty salad bag and tied it with a hairband to take home. *Swim on your birthday next week?* she asked, scrubbing at something on the hob. *Yes please.*

And who will you be seeing in the evening? I flinched from the arrow of her judgement. *Er Jem. I think we're going for dinner,* I said. *Two boys for the birthday girl,* she replied, *very lucky.* I stopped what I was doing. Miri had recently ended things with someone and I'd overheard her tell Orla the most action she'd gotten that autumn was when someone accidentally sat on her on the tube. I used that knowledge to imagine a tone in her voice that wasn't there. My guilt was hearing things again.

What's that supposed to mean? I said. Miri also stopped cleaning. Lauren walked into the kitchen, sensed a shift in atmosphere and picked up a glass like that was what she'd come in for. *It wasn't supposed to mean anything. I was just teasing. Last night you were joking about it like it was funny,* I silently objected to the use of like, *and now it's not?* I could've told Miri I'd decided it was over with Flip, but I didn't because it was less of an ending and more that I just wouldn't be continuing. I decided the kitchen was clean enough and put the Mr Muscle away.

You know there's never any judgement in what I say, Miri paused like she wanted to redact her statement, *and even if there was, I love you. I love you regardless of any of that.* I looked at her and hated her for a moment. Not because I thought she was lying, but because she loved me and she was wrong to.

Flowers from Flip arrived for my birthday. I felt unmoved, and then moved that I felt that way after sharing so much time with him. I thought about his film idea and our writing retreat. The woman who made those plans felt like an acquaintance to me. The card read:

Poet. All the best on your birthday,
Flip x

I messaged him to say thank you for the flowers. Flip asked when I would be free to celebrate properly and I said I wouldn't. He called me and I didn't pick up so he replied to say he understood. Then we embarked upon an extended period of not speaking.

Screen Time told me my social media usage went up twenty-four per cent once I'd ended things with Flip. I wondered which had been a healthier distraction. My favourite Sunday activity became sitting down with a cup of tea and a book, then scrolling on my phone for an hour. I decided I should try to put the time into something good and deleted Instagram, but I kept opening my phone and moving my thumb to where the app used to be. Phantom limb syndrome. I subscribed to the Poetry Foundation newsletter and tried to read a poem a day when I got a craving. I told Miri about all this, then heard my own voice and thought I was so boring I could die. However pretentious it was, poetry did wonders for my creativity and I entered a new honeymoon period with my writing.

In my Cambridge cohort, I was the second to get a literary agent and was exceptionally embarrassed by the whole thing. It all happened quite accidentally. I'd released a swimming podcast and a literary agent got in touch. She looked at the manuscript of my failed novel and told me I wrote well. We chatted about my adventure swimming in tidal pools and she said I should send her a pitch for a book about it. Then I had a publisher.

An old university friend said, *you must be so happy. You've got everything you ever wanted.* I said thank you then thought, *what a hateful bitch you are,* and vowed never to speak to her again. All of my dreams coming true felt like a threat. A threat that I might have to accept that if I got everything I wanted and was still unhappy, it was me that was the problem.

The book was a trapdoor into a part of me that was dark, shadowy and I didn't like to visit often. My desk was a graveyard of failed stories and poems about grief. I experienced the book deal as a promise to myself. A promise that propelled me forward with great urgency and intention. I never doubted my ability to complete a book. Although I was self-conscious about my skills, I had confidence in my ability to finish. I am, above all else, a ruthless finisher, which is terrible when it comes to drinking, desserts and disastrous relationships. Writing about Tom, on the other hand, was something I'd never been able to do. Suddenly, I had this promise. And the thing had to be done.

Chapter Fifty-Four

Lordship Lane: 51.45631° N, 0.07599° W

It's odd that happiness seems so hard to find, then happens all at once. The confidence of getting an agent laid roots in my life that spread far and fast, burrowing into a commitment to the page and people around me. There was an irony that the confidence Flip had instilled in me was energy I converted into my relationship with Jem. It was recycled love. Was everything not recycled love for Tom? At the start of my journey to swim in every tidal pool, I'd thought that Tom's death had left a hole in my heart and I had to look for something to fill that empty space. I was beginning to realise that the love I had for him was still there. It was love I could give to others too.

I tried to put the work into being in love and to feeling that I deserved how good it all was. I gave myself homework. Exercises, if you will. And it helped. It truly did. My brain needed training to believe it all. What helped most was writing down the kind things

Jem did for me and reading them when an unhelpful thought tore through my mind. It started with actions but, as time moved on, I just wrote down words that reminded me of times I'd felt particularly in love. Because love happens like that. Not a slow, gradual process but in moments struck like matches. The click of his jaw as he yawns. The quiet of mornings in bed. The tenderness of his touch. The sea-gifts collected together. The shell he kept.

One weekend we went to the East Dulwich Picturehouse to see a film with his friends and walked around town in a four. I was part of one of those couples now. We were progressive and called each other 'partner'; he borrowed my clothes more than I borrowed his; he persuaded me to go pescatarian. We watched indie films with couple friends and discussed them afterwards while we drank Gipsy Hill craft beer and ate Perello olives. When it was just us again, we walked Lordship Lane and picked up fruit from Bora & Sons. Jem asked what was in season and bought pears, sage, chicory and nuts. With our bag full of fresh vegetables, we bundled ourselves into Mons Cheesemongers and tried not to look too surprised that the parmesan was eleven quid for a slab and settled on an oozing white medallion of goat's cheese instead. I offered to help, but Jem was a better cook, so I set the table, lit candles and worked on my book while I waited for him to reappear. An hour went by. There was clattering and an occasional yelp from a cut finger or a burned wrist, then he appeared grinning with a delicious chicory, goat's cheese and walnut salad and every pan thrown in the sink. I added to the list:

Chicory

As the weeks went by, I mostly forgot about the list. The beautiful thing about its creation was that, more and more, I found I didn't need it. Eventually, it was archived to the bottom of my Notes beneath shopping lists and jottings-down of curious things I'd overheard people say on the tube. Last week, for example, a woman with large hoop earrings had said to her friend: *how could you let me fall in love with a Gemini again?*

Jem liked to cook with my iPad and streak his marinade-covered fingers over the screen while he read recipes from BBC Good Food. As I poured us a glass of wine, I saw him copy and paste an ingredient list into Notes. Beneath it was 'Nice Things from Jem'. My heart sank; he must've seen it. I saw his eyes hover for a second, then he clicked back onto the recipe and squeezed a lemon into a bowl. He never mentioned it. Jem didn't need a list, but I don't think he ever minded that I did.

Winter

Chapter Fifty-Five

Am-Nawr: 51.85996° N, 3.13642° W

Things felt like they wrapped themselves up for me ahead of Christmas. On my last day in the office Annie and I used our lunch break to buy fancy wrapping paper from Liberty of London. Before returning to our desks to put our Out of Offices on, we sat in the kitchen with two black coffees. She asked me if I was excited for the holidays. She was excited. Most specifically to dress up her dogs in the Christmas-pudding outfits she'd bought them. I tried to explain why Christmas in my house feels sad and kept accidentally kicking the bag of paper, tags and ribbons beneath the table; it jingled awkwardly.

Of course. It must take a long time, she started and I clenched my teeth, mentally preparing for her to say 'to move on' before she continued, *for everyone to adjust to the change in you*. My eyebrows raised in surprise. Annie assumed it was everyone else's responsibility to accept me as I am now. The burden was not on me. I felt guilty that I'd never acknowledged how much she'd done to adjust to me since grief, and how little I'd been willing to do the same for her. I smiled. Our hands around our coffee cups felt very close. I thought about reaching out to hold her hand. Then she got out her phone and showed me a picture of the dogs under one blanket. *Have I shown you this one before?*

December used to be the noise of five children, moulting tinsel, the smell of pine needles and Dad placing presents on the branches of the tree for after dinner. Now it was not talking while watching *Gavin & Stacey* reruns, drinking too much and boil-in-a-bag salmon because no one could stomach any attempts to recreate our old traditions with Tom missing. There was a weary desperation for joy in our house.

Sitting on the sofa, the four of us opened our presents. I watched Dad's foot tapping among the discarded tags to Wizzard's 'I Wish It Could Be Christmas Everyday'. Mum hates this song. I observed a tightness in her jaw, but I knew she wouldn't complain as Dad's tapping was the brightest he'd been that day. Mum once told me she'd paid extra to get the sofa made shallower because Dad is so short. I thought about the lengths she goes to to make our lives comfortable.

Mum's gift for Dad was a training course from the Dry Stone Walling Association. My gifts were awful compared to Emma's thoughtful and beautifully wrapped presents, so I panicked and spent five minutes making a DIY voucher on Microsoft Word for us to all spend a weekend in Cambridge together.

Mum worked hard to invite Tom into the days. She said things like *I wonder what Tom would've got you* or *oh wouldn't he find that funny* at every passable joke on *Big Fat Quiz of the Year*. Then we all ignored her because it was too painful to acknowledge so she'd drink a bottle of Sauvignon Blanc and cry while saying none of us cared and she felt so lonely in our family. I felt guilty about my refusal to participate in her fantasies, but not enough that I joined in. I'd already paid a major emotional dowry by being there for Christmas.

It was important to Mum that we keep Tom alive by imagining his future. To me, that was excruciating. The injustice of it was intolerable. To imagine a job he'd have with a company email address. To imagine a wife and small children that he'd pack into a Volkswagen Golf on weekends. If I thought about the 'Merry Christmas from your Uncle' cards my sister's children would never receive, I couldn't cope. If I imagined that future, and knew I couldn't have it, why would I want any future at all? To imagine it was to create new mini losses that I'd have to grieve. Imaginary people and moments and places. All gone. Things that were destined for Tom that cancer had stolen from him. Life's cruel little thieves. Instead, I imagined the book of Tom's life. Perfectly complete.

When I'd been Christmas shopping I'd bought an extra card, *Merry Christmas to my Brother*, and decided I would write to him. Christmas came and went and I hadn't removed the cellophane wrapper from the card.

I'd intended to stay in Wales between Christmas and New Year, but couldn't quite face it and escaped by visiting Jem at his parents' house. I waited for Dad to return from playing golf so he could drive me to the station.

Mum asked me to stay longer and I was angry she'd made things difficult when they were already hard. *At least one last cup of tea*, she opened the fridge to get the milk and the light illuminated her face. She is gorgeous. In noticing, I realised how often I forget this. I also realised how beautiful I am, in her making. Her hair, her eyes, the ease of her smile and how quickly it thunders. I wondered what it's like for her to look at me, and see herself, but with a life ahead of me full of second chances she didn't get. I stared a moment too long and she noticed. In that second, I felt incredibly distant from her and wondered how mothers and daughters get this far apart. I felt that I'd taken something from her by being this far away when once I was entirely hers and called for only her. Now I call for other things.

I wanted to say *you're beautiful* and offer her the love that I hope a daughter will give me one day. I thought about how much I want a daughter and how much Mum wanted me. Did she ever think it would be like this? The closest stranger she'd ever know. I could tell her all my hopes and dreams, but I worried she'd consider it an insult to have dreams after Tom's death. When will my dreams run out? Will it happen when I have a daughter and have to hand my dreams over to her? Maybe I could ask Mum this.

I thought of Christmas, then the next Christmas and our birthdays in between. How many days do we spend together a year? There were probably only weeks left in my life with my parents. That scared me. I thought of asking her to go on holiday with me, and knew I wouldn't. I could offer her a chance to get to know me better. I could ask questions and get to know her, but I feared we might be more similar than I already knew and I didn't want to look too closely at how things might turn out for me. I wanted to offer that she's doing her best, and so am I. That was something to celebrate. Maybe we should drink gin instead of tea. Ah, there it was. My mother talking inside me again.

She poured the milk and I didn't say anything. I felt all her pain against all of mine. I understood that it's very hard. I understood that I inherited some of this, and some of it we lived together. Some of it will be inherited by my children one day, and I'll be as much of a mystery to that daughter as my mother is to me, and I am to her.

I said I had to leave again and this time she said ok. *You know*, she tapped her nails on the counter, *you're only ever as happy as your unhappiest child. And you're always so unhappy.* I readjusted my bag on my shoulder. *That's a good way to blame me*, I said and just as quickly she replied, *that's a good way to misunderstand me.* Her phone lit up with a Facebook notification. She stared at it for a moment, then put it back down and looked towards me as if she'd forgotten what we were talking about. *It's not blame. It's responsibility. I'll always be responsible for you. That's what being a mother is.*

Dad turned off the radio as he drove me to the station, *that's enough Christmas songs for one year.* I felt him giving up on the holidays and thought I wasn't far behind him. I boarded the train and carried the card for Tom with me like it was a talisman. I hoped eventually I would have the strength to wish Tom a Merry Christmas.

Jem's mum had a soft openness about her. She brought out photo albums and showed me baby pictures of Jem, or Jeremy, as she called him occasionally. I was most drawn to the photographs of them as an attractive young couple with two boys and their whole life ahead of them. I loved the shoulder pads and chintzy rose-printed sofas. There was a photo of Jem's brother tenderly holding him as a baby. I had a similar one of me and Tom. I thought it was a very precious thing.

We talked about how funny it is that children show us so quickly who they are, as if we could doubt how fast they become full people. I asked her what she knew about him when he was little. *Quite an angry little boy*, she said, *he used to have these rages*. I winked at Jem. He seemed quite far from being an angry little boy now. I wondered where his rage had gone, or where it was hiding. She continued, *I remember once we were having lunch outside and locked him in the house because he'd been naughty. He stuck his head through the cat flap and screamed so loud.* She laughed, which made me laugh. She has a gorgeous, wicked laugh that I thought I'd like to hear more. Jem nodded, *that's true.*

I thought about my mum calling me frigid and Jem's mum calling him angry. Did our mothers know us better than anyone else? Our truest selves. The stories that they'd told us about ourselves for as long as we'd been old enough to listen. I used to think that I was a story and that to love and understand me, someone would have to read every page of my past, learn my plot-points and study the footnotes. Now, I wasn't so concerned with what had been written before. I wanted to write new chapters and knew that Jem was there to help.

I wanted to believe that we could change, but maybe we all come back to the qualities we try to outgrow. The things that we try to bury are the things that need soothing. I hoped that I could be Jem's hiding place. The place where things are safe. Where he is safe. I wanted to hold him until his rage resurfaced, to kiss it and stroke it and say, *it's ok*. I didn't know what he'd find if he held me long enough. I trusted that we'd find out together.

It was comfortable being curled up in Jem's childhood room. In bed, I played with his hair and saw a faint scar that I'd never noticed before. *Was this the cat flap?* He smirked. *Postbox, actually*. I stroked it and it was smooth, barely noticeable by touch alone. *What were you trying to deliver?* He touched it too. *My head, I suppose.*

362

I looked through the shelves stuffed with books, board games, a marble run and old football and *Beano* annuals. We flicked through a dusty encyclopaedia. I yawned and wanted to fall asleep dreaming of gods, sirens and centaurs. *Look up Helen of Troy,* I said. *It's funny you should say that.* He put down the encyclopaedia and passed me a gift wrapped in gold paper. It was rectangular and weighted, exceptionally book-shaped. I sat up in the bed and shook it, *is it a tennis racket?* I unwrapped the hardback copy of *The Women of Troy* by Pat Barker. *Open it,* Jem tapped the cover. I flicked the pages and ran my fingers over the creamy paper. There, on the title page, he'd written:

To my Helen, but somehow more beautiful. Merry Christmas,
Jem x

I nestled into him, my face on his neck where his pulse quivered beneath his skin, as he read me the story of the captured queen Briseis. Perhaps there could be new Christmas traditions.

Chapter Fifty-Six

Walpole Bay: 51.39339° N, 1.39960° E

For New Year's Eve there was nothing I wanted to do more than visit Margate so I could be reunited with my screensaver and the coast that I'd stared at every day for nearly a year. For reasons I can't remember, Miri's flatmate decided not to join us at the last minute so it was just me, Jem and Miri. Jem joked that he felt more like he was tagging along with me and Miri, rather than the other way around. I said he was correct, as Miri had made the same joke acknowledging that it would indeed be him who was the third wheel.

On the journey to Kent we made a stop-off at Minnis Bay tidal pool in Birchington-on-Sea. While slamming the boot shut I overheard Miri say to Jem, *Desert Island Discs is the Millennial Church* and start talking about episodes with Lucinda Lambton and Maggi Hambling. Having spent too long faffing and packing the car, we arrived when the sky was already a blueish black. Clambering into the semi-circle-shaped tidal pool in the dark, I slipped on an algae-covered rock and landed on my side. My fall revealed that the Victorian pool was only knee height. Miri and I attempted to swim while Jem stood by the edge and looked at his phone. *Get me a postcard?* Jem said. I looked at him quizzically while he put my towel around me. *From your trip!*

We were staying in an Airbnb behind The Flamingo amusement arcade and cooked puttanesca for dinner. By 'we' I mean Jem cooked while Miri and I drank wine and laughed our heads off at our own jokes. Jem offered to set Miri up with one of his friends, but she said he looked like he would spend all night telling her about the microbrewery he was going to launch in De Beauvoir Town. She was weary of self-proclaimed IPA enthusiasts or coffee aficionados. *If anyone lists an inanimate object as part of their personality, it says a lot about their personality.* While I grated parmesan onto my pile of spaghetti, Jem tickled me on his way to sit down. Miri lifted her glass and used it to point at us, *I get the impression you two are the kind of couple who wrestle.*

When the three of us had had enough to drink that we could leave without needing coats we stormed past the harbour to Bar Nothing, a speakeasy on the seafront. There, we jostled at the bar to order gin and tonics. Miri leaned in to say, *I put my Converse in the washing machine last night. I'm ready for a sticky-floor dancing kind of night.*

Everyone there was dressed like they could've been Jefferson Airplane groupies. I chatted to a woman wearing a sequin dress and gold thigh-high boots. While she spoke she blinked to keep her blonde fringe out of her eyelashes. Her boyfriend was wearing a grey suit with lapels reaching out towards his shoulders. The salt from his margarita kept getting in his moustache. *How did you meet?* I asked with wide eyes. He wrapped an arm around her, *her ex-boyfriend was supporting my band.* I thought that was the coolest possible way he could've answered that question. *We got married here three weeks ago,* he said and they started snogging. *He DJed,* she pulled away from their kiss to point to a man with a handlebar moustache leaning against the bar with a beer in one hand and record in the other. Moustaches seemed compulsory in Margate.

Midnight came about with little fanfare. The DJ was playing 'Beast of Burden' by The Rolling Stones and wasn't interested in interrupting it. The barmaid gave him a shove so he rolled his eyes while turning the track down a little so everyone could sing 'Auld Lang Syne'. Disco lights circled the room, transforming the space into a rockpool. The light refracted above us and bounced off old pianos, church-pew seating and megaphones. I moved my hands above me so my fingers shimmered in the light and thought about being a mermaid at Treyarnon tidal pool. When I was so drunk that my eyes couldn't focus on the disco ball anymore, the others pulled me away.

We debated chips or a kebab but settled on neither and walked along the beach. Far, far on the horizon I could see lights. Specks of gold, ruby and humming amber. The waves were gentle and distant, like a whispering drunk couple in the back of a taxi. Suddenly I was tired.

Goodnight! we shouted to Miri, who was already kicking off her shoes and waving behind her as she drunkenly slammed her door shut. Jem and I stayed up kissing and whispering to each other quietly so Miri wouldn't hear through the wall. He started laughing. *What?* I said. *You spent most of this evening staring at that spinning light.* I wriggled the sheets around me. *It was magic*, I said smugly. *Happy new year*, I pressed my palm against his cheek and he kissed my wrist, *another year of getting to know your complex, strange, wonderful brain.* We carried on like that, whispering into each other's ears with his fingers inside me. Both too drunk to finish but too drunk and happy and in love to stop.

In the morning we saw that the lights from the night before were a shipping container and a wind farm. By the time we'd walked to the beach the sea air had just about cured me of the worst symptoms of my hangover. Miri didn't look much better, her eyes weary and her tongue still blue, though from what drink even she couldn't recall. There was no time to waste. There was a tidal pool to visit.

Walpole Bay is Britain's largest tidal pool. It's around four acres and is made of a four-sided concrete wall and many metal ladders. It was built in 1937 and is Grade II-listed. Miri and I realised that the tidal pool we'd visited on that first trip to Margate wasn't actually Walpole Bay, but another tidal pool near Marine Terrace, which is Victorian, but much smaller. My screensaver wasn't the pool I thought it was at all. Another unexpected adventure from our trip. Margate had not one, but two tidal pools.

We walked through a break in the cliffs that was created for farmers to bring seaweed into town. On New Year's Day the strip of beach before the pool was packed with couples and their dogs, families with small children running into the water in their wellies and circles of friends toasting with schnapps. Someone was cooking bacon on a small campfire and the smell of honey-smoked meat filled the air. I recognised a few faces from Bar Nothing and we exchanged good mornings.

Buoyed by the joyous energy along the seafront, we rushed along the tidal pool wall to get in. It was impossible to hesitate with a queue of people waiting behind us. First Jem, me next, then Miri. We splashed in and yelped at the shock of winter water. Impatient to experience the thrill, people gave up with the queue down the ladder and started jumping from the pool wall. A scruffy Bedlington whippet guarded his master swimming. With the dog blocking the steps, a more cautious man looked like he had no choice but to jump too. He second-guessed himself and went to crouch and slide in, but at the last minute gripped his nose and did a flat-footed jump. Everyone cheered! Swimmers were just the loveliest people. I looked at Miri while I treaded water and knew she thought the same.

After a few minutes, the tension in my neck melted away and the cold became glorious. Jem, not as used to the chill and perhaps sensing that he should give us a moment, returned to get changed. The weather was mild enough that Miri and I decided we could swim the width of the pool and back. *Thank you for this year,* she said. I thought about how to possibly thank Miri for her friendship. A moment passed and I heard bottles being opened and dogs barking on the beach. *Thank you for everything Miri.* The seagulls above us were like white gloves applauding.

We emerged with little pieces of seaweed clinging to our arms and legs. I rubbed one between my fingers, rough as cat tongues, before flinging it back to the sea. Seabitten and shivering, we rushed to return to our things and passed half a dozen swimmers on their way in. Those of us that had been in the water were differentiated by our glowing red bodies. *Happy New Year,* I said to each of them. And I truly felt that it was. I had enough happiness left over to pass on to Miri and Jem and all the swimmers there. This year would be happy too, maybe because finally I could accept that sometimes it would be sad and hard and raining, but there would also be sun.

Miri and I had our routine for getting warm rehearsed to a fine art. She poured us a cup of coffee from her flask while I whipped out two hot water bottles and pressed one against Jem's chest. Miri, as she usually does, put her hat on first while I stripped off completely then rubbed myself dry with a towelled robe. Jem teased us for our matching towels, swimming bags and hot water bottles. *You two are cute,* he said. *It's nice to share things,* I replied. Meaning not just the towels, but this swim, this day, this memory.

I'd expected our hangover to last all day, but I was energetic after the adrenaline of a swim. The three of us queued for Peter's Fish Factory and ate our cod and chips on the harbour steps, then walked through town, popping into antique emporiums. There was a vintage store with a woman sitting at the back, unpicking the seam of a dress while her French bulldog sat on a fur coat being used as an improvised pet basket.

We moseyed around Turner Contemporary and I stared at a piece in a glass display case called *Keep Collect*. It was a plush grey box with sixteen souvenir pens carefully laid on top. The artist's grandma had never left England but was a keen diarist; her friends and family had brought her pens from their holidays. Isle of Wight, Praia da Rocha, Lanzarote.

I thought about how lucky I was to travel and have an adventure. There are two routes of travel in Britain. Those who have freedom, choice and resources like Miri and me. Then those who travel because they have no choice, those who are escaping. Choice was something to be thankful for.

Miri returned to London, so then it was just Jem and me in Margate. Jem and me. Me and Jem. I hadn't quite gotten used to that. I ran a bath and soaked in the tub with the door open, listening to him play the guitar downstairs. He was singing softly, but I could tell it was 'Blackbird' by the Beatles from the way the chorus lifted and dropped. I'd never heard Jem sing before and delighted in this new detail about him, this evidence that, of course, there were new things to discover and I would keep unearthing more treasure if I kept digging. I walked downstairs and told him to get a kitchen utensil of his choice and bring it to the bedroom. Jem returned with a silicone fish slice. He chose well.

There was no TV so we read the paper with our heads on either side of the sofa and our legs intertwined, then had more sex and stared at our phones. I saw a post that said New Year didn't mean anything. That 365 days was purely a unit of measurement. It was just another Saturday. To me, it did mean something though. It meant a new chance to do better at living. What I'd been doing for the five years since Tom's death felt closer to just existing.

I promised myself 2022 would be the year I started flossing and stopped buying clothes from Instagram adverts. I would stop being so easily swayed and gullible in general; that way the ads wouldn't have a chance against my willpower. I would be more compassionate and less critical. I would stop drinking alone and keep dancing with Miri. I wouldn't waste any more time Googling: *get rid of freckles* or *laser hair removal for chin*. I would open an ISA. I would understand what an ISA was. I would start donating to the *Guardian* instead of clicking the big X when the pop-up bar told me how their journalism stands for truth and integrity. In fact,

I would read more of the *Guardian* than just the agony aunt column. Or maybe just start by reading any news longer than the 180-character summaries on Twitter. I would stop being so judgemental. I would apply that to judging myself too. I would call Mum more. I would call Emma more. I would be more of everything to Emma. I would keep swimming. And all these promises felt possible, felt promiseable.

Trevone tidal pool

Chapter Fifty-Seven

Our tidal pool adventure had put me in touch with Chris, an architect who was working to restore lidos and build a new one on the Thames. He was passionate about giving the river – which he viewed as a public resource – back to the people. We'd exchanged lengthy emails and I delighted in having a new penpal. In a city that was often isolating, swimming gave me neighbours. In a world that didn't care, swimming gave me community. In an age that was unkind, swimming gave me friends.

Chris was researching a book on sea pools and we'd shared thoughts on our definition of what a tidal pool was. Initially, Miri and I had said it was a pool filled with seawater by the tide, but if that was true then there were hundreds of small rockpools that fit the description. Chris suggested that the unique combination of a natural pool filled by the tide that had man-made elements was a tidal pool. Man-made elements could include concrete walls (Bude and Devil's Point), metal ladders (Walpole Bay and Clevedon Marine Lake) or even the use of dynamite to create the pool (Dancing Ledge and Blue Lagoon). This meant that our first swim, Blue Pool Bay, was technically a rockpool and didn't count towards our list. I viewed it as a warm-up. Miri and I added the caveat that our adventure would only include swimmable tidal pools and paddling pool depth didn't count. This saved us trips to Shoeburyness, Woodup and Chalkwell in Essex, which were all scenic but small pools used for children or boating.

I invited Miri and Chris for a boozy lunch in Soho where the three of us could compare our research. It was a short walk from the underground but long enough that the cold wrapped itself around me. Frost candied the grass in Hanover Square and smokers huddled outside offices on their cigarette break. Inside, the restaurant had a low linen curtain that half-covered the steamed-up window.

The three of us merrily shared anecdotes about the complex politics of community fundraising groups and people we'd met on our respective travels. *It's a shame you didn't have a chance to meet Pat*, Chris got the waiter's attention to order another round. Pat looks after Tarlair, an abandoned lido in Macduff. We'd tried to meet when we were in Scotland, but hadn't been able to. *They're a great team. You have to be patient with these things, but it looks like the restoration is happening. What did you think of Saltcoats?* I looked at Miri, who grabbed the olive from her martini before the waiter took the glass. *The pool in North Ayrshire*, Chris pushed. *Oh*, I blinked, *I don't think we knew about that one.* Chris explained he'd been working to restore the tidal bathing pond there. It was built on Scottish salt pans in the 1930s, but had since fallen into disrepair. He got out his phone and showed us a few people we should follow who share their swimming travels or coastal drone photography. As he scrolled through, a post of a turquoise tidal pool hemmed with boulders in Keiss appeared. *Been here?* I shook my head. We were quiet and Chris awkwardly placed his phone back in his jacket pocket, *oh well. Good to know about them now!*

We stepped out of the restaurant and the traffic fumes made me feel lightheaded. I thought about the expense of returning to Scotland for two missed tidal pools. It'd been cold enough in August; visiting this time of year would surely only result in a five-minute dip. It was a long way to go. I considered suggesting a night in with Miri to look at Google Earth together, but the thought depressed me.

Miri was already heading towards the tube. *I think I'm actually going to walk for a bit*, I called after her. She gave me a hug and I pulled my coat around me a little tighter. It was January and we only had two months to go before our year would be up. My research told me there were pools in Northern Ireland, Jersey and Guernsey. We'd kept them on our list of To Travel, but I'd been avoiding booking ferries or planes because of the expense. Looking at my bank statement, a flight seemed ambitious. I felt the adventure slipping away from me, but rather than holding on too tight, I tried to let it go.

I sat on the same bench I passed on the way to the restaurant. There was no dedication. It was just a stopping place. Two strangers tried to avoid each other on the pavement and did a tango of sorts. Jem had told me once about a performance artist who followed people in the street for days, hoping to find a new direction. Hadn't that been what I'd done? I'd spent so much time thinking about a memorial bench for Tom and if it would be possible to find a place for me to feel connected to him. I thought about the coordinates I'd collected on this journey. I'd like to say I found him in each tidal pool, but the truth was that I was still searching.

Although I hadn't found the resolve I was looking for, I'd found more reasons to live and a way to justify the time I have that he didn't. Because really, this stopped being about place a long time ago and became about time. I didn't know how much time I had left. Hopefully, it was enough time for one more swim with Miri, one more kiss in the park with Jem and one more phone call with Emma where I would have the courage to say *I love you* before I hung up.

How else could I make my limited time on Earth special? Swimming taught me I could travel far, or I could look at my environment and think about how to make it somewhere I could find whatever I was looking for. On my next swimming trip, I promised myself I'd wave hello when I passed someone on the street. I'd think about how I touch the lives of those around me and the nature too. I'd pack a lunch, then sit and share my picnic with the wildlife. I'd listen to what birds I could hear. I'd learn the name of a plant that borders the water. I'd water it. I'd read the dedication on a memorial bench when I sit down.

The morning view in Durgan

Chapter Fifty-Eight

Durgan: 50.10367° N, 5.11567° W

It took Miri and me eight hours and twenty-seven minutes to get to Durgan. Another way to look at it was one bus, three trains and one taxi. Or only two cups of coffee. Durgan is a hamlet in Mawnan, South Cornwall with a small beach wide enough for just a handful of cottages. The shingle beach is a small horse-shoe sheltered from Atlantic gales. *Mildest corner of the country*, the taxi driver proudly told us. We'd passed the hamlet on a hike last year and fallen in love with how picturebook-perfect it was. The National Trust cottages were drastically cheaper for the month of January so we booked a week to visit Polperro tidal pool. The cottage was as pretty as I remembered it. An eighteenth-century stone and slate cottage with small dormer windows from which the beach was visible.

Back in London, everything was grey and didn't match my mood, which was all yellow that January. Library card, buttered toast, freshly sharpened pencils,

Jem's kettle, early flowering daffodils in Myatt's Fields. I had endless energy and enthusiasm, but not the time for all of it. The winter days were sharp and short and trying to write a book, keep my job, be a girlfriend to Jem, stay a friend to Miri, start being a sister to Emma and stay sane was a lot. Being in Durgan was a way to invent more time. I never wasted a moment. I got out of bed as soon as my eyes opened and rushed to the window to inspect the sky. Beautiful, again. Light broke through the clouds. Spring didn't feel too far away.

It didn't take us long to create a routine in Quay Cottage. In the mornings, I put the kettle on to make hot water bottles while Miri laid out our beach shoes by the door, still wet from yesterday. She spooned three heaps of coffee into the press and left it brewing for our return, then we pulled on our hats and left the door slightly ajar. We walked barefoot down Durgan beach. Rocks dug into our footsoles and we howled like dogs into the morning air. I waded in until the water was up to my calves. I clutched my elbows, arms folded across my front, and noticed the hair on my thighs prickle and my nipples harden. When I was finally waist height, I propelled myself into the water.

The water there is brackish – saltier than fresh water, but not as salty as the sea. It's a secluded part of the Helford Passage and the surrounding hillside is covered in bracken, moss and foliage, all the deepest of greens. From the beach, the water appears as an inkwell; the shade of poison ivy. *What green would you call this?* I asked Miri and we tried on colours: ivy, emerald, crocodile, pine. None were quite right. We settled on a new shade: Durgan Green. *Apparently,* I started and Miri looked towards me patiently because she knew I was about to recite a fact I half remembered, *in countries where there are more words for the colour blue, they see more shades of it. Doesn't it make you feel funny knowing you might see the world differently, just because you have more words?*

Miri swirled her hands in a figure of eight. *It's a little like love, don't you think? Not enough words to describe the kinds. Especially friendship.* I thought of *The Fisher King* and *The Handless Maiden. That's a very good point. I wonder if that's why British people are emotionally constipated. Because we don't have enough words to express ourselves.* I looked at the horizon and decided it was time to head in. Miri was still drifting when she said, *or maybe we don't need other words. You know what I feel, when I say I love you.*

We didn't rent a car because the nearest pub, The Ferryman, was only a twenty-minute walk away and from there we could catch a small passenger ferry across the river to Helford village and the Lizard peninsula. At least that had been the plan. When we arrived, we realised the pub was closed for maintenance and the ferry had stopped running for winter. There was nothing to do, and nowhere to go. It was perfect.

In the evenings, we got drunk and went skinny-dipping in the moondark then danced naked to Robyn in front of the fire. When we ran out of wood for the log burner, we walked to Mawnan, filled our backpacks with as much as we could carry and lugged it back. The next beach along from Durgan was Grebe, where we skimmed stones or, more accurately, Miri skimmed stones while I threw them into the water. A yellow-signed buoy bobbed in the distance and we decided we could swim out to it, but only realised when we were close that it read: 'Danger Eel Beds'.

I wrote in my bedroom with Miri's voice, delicate as silver bells, still audible from downstairs. When I got writer's block, I strolled along the beach and collected rubbish like I might pick up some good ideas. The first day I felt so proud of my bag filled with bits of plastic. Then I returned the next day and the beach was littered again. Moving up and down the shore, I leaned into the meditative practice and accepted starting over. I placed my treasure on the bedroom windowsill – sea glass, milk bottle cap, disposable lighter and barnacled plastic toothbrush

– and said goodnight to them before sleep as though they were good luck charms.

All these things were very special, but the most special thing about that week in Durgan was the trees. Often the prettiest parts of Cornwall look like the Mediterranean, with the same azure water and sandy beaches. The mossed woodland surrounding Helford, however, could only be British. It feels ancient and powerful, mysterious and timeless. High above the coppiced oaks along the coast there are taller trees that knife the horizon. These are Monterey pines, natives of the California coast. I wondered how they'd arrived here. When I walked barefoot on the beach, I often noticed their dark green needles pressing into the fleshy part of my sole. Their pinecones are serotinous and stay closed until opened by the heat of a forest fire when their seeds regenerate on burned forest floors. There are rarely forest fires here, but the cones burst open in hot weather.

For five years, there had been a fire inside me. It raged and it burned. Being in Durgan was the first time it occurred to me that fire can be good. It can also mean rebirth.

Chapter Fifty-Nine

Gyllyngvase Beach: 50.14437° N, 5.06776° W

Miri and I went to meet author Cathy Rentzenbrink for a swim on Gylly beach. Cathy's book *The Last Act of Love* was the first grief memoir I read after Tom died and it remained on my bedside table long after I finished it as a reminder that someone else had lived what I'd lived. I wasn't alone. She wrote it twenty-five years after her brother Matty was hit by a car. Twenty-five years felt a lot longer than the five I'd had since Tom. I avoided imagining what it would feel like to be nearly fifty and for Tom to still be stuck at nineteen.

It was sunrise when we saw Cathy, already waiting on the beach. She was speaking into her phone. *I find a voice memo is much nicer than writing a diary*, she told us. I scrunched my toes inside my trainers to force some feeling into them. It was icy that morning and I'd been able to see my breath before me on the bus. Cathy's shoes were already off. *Now Freya, I have a habit of talking myself out of doing things that are good for me. So I hope you two are going to persuade me that the water will be lovely.*

I circled my hips as we tangoed through the waves. We pushed ourselves towards the sun, which lit up the water. *Mind,* she warned, *there's a ledge,* just as my feet fell through the water like I was expecting another step at the bottom of the stairs. There was a long road of light dancing on the surface, wide and open-mouthed at the shore. It narrowed towards the horizon where the sun hovered cautiously. I stared too long, then all I could see behind my eyes was red. When I blinked, the world went black and white. When Jem was in Sweden, he'd told me they have a word for the trail of light the moon's reflection creates on water. *Mangata,* meaning Moon Road. I thought that this must be Sun Road and I wanted to follow it. We stepped forwards, deeper into the illuminated sea.

I always find, Cathy said, *that when the waves are rough you're so preoccupied getting past them that you don't mess about worrying that it's cold.* She was right, as we'd skipped my usual two minutes of nervously hovering in the shallows while exclaiming how freezing it was.

After a swim, we bustled ourselves into Gylly Beach Cafe. Ribbons of shudders furled through me and unwound themselves from my chest and arms. The sensation stayed for twenty minutes or so then gently eased away. We talked about grief, swimming and writing. Acceptance and persistence were present in all three. I said I was writing a lot, and worrying about the book's release before I'd even got there. *Enjoy the process*, she said, *it's all we have in the end*. I asked what it was like to be a 'real author' and Cathy said she didn't think she was one yet. *Maybe you never do*. We spoke about how as women we neatly fold ourselves into the role of administrative assistant for our loved ones. It's such a comfortable and snug position to occupy. It's so learned. So it's no surprise that at book festivals male authors might have their wives helping run the show and cheering them on from backstage, while the female authors are either alone or apologising to grouchy partners that it's all going on so long and they might miss the cricket. We suspected that the male authors who travelled alone came home and left their suitcase at the door to be unpacked later, but the female authors came home to do everyone else's laundry. It felt like we weren't really talking about book festivals at all. My mum packs for my dad on every holiday. There've been many times when I've watched her fold freshly ironed shirts into a holdall along with the Rohan trousers she gets specially tailored shorter for him as he's too small for the standard outdoor trousers with zippable pockets on the leg. I hoped I was part of the first generation of women who didn't have to iron.

Our conversation began with writing habits, then detoured to self-doubt until we arrived at agreeing social media was the devil, but there wasn't much we could do to avoid it. Cathy said, *I'm only ever a few steps from depression. My son points up at a plane and asks what the white clouds are behind it. I think about pollution. I eat a blueberry and remember reading they prevent Alzheimer's.* We hugged goodbye and I was so pleased we'd shared the sun road that morning.

In Falmouth, everyone seemed friendlier than usual and I don't know if that was because we weren't in London or that a sunny day in January brings such unexpected joy. *Glorious day*, a pleasant-faced woman with a rolled-up newspaper under her arm said as she passed, *just glorious.* I imagined I lived there and enjoyed the daydream. I thought that my time in London was running out. I told Miri that when our husbands died we should move here and it would be the happiest phase of our lives. She nodded, and I felt she understood I was not only joking but also expressing a yearning for a life outside the city and a hope that growing older wouldn't have to mean the fading of friendship. We passed a man in the harbour selling Cornish daffodils from an upturned bucket. They were still buds, the most perfect of yellows, ready to bloom when someone took them home. I remembered that nothing about that day felt close to depressing.

Have you been thinking about what Cathy said? Miri asked me on the bus back to Durgan. *Constantly, I'm a bit worried.* She crossed her legs, *we can keep each other in check. Let's be honest, I think you'll always have to unpack your own suitcase, but we'll never let anything go uncelebrated.* I imagined walking into the kitchen from a future home office I might have one day and asking my husband if he'd listened to me on BBC *Woman's Hour.* The thought depressed me. It was a special talent of mine that even my own fantasies disappointed me.

As she searched her backpack for gloves, Miri asked if I thought Jem would be a good husband. *I'm not sure. I need to rethink what that word means to me. If I was on the radio for my book, I'm not sure he'd even listen. It wouldn't impress him much,* I nibbled my bottom lip, *maybe I don't need someone who's impressed by me. I'm not sure,* I repeated and handed Miri my gloves.

I contemplated the tallying I'd done between Jem and Flip as potential suitors. I felt ashamed for treating them like they were commodities, which, in some ways, they had been to me. I'd been shopping for men. Trying them on for size. Hoping there was a satisfaction guarantee. I'd compared them as mechanisms for feeling better because it was easier to be near people who represented the change I wanted in me, rather than change myself. That didn't feel so true anymore.

I felt thankful I wouldn't be packing Flip's suitcase for the rest of his life, with no one to pack mine. Guessing what was on my mind, Miri asked: *how are you feeling about seeing him again?* A wave of adrenaline bolted through my body like the last surge before a power cut. When we'd been more of a we I'd suggested to my course-leader that Flip speak at Cambridge. I found myself in a strange situation where he'd be presenting in our 'Writing for Performance' module. I say 'I found myself' as if I hadn't orchestrated the whole thing, but it often felt that way. Like, how did I get here? How did I let this collision of circumstances happen? Flip and I would be overnight in an old, bricked manor with secret staircases, quiet corners and hidden libraries. I was nervous I'd be tempted. At that moment, I felt stable and didn't need distracting, but I never knew when things would turn inside out and I'd be at sea again. Grief came in waves and what if one swept me into his arms?

I rang the bell; our stop was next.

Polperro tidal pool

Chapter Sixty

Polperro Tidal Pool: 50.32983° N, 4.51615° W

Miri's fall meant we'd missed Polperro tidal pool on our last trip to Cornwall. Now it was time to tick it off our list. The path to Chapel Pool went right behind The Blue Peter Inn so we stopped for a fish stew lunch before our swim. The wooden rafters of the pub were painted black and quotes had been carefully chalked into them. They were an odd selection. One said: *the more people I meet, the more I love my dog.* Another: *the older I get, the wiser I was.* There was one I quite liked: *the time you enjoy wasting is never wasted time.* It seemed an outlier in being quite earnest.

From above, Chapel Pool is a geode. There's an almost amethyst hint to the rocks that gives it a bruise-like hue. A fuzz of heathery seaweed hugs the rockpools, radiating this heliotrope glow. I took a picture and it came out all blue and grey, not at all like how I saw it. I thought it was probably better that way. I'd have to remember this just how it was. There was a railing from the cliff to guide us on the walk down and twelve or so stone steps had been added to make the descent safe. A concrete bung had been placed at one end to keep the water in, but it was otherwise natural. Small shells glinted from the bottom of the pool like silver coins in a wishing well.

There was no one around, so skinny dipping didn't feel too risky. We bundled our clothes into a pile on the rocks. I stood and felt like a tiger, wild tufts of hair emerging from between my legs and striped marks stretching across my bottom. Slipping into the icy waters, my skin blazed. So cold it was hot.

When I turned onto my back, we saw a couple walk down the steps. They clocked us, froze, then bumped into each other as they hurried to clamber back up the steps. *Sorry!* I yelled out, as Miri turned over to protect her modesty, *we didn't mean to hog the pool.* The woman tried to hurriedly walk away, but her partner was stationary so they bumped into one another again. *No worries! We were going to take some pictures, but decided we better not.* It was hard to tell who'd been more flustered: them or us. *Very kind of you!* Miri cried out. She looked back at me. *Well, that was the most British interaction I've ever had.*

My social-media detox hadn't lasted long. It never did. I was mindlessly scrolling through Instagram to make the bus journey back from Polperro pass quicker. I looked out the window where children had drawn snakes and ladders on the pavement in chalk, then back at my phone. A post appeared. I paused. It was Nicole's twenty-third birthday. She'd posted a selfie with the caption *feeling 23* and a glitter emoji. Her hair was shorter than when I'd last seen her. It suited her. I thought she was a bit old to be using filters like that, but had to admit it did make her eyelashes look long.

Tom had had a crush on Nicole for a year before they got together. I knew as much as most sisters do when it comes to their little brother's romantic relationships: she was around the house a lot. They were a couple for the three years that he was ill. I don't remember how or when that started, but I think it was shortly before the diagnosis. They were in love in that way only young couples who haven't had their hearts broken are. It was so intense and all-consuming. They were also in love in that way couples only are when one is going away, when one is dying. It was them against the world.

Every now and then I'd be in touch with Nicole. Last time I saw her, she was wearing a very business-like blouse with a tulle collar and I wondered where the time had gone that she'd become a woman who wore something like that. She tapped her shellac nails on a vodka slimline tonic. Same drink as Emma. Was that a coincidence or just being in your early twenties? She sat cross-legged with her car keys looped through one finger, resting on her lap. She's an executive sales assistant for a rental car company and it sounded like she liked it. They'd both liked cars. She used to sit watching him play *Grand Theft Auto*. I'd say, *isn't that boring,* and she'd just shake her head.

Nicole'd wanted to read something at the funeral, but when she approached the lectern and opened her mouth no words came out. Eyes on the floor, she shook her head and passed the sheet of paper to her form tutor. It was a discussion she'd had in advance with my parents, that it might be too much on the day, but that she'd like to read. Looking back on it, I find it astounding that she was eighteen and brave enough to speak, but compassionate enough to prepare an out for herself. I should remind myself that next time I feel guilty that I 'should' meet up with Nicole. She probably has a lot to teach me, that I couldn't teach her.

I hovered over Nicole's profile, and thought about messaging her happy birthday. Then I thought that hearing from me, and being reminded of Tom, wouldn't make her birthday so happy. It was probably true that she'd be thinking of him anyway, regardless of whether I messaged or not. I put my phone away and sighed loudly, but Miri was too engrossed in *Persuasion* to notice. The bus wound around the tight Cornish country lanes and she remained transfixed on the page. I looked out the window and noticed the names of the cottages we passed: Muggles End, Penwarne Lodge and Buttercup Barn.

Nicole must know Tom in ways I will never. In the same way that I know him in ways Mum will never know. I thought what a singular moment in time a relationship is. The moments, revelations and changes intimacy provides you the opportunity to witness.

I felt compassion for the woman that Marlowe knew. It was only the briefest of time together when I was a person trying to search for something I didn't know the name of, gripping my fingers to the ledge of an existence I wasn't sure I wanted. The fragility of everything I had then, compared to how strong I felt now. I also felt compassion for the parts of me that Flip had seen, the hunger he recognised in me. How openly he witnessed and nourished it.

And I felt compassion for all the parts of all those men I had seen. The dreams they told me as they momentarily loosened their grip on the cage of masculinity. The intimacy our bodies shared, shattering some kind of wall between the foreign lands of our existences.

I hoped that there would be a future for Jem and me, but I tried not to let my fear of it not happening be shadowed by how grateful I was for our time together. A time in which I'd grown a lot. I knew Jem had a part of me that was raw and vulnerable and changing, and that part would forever be his.

It was that week in Durgan that I considered contraception for myself more earnestly. I read about the pill, coil, injections and got lost in folklore from friends and women online about their experiences. I read about the thickening of the mucus lining of the womb and realised how little I knew about female anatomy except for how I thought it was supposed to look and taste and feel and smell. Pink, hairless, feminine, soft. I still didn't really know what or where my Fallopian tubes were.

I looked at pictures of the coil and thought the bit of plastic and metal looked like something I might find washed up on a beach. A bit of broken fishing line. Was my body something where things washed up? I'd treated it that way for a long time, loaning little parts of myself out to men and hoping they'd leave meaning in their wake. Now sex was something that made me feel precious, treasured.

The side effects of the coil were: headaches, nausea, pelvic infections, damage to the womb. I mentally shrugged. That was all expected, part of the toll of being a woman. I went to a sexual health centre and they implanted the coil. I chose it because I thought it was least likely to cause me hormonal mood swings and cramps, so I wouldn't have to risk losing days of productivity. My commitment to capitalism was clearly strong.

I still thought about a baby a lot. Sometimes I stared in the mirror and pushed out my stomach, then cupped it like I was an actress doing a pregnancy announcement in a magazine. I told myself one day I'd be ready for that new relationship with my grief and tried to work towards feeling excited about it. Feeling closer to Tom. Feeling closer to Mum. It was something I carried tight inside but knew that, for now, there were other dreams to come true first.

Quay Cottage! a neighbour cried out as we exited the house on our last day. *Are you leaving?* Everyone in Durgan was referred to by the name of their cottage. There was Rose Cottage, Postbox Cottage and School Cottage. Some were permanent residents and others holidaymakers. Visiting in January's hush meant we'd got to know people. That week reminded me that the longing we have as adults to relive our time at university is not a rejection of adult life, but a desire for a time in a community where we recognise one another, wave in the street and know each other's names. That week I loved not getting in a car, but just walking everywhere, and the days having smaller, more meaningful purposes.

~~

On the train back to London, we sat at a table opposite an older gentleman wearing circus-red trousers and a pinstripe blazer. He spent the entire journey with a bag on his lap that had sand in the zip. We didn't speak except for when he said, to no one in particular, *why is it that time goes so slowly on a train, but very fast when you're waiting for one?* It did go slowly and gave me time to practise the motion of turning pages of a book while I thought about other things. I missed Jem. Soon, I'd be back with him and I could touch his hand, his face, his hair. I'd typed out messages then backspaced them all so I could tell him with our heads on the pillow, his eyes closed, listening, while I traced circles on his arm. I thought about what I'd say into his ear when I hugged him. *I missed you. I love you.* How lucky to travel home to someone I missed, someone who would listen to me when I talked about the man selling daffodils from an upturned bucket, the biggest fish stew I'd ever seen, rocks so purple they were amethysts from the ocean, sleeping in woollen socks and seven days of filling Miri's hot water bottle. That week in Cornwall gave me a lot, but the greatest gift it gave me was knowing I could miss someone who I would see again.

⁓

I missed Tom. How lucky to love someone so much that it hurt to miss them. So lucky. I am a very lucky girl.

Chapter Sixty-One

Tate Britain: 51.49081° N, 0.12693° W

I rarely go to Tate Britain, but every time I do I think *I should do this more.* I could get lost in the permanent collection and – however many times I visit – I never feel like I've finished looking at all the paintings as room after room presents itself. There's something childlike about having to crane your neck to look at the paintings at the top of the gallery wall. Plus, there's a much better chance of having a bench to yourself than in Tate Modern. When Flip suggested meeting at Tate Britain I first thought, *strange. Why not the Modern?* But said yes, and called Natalie in the hope she'd join us and support me in establishing a new friendship-only relationship with Flip.

Natalie and I were staring at a still life of a bowl of pumpkins and gourds when Flip texted to say he'd meet us in the members' cafe, which is nestled around the rotunda in the top of the building. While we waited, I peered over the railings to spy down at the gallery below, then up at the glass dome above. It was like being inside the whorl of a shell. Flip removed his hat and ran his palm over his head as he came towards us. He had a slight shuffle to his walk, probably his bad knee. I went to touch his arm and ask if he was ok then remembered I wasn't that person, his person, anymore. Redirecting the flight-path of my hand, I gestured to Natalie instead. *This is my friend Natalie! She's on the course with me so I thought I'd bring her along.* I tried to force enough enthusiasm into the greeting to mask the fact that I'd ambushed him by bringing a friend. We all exchanged hugs then sat down with our teas: English breakfast for me and Natalie, and something herbal-looking for Flip. After a few minutes of awkwardly guiding the conversation, we were all getting on and I stopped worrying about the teacup slipping out of my clammy hand.

Via screenplays and New York's dating scene we were somehow on to the topic of Natalie's love life when she said, *sometimes it's not clear straight away if you wanna be with someone or be them.* Flip turned towards me and our eyes met. I knew that he was expressing an admiration between us, that I was glad was mutual. I'd forgotten what it felt like to be seen by him. How happy it made me to be acknowledged and respected by him. Suddenly, I realised I'd been holding on to a sadness that I wouldn't be able to experience again and there it was. A new way to know one another.

I was dreading the family meet-up in Cambridge. I'd organised it at Christmas when I was in a dead-end of believing I was an awful daughter and sister who never called and should organise a weekend away for the family as a gift. I was also secretly hoping it would be an opportunity to show off that I'd got into Cambridge and my parents would tell me how impressed they were with me and that I was a clever girl. The week before, I'd texted to say I'd booked a pub for dinner but hadn't planned much else. *Very busy with work, writing and studying, would anyone mind if we keep it a chilled weekend?* I sent an emoji where the eyes look like whirlpools and the mouth is a squiggly line.

When we met in the hotel car park Dan did the greeting nod men do towards Jem and placed a ticket on the dashboard. Emma pulled a heart-shaped balloon the colour of a maraschino cherry from her car. *Here you go*, she pushed it towards me, *I know you were stressed this week. A balloon always cheers everyone up.* I received it in my two hands, which seemed like body parts from someone else's memory. The glitter rubbed off on my coat and for the rest of the week it sprinkled from me wherever I walked.

We took a punt from Scudamore's and learned about the bear Lord Byron kept as a pet while studying, then we ate Chelsea buns from Fitzbillies and stopped in at The Mill. Dad and Jem seemed to get on ok when Dad wasn't trying to corner him in a debate. We returned to the hotel and had some time apart before dinner.

All day I kept thinking about the pink balloon and wanted to cry. I'd been actively dreading seeing Emma and being reminded that she deserved so much better than me. Sensing I was preoccupied by something, Jem did his usual thing of moving towards me to try to make eye contact then asking if I was ok, so I did my usual thing of trying to have sex with him by pulling him towards different, exciting-looking parts of the hotel room. He was cleaning a gelatinous glob of semen from the bathroom's marble floor when he asked me if I was alright again. Then, when I nodded my head, asked if I wanted to talk about Tom.

Can you stop, I surprised myself with the strength of my voice. Jem moved the hairdryer off a footstool and tried to get comfortable in the armchair. I gave in to his expectation that we would 'talk it out' and said, *I'm just a shitty sister. The balloon really fucked me up today*. I looked at it, bobbing cheerfully by the minibar. With a sigh, I sat on the end of the bed holding a towel around me.

That's so far from the truth, Freya. Surely you know that? I thought about explaining what I'd promised Tom and how I was so scared of letting Emma down as well that I barely tried. *It's not. Anyway, I should get ready,* I raised two dresses on their hangers, *shall I wear the orange or the blue one?* Jem checked his phone, *we're not leaving for another hour and don't 'anyway' me,* he said, making air quotes with his fingers, *we can talk about this stuff.*

Jem was sentimental sometimes and it irked me. What he called communicating, I called wallowing in unearned emotions. He thought everything could be fixed by talking, which I didn't believe. I feared that talking about things too much would affect my ability to move through the world. He didn't understand how hot and red grief felt inside. Why would I stoke that fire? Sometimes I was mad about the big injustices of it all. The pain, the loss, the knowing I'd never see him again and that the last time I'd seen him he'd been suffering. Then sometimes I was mad about the smallest of injustices, like Tom dying before the *Fast & Furious* saga ended. Some days, just knowing that he'll never go to a cinema to see one of those awful, bloated franchise films again is enough to send me into a fit of rage that could trash this whole hotel room. I'd been doing so well at keeping myself together recently. I didn't want to go backwards.

If I sit here and think about it, what good does that do? I need to not do that, so we can all have a nice time at dinner tonight. I threw the blue dress onto the bed.

Maybe it's ok to get upset. What would happen if you went to dinner feeling sad and told Emma you were having a bad day? She loves you. You have permission to have feelings around her. I chewed my bottom lip as Jem continued, *just the same as me. I want to get to know every part of you, Freya. Not just happy Freya. You don't need to be fake around me or around Emma.*

I'm not fake, Jem. I bit down on the inside of my cheek. *Ok, I didn't mean that. I just mean it'll make you feel better,* he said.

I undid my hair from its messy bun and replied: *you don't know that. In fact, you don't know anything about this.* Aggressively combing my hair, I glanced at Jem's reflection in the mirror. He was watching me. I wasn't sure why I was fighting him. I took a breath, lowered the hairbrush, and sat back down on the end of the bed. *Maybe I'm just not ready. I'm not ready to be angry all the time. I'll stop caring and be awful and bitter. I want to be a person who hugs. If all of this sinks in, then I won't think anyone deserves kindness from me, because they don't.*

Jem smiled softly and reached through the distance between the bed and chair, *there's not any world where you wouldn't be kind. You tell yourself you're not, and I don't know why. You are.* I looked into his eyes, *I'm not*

407

kind. Jem rubbed his temples, *that is far from the truth and you know—*

I interrupted him: *I've not always been kind to you either.* The sound of teenagers jeering outside drifted up from the street. Jem's eyebrow twitched, *what does that mean?* Guilt shuddered through me. I pulled the towel tighter around me. *Flip's speaking at Cambridge this week.*

Flip? Jem asked. *The man I told you about.* Jem blinked, which I took as an invitation to continue. *When we'd been seeing each other,* he closed his eyes, *I put him in touch with a tutor and he's doing a talk. So he'll be there this week.* We were both quiet and I wondered when Mum would come knocking so we could all go to dinner. *I actually met up with him recently. With Natalie,* I added. *I didn't want things to be awkward when we were here, but I thought you should know.*

Awkward? It's a course, why would that be awkward? What was the real reason you met him? I didn't reply. Jem leaned forward in the chair and placed his head in his hands. Eventually, he sat back up. *Obviously, I trust you Freya. I'm just wondering, why you would really do that?* I played with the towel, and thought that I'd spent a long time wondering why I ever did anything.

Jem said, *you know I've been thinking about what you said. That you carried on seeing him because you weren't sure about how I felt about you. And I took that on at the time. I thought maybe that was my fault and I could've done more, been more verbal. But since,* he shook his head, *I'm not sure that that's true. I did show you how I felt. I just showed you in my way.*

Since meeting Jem, I'd thought that he was putting me back together and I never thought that in the process I'd broken him into pieces.

I'm sorry. I can't explain. Maybe sometimes I want to run away from you. I'm scared you'll leave first because I don't deserve this. I'm sorry. I curled my toes into the carpet.

Jem looked out of the window; the teenagers were still shouting. *We're all scared of being left, Freya. I feel like that all the time, but I'm still here,* he offered his hand, *and I'm not going anywhere.* I looked at his palm and thought of Emma's balloon. These people trying to reach me. I tried to reach back.

Chapter Sixty-Two

The next morning, the six of us had breakfast at the hotel. Mum, Dad, Emma, Dan, me and Jem. I was getting used to the idea of us being a six. We'd found new ways to grow. Jem was still being interviewed by my mum for a permanent position in our family. She cut into her Eggs Benedict and asked Jem what his ambitions were. My lips curled thinking back to when I'd asked him the same question. I was most definitely my mother's daughter. He looked down at his avocado and thought for so long that Mum cleared her throat to prompt a response. *To be nourished by friends, family, work.* She stared at him quizzically as her egg yolk bled onto the muffin. I could tell she was musing on his use of the word nourished. *And to be fully present to support Freya while she writes her book.* My mouth struggled to contain both my breakfast and my smile. Mum blinked. *Well, that's very nice,* Dad said finally.

I looked towards Emma, who mimed being sick, then squeezed my knee under the table. I'd spent so much time working hard, getting the degree, writing the book. It was the first time I realised that Jem's love, my parents' love or anyone's love was not improved or altered by my attempts to impress them. Love existed in a realm that was not touched by such things and my confusion that it was had led me to some dark places.

That afternoon we went to the botanical gardens and Jem filled my pockets with pinecones.

Flip's talk was a success. A last-minute schedule change meant he delivered it virtually. He spoke about what acting taught him about writing, directing and persistence. I watched him talk through a 16:9 digital window. The Recording symbol blinked red on the screen. It twitched and pulsed like my body had beneath his once. He didn't look real. The face that I'd touched was now just a collection of pixels. I'd submitted a question about stage directions in advance and when the tutor read it out, a flash of recognition moved across Flip's face. Watching him say my name sent an electric shock through my body. I missed the times I'd earned being called poet. *Freya*, he smiled easily, before answering the question and moving on.

To: follertongreen@mac.com
From: frey.bromley@gmail.com
Subject: RE: Your Talk
I wanted to write and say how much I enjoyed your talk. It also meant a lot to me when Natalie said: *sometimes it isn't clear if we want to be someone or be with them.* I have always, and will always, admire you. I'm glad you recognise that.

All the best,

Freya

To: frey.bromley@gmail.com
From: follertongreen@mac.com
Subject: RE: Your Talk
It wasn't quite like that. I want to be you! If I'd been half as talented as you at your age . . . anything is possible for you poet x

Anything was possible for me. That was true. So I chose the hardest thing, I chose joy. That month I ended my tenancy, left my job and decided I would try to make writing work. I'd read once that 'the novel can do anything' and if that was true, then maybe it could do anything for me.

Spring

Chapter Sixty-Three

Tom's Bench: 51.27013° N, 0.39391° W

Suddenly there was not as much of a reason to swim anymore. Jem and I were together. I was writing. People were interested in my writing. Life was calm. Weekends were for walking, and living in the city like it was a village. On Sundays we walked to Herne Hill market for takeaway tubs of tartiflette, spinach rolls curled up like snakes and cartons of Braeburn apples and field mushrooms. *Spring is nearly here,* I said. There were crocuses everywhere; these pretty purple buds bordering the park. Volunteers gathered by Brockwell community garden to saw logs for new benches beside the herb planters. The smell of thyme filled the air. *Remember our date here?* I rubbed some between my fingers and brought a sprig to Jem's nose. *We've come a long way.*

Miri and I texted each other sporadically: *I miss you* or *swim soon?* We only met at the lido occasionally. The cold was the excuse we told ourselves, but we were happy too. And like all things that keep you well, you forget that the reason you're in the place you are is because of the thing you neglect as soon as you've arrived.

The week we planned to visit Broadstairs tidal pool, Storm Eunice arrived in England. Everyone was outraged by the weather and exclaimed it was the worst wind since 1984, but no one talked about climate change. I saw a video on Twitter of a wheelie bin flying through the sky like an urban revival of *The Wizard of Oz*. Jem messaged to say he was worried about everyone's cats. When a neighbour asked if anyone had found the outdoor furniture that had disappeared from the building balcony, I called Miri. *What do you think about tomorrow?* I tied my dressing gown and walked to the window, where I could see someone in flat sixty-four spreading jam on toast. *What about it?* Miri replied. *Isn't it a bit . . . windy?* I heard her turn down the volume of a conference call in the background. *It's all copy, right?* We agreed to meet at Paddington station, but I wasn't excited by the prospect of our swim. I didn't fancy running after my knickers if they blew away, and I thought the sea would be full of leaves and branches. An hour later, Miri called me back. *My fence has just fallen down. Let's postpone.*

The following week Jem called to say I should go outside; it was raining sand. A cloud from the Sahara had carried dust over London. I looked up, and the sky didn't look unusual. I stood outside. It felt like normal rain. Then that evening I saw sand swirling down the drain as I washed my body. Drying my hair with a towel, I thought about Tom's ashes. I imagined the weight of them in a box or in the clouds or down the drain.

I'd once read about the man who tried to weigh the human soul. Duncan MacDougall measured the mass of six patients at the moment they died. They lost three-quarters of an ounce. Twenty-one grams. None of that really means anything. When you die, your lungs stop cooling your blood so your body temperature rises to make sweat. I thought about the sweat in the beds of dying patients. The wringing of hospital sheets. The precious last drops. I wondered if I would've liked to touch them. The last beads of Tom's exertion from trying so hard at being alive. My friend told me that when her mother died, she had to go and clear her room. There was still an imprint on the pillow where her head had been resting when she'd died, as if she'd just got up to brush her teeth and would be back soon to ask if someone was going to put the kettle on. I thought about the evidence of life people leave behind. The patina of the dead. Handbags left on hallway hooks, sweat on sheets and dents on pillows.

Was it twenty-one grams whatever age you were? How does a soul look at nineteen? Lighter? Darker? Mine felt heavier somehow. That seemed unfair. Like a cloud carrying rain. A cloud carrying sand. A cloud carrying ash. I was still hurt knowing Tom's ashes had been spread at the bench without me. I didn't like the idea of them being separated. I hadn't been asked if that was ok with me. I didn't think it was. He would be less than the sum of his body minus twenty-one grams then. Harder to keep account of the soul. Mum was probably still upset with me for not going. We were hurting each other, but we were the only ones who knew our hurt. That felt just in some way. A weapon that we'd earned the right to use against each other.

I was upset, but if I was honest with myself, it had nothing to do with the ashes. I didn't believe that he was in there. Perhaps it would've been easier if I did. I was learning that grief contained many new moments of loss. Lots of ways I had to let go of things I'd not realised I was holding on to. The bench was another thing I'd hoped might make me feel better, and now it was time to acknowledge it wouldn't.

With one towel on my head and one around my body, I walked to the kitchen to pull my phone from the charger. I played a video of Miri jumping into Trevone tidal pool and dragged my finger across the screen so it played back and forth. She swung her arms behind her, bent her knees, then leapt. A moment of freefalling followed by a splash and total absorption in the water. The ripple disappeared. The water had healed itself. The possible innocence of sorts, the undisrupted water, no sign of the dive.

I wondered if Tom had never died, if the ripple had never begun, who I'd have had the courage to be and what life I'd be living. It would be a blameless life. It would also be a life without perspective. My finger hovered over the screen and I knew I wouldn't change any of it. This feeling that I had to heal myself, like the water, would go on forever. *Grief is endless,* I said to myself because there was no one to say it to me. I removed a pin from the corkboard and took down the tidal pool list, rearranging the photograph of me and Miri at Priest's Cove to cover the empty space.

The week of the sand cloud was also the week Miri and I decided to finish our adventure. I'm sure that timing was no coincidence. We gave up on the challenge to swim in every tidal pool in Britain, in the hope that it would strengthen our ability to continue it more freely. Every time we'd thought we were done, we discovered a new one. It simply wasn't finishable. And I hoped that that would remain true. I hoped that

I'd spend more time in new places with new people trying to save tidal pools from ruin. There didn't have to be rules or limits. The journey could go on forever. It was endless.

～～

Finally, I had enough space that I could go to Tom's bench. Or perhaps I had enough happiness to cushion it. I took the train to the park and sat there for a while. It's close to the Scout hut as Tom was an Explorer; good at tying knots and lighting fires.

Something about the view seemed off. The vista over our old school playing field meant I ended up inadvertently watching the rugby and wondering if people thought I was enjoying the year nine touch tournament rather than sitting in silence thinking about my dead brother. I wished there were badges for this kind of thing. Not quite 'Please Offer Me A Seat', but perhaps: 'Please Offer a Condolence Nod for My Seatedness'.

It was the Feng Shui of it too. The proximity to the facilities is convenient, but it's also in the flightpath of a bin so I could hear when dog-walkers dropped plastic-wrapped shit in the metal barrel. Depending on the weight – and I mean of the shit, not the dog, as they don't always correlate – it sounded different. Sometimes a ding. Sometimes a thud. Either way, it distracted me from focusing on my death ritual. I thought how much I would rather be at the sea searching for Tom than sitting somewhere I knew he wasn't.

I held a bouquet of white roses on my lap and wondered if anyone was watching me. Then I stood up and left them behind. I didn't check the time, because I thought I'd be ashamed of how little of it had passed. I was hoping to avoid any acknowledgment of time altogether, but the departure board at Effingham station mockingly blinked bright orange.

An old school friend texted me to say the roses were gone the next day. Maybe it was badgers. The next time I visited the bench I removed the blue elastic tying their stalks, just in case they visited hungry again. Now when I think about Tom's bench, I think of the roses. And when I think of the roses, I try to think of the badgers and their warm bellies full of petals, rather than the dog-waste bin. Sometimes I still visit Sami's bench.

Walpole Bay tidal pool

Chapter Sixty-Four

Since our first swim, Miri and I had swum in thirty-five tidal pools across mainland Britain. On a Saturday in April that smelled like newly cut grass, we visited Viking Bay, Broadstairs. It would be the last swim in our year of counting tidal pools and beyond that, we'd be exploring. We couldn't count forever. *Our last tidal pool for now*, Miri kept saying. *Am-nawr. For now.* Maybe where we'd started had been a clue all along. This was, of course, still sufficient cause for celebration, so we'd invited friends and family. The plan was that Miri and I would swim in Broadstairs tidal pool together, then walk to Walpole Bay where we'd meet everyone for a swim.

Charles Dickens wrote many of his novels while on holiday in Broadstairs. Every summer there's a Dickens festival where people dress in Victorian bathing costumes or as characters from his books. There was something dream-like and literary about the beach

423

too. It was dizzyingly beautiful. There were so many daisies the grass was full of stars and, above it, a broad blue sky that touched the tips of the white clifftop houses in the distance. We tried to guess which one Dickens had written *David Copperfield* in.

Around Viking Bay the seabed was covered in white, chalky rocks punctured with perfectly round holes. These tiny tunnels are made by piddocks, a clam-like shellfish also known as angelwings. They use their toothed shells to burrow into soft rocks. As they grow from larvae their tunnels deepen, locking themselves in. When they die, it's these empty holes that are left behind in the rocks. I found one with a shell still inside, but the burrow entrance was too narrow for it to fall out. I shook it like a rattle.

Propelling myself from one wall to the other, I tried to feel present in the familiar weightlessness of my body. The cleanness of it. The total absence of pain. *Don't take it for granted*, I told myself. Watching Miri's toes and elbows take turns emerging from the water, I reminded myself not to take her health for granted either. Afterwards, we sat on the pool wall and dangled our feet in the water. Pinching my toes around some seaweed, I tried to pop it like bubble wrap. I let a half-formed thought fall from my lips: *I said to Jem that I wished he communicated how he feels about me more, and he said that he feels I don't listen. That it's never enough for me.*

Do you think that's true? I readjusted to avoid a wave and Miri replied: *what I think doesn't matter. Do you think it's true?*

I leaned back on the pool wall. *Maybe a little. Somehow, I feel like we've been here before. Like we're starting the same circular walk from our house that we've done a hundred times before.*

Three children with blue and yellow fishing nets approached. Miri said wistfully, *the arguments that you have at the beginning are the same arguments that you have at the end.* The sun was bright. I closed my eyes and opened them again. Everything looked monochrome. *I guess I could be better at listening. I'm an awful listener, and the problem . . .*

She tapped me on the thigh, *none of that matters though. It's more about deciding if this is the argument that you want to have for the rest of your life. And if this is the person you want to do it with.* An undulating reflection danced across the hollow of Miri's throat.

How did Miri get so smart, I thought. I didn't know how smart I was. I wanted to be kind, but I didn't know if I was that yet either. Maybe I could be kind enough to try for him. To do something really kind and hard like love someone consciously. Love someone by committing to the whole experience of them, with space for all the shadows and hiding places. It would be nice for there to finally be space for my shadows. Miri and I stayed like that for a while at Broadstairs tidal pool.

From the pool, it was a long walk along the Kent coastline. I tried to relax, enjoy the scenery and concentrate on talking to Miri. I wanted to savour it. That 'last for now' walk. I was distracted knowing that our friends and family would arrive soon and wondered if any of them were lost. I put my phone in my backpack and we walked in silence for a while.

Miri seemed distracted too. She kept looking left and right when we crossed the road as if her mind forgot it was clear as soon as she turned the other way. When I'd last been at her house I noticed new Pilates bands on her table as she told me about a pottery course she'd started. Two tell-tale signs that she was feeling down. She often tried to Marie Kondo her feelings into action, as if uncertainty and anxiety are avoidable.

When we approached Walpole Bay, I saw the shore was busy. A pair of hands waved towards me, was that Orla? She must've been looking towards the cliffs for us. Miri slowed behind me. *Promise me there'll be more?* Her teeth bit down hard on her bottom lip. I thought back to our first swim on the Gower coast. How close I'd stayed to her and how much I needed to be on my way to somewhere, anywhere. Miri was gripping her backpack straps as though she might take off, thumbs looped and fists facing forward. Now it was her time to need. The pendulum of our friendship had swung the other way. I would stay constant to her. Not fall away when I am hurt or lean too close when I am well. *There'll always be more. I promise.*

Our stride quickened as we walked towards the others, who were cheering in the distance. Jem ran over to give me a kiss then leaned in to hug Miri. He pointed to the water, *have you been to one of these before? I hear it's something called a,* he scratched his chin, *tidal pool?* I shoved him and he ran back to his friends, who were tying beers to the pool ladder to keep them cool. I watched Jem bend to tickle a bearded collie behind the ears.

From the graffitied clifftop I glanced at the path, where I saw Doug from Owl Valley talking to Eileen from North Baths along with other wild swimmers who'd joined the party. The girls were there too. They probably wouldn't swim, but they had lunch and looked content chatting by the sea wall. Natalie was trying one of Nikia's chips. I wondered if she'd had fish and chips before and knew she'd enjoy learning Welsh slang from Ellen. I looked forward to the first time she'd say 'cwtsh' to me. Orla and Miri were already pulling towels from their bags as they prepared to swim.

The metal ladder of the pool glinted and a memory of Tom's wheelchair crossed my mind. We'd taken him from the hospital to the pub, but the door had a ledge and getting in was difficult. It took multiple attempts, which Tom begged us to abandon. He'd covered his face with his hand in utter embarrassment. I wished I could go back in time to kneel before him in the wheelchair, grip his arms and say: *don't be embarrassed. Fuck everyone. You're a superhero. Let's get a pint.*

Tom had suffered so much. I suffered by remembering any of it, all of it. It happened. All I could do now was choose to change the landscape of my life. Choose trust. Choose joy. It pained me knowing how hard that would be. How much strength it would require. It would be the closest I'd ever get to having courage like Tom.

The light shifted across Walpole Bay and caught Mum's hair. It glistened blue-black. I raised my hand, as if to be called on at school. She did the same, wanting to answer the same question. We both waved and it was like staring at my reflection in water. Mum turned back to talking to Dad and John as Jem appeared behind me. He placed his hand on my collarbone and kissed the top of my head, hot in the April sun. Letting his hand fall to meet mine, he pulled me towards the tidal pool. I looked at Jem in front of me and Mum behind me, knowing we were joined in our continuing effort to return to each other. *I'll follow you in*, I said, then watched the shore with all my friends and family, all this love. Emma walked towards me and I took her hand. *Want to go for a swim?*

Chapter Sixty-Five

Am-Nawr: 51.85996° N, 3.13642° W

I stopped typing. Finally, it resonated as the end of something, rather than a beginning. Once, I'd believed I needed to hear that from a man. And now I'd found the answers all on my own. The answer was that I knew I wouldn't arrive anywhere. I thought about how much I missed the characters of my life. Mum driving to pick me up, Miri pulling off her neoprene swimming socks, Jem placing a pinecone in my pocket, Emma bringing a balloon.

Life is very short. Everything passes by. Everyone passes.

I closed my laptop and looked out the window. Contrails were purling and lacing the grey-blue sky. I was hopeful the sun would break through that afternoon. The postman walked by, delivering a letter to next door. I wondered what words were inside, and what meaning they carried. What should I do with my day now that the book was done? A swim would be a good start. I opened the internet and nothing excited me. I looked at my emails. *Inbox: One.* An article about tidal pools in Northern Ireland from Miri. *Our next adventure,* she wrote.

Two weeks later, I went to Wales to meet Emma and told her I'd finished the book. *What happens in the end?* she asked. *You'll have to read it,* I joked, then thought about the manuscript I'd brought her, which was sitting in my bag. I'd gone to the library to print it out and irritated a schoolboy by occupying the printer for so long. Now I was too shy to get it out and see the weight of the 90,000 words I'd had to write because I didn't know how to say to her, *I'm sorry. I love you. It hurts me too.*

We were all there for the final swim. You were there. We held hands and went swimming together in the last tidal pool. Saying it aloud made me feel a pang of embarrassment. *Was Tom there?* I shook my head. *It's as if my heart was so full with this wish to write an ending where you were there and happy that I didn't have space to imagine that.*

Emma had her chin placed on her folded hands. She looked outside where our dad was bent over a tub of primroses, inspecting and occasionally pruning. *And anyway, I don't know if I could imagine his face. It doesn't come clearly to me anymore.* She seemed surprised, perplexed, even, by this. *Really? I dream about him all the time. Can I give you a new wish?* I nodded. *I hope he comes to you in dreams.* I reached out and held Emma's hand. It was heavy, and mine slick with sweat, wet as a stone from the shore. We pressed them together for a moment and a tide moved inside me. I knew that, soon, I would have space inside me for a new wish. A new dream.

Acknowledgements

Thank you Joelle Owusu-Sekyere, my editor, for believing in this story and thank you Jo Bell, my agent, for believing in me. I'm so grateful that you both took a chance on me. Thank you to Sophie, my copy-editor, for making this book better in so many ways. And to the Society of Authors for the grant to complete this work and for supporting so many aspiring authors like me.

To all my work family. Thank you for your support. Especially Martyn; the confidence you helped me develop at work touched everything else. To my mentor, Cathy: writing about a loved one no longer here wouldn't have felt possible without your warmth and encouragement.

Thank you to my tutors at Cambridge for being so generous with your time and wisdom, particularly Derek and his spectacular nature notes. And the MSt writers who taught me to be a good reader, as well as a good writer. Most of all thanks to Natalie and Angelica for their notes on my early drafts. Our friendship – and that writing trip to Greece – was the first space where I felt like a true writer.

Thank you to my parents, for teaching me to fall in love with nature. And my big brothers Lawrence and Howard for making me a loud and fearless woman. To the wonderful women in my life who provided more romance than I could write in a lifetime's worth of romcoms. All my readers: Agathe, Jess, Becky, Jo, Nick, Elsa, Ed and the Book Club.

Thank you to the kind strangers I met in the water and to the many councils, charities and the National Trust who fight to keep these magical places open. Thank you to nature for coming back, even though we've treated you so badly.

Thank you, Jem, for the love.

Thank you, Jo, for the adventure

And Emma, for everything.

Staff Credits

Commissioning Editor
Joelle Owusu-Sekyere

Publicity
Kimberley Nyamhondera

Marketing
Katy Blott

Production
Rachel Southey

Cover design
Sarah Christie

Copy editor
Sophie Lazar

Proof reader
Jacqui Lewis